VICTORIAN IDYLLIC FICTION
PASTORAL STRATEGIES

VICTORIAN IDYLLIC FICTION

PASTORAL STRATEGIES

Shelagh Hunter

Humanities Press

Atlantic Highlands, N. J.

NEH

PR
878
.P3
H86
1984

First published in the United States of America in 1984
by HUMANITIES PRESS INC.
171 Atlantic Highlands, NJ 07716

Printed in Hong Kong

Library of Congress Cataloging in Publication Data

Hunter, Shelagh.
    Victorian idyllic fiction.

    Includes bibliographical references and index.
    1. English fiction — 19th century — History and
criticism.   2. Pastoral fiction, English — History and
criticism.   3. Country life in literature. 4. Labor
and laboring classes in literature.   I. Title.
PR878.P3H86   1984   832'.8'09321734   83–22721
ISBN 0–391–03032–9

To my parents

Contents

Preface

The idea of a transaction between text and reader with results as indeterminate as those of good conversation is at the centre of the present critical study, which sees genre as more importantly a guide to reading than to writing. There are clearly other ways than generic of looking at the novels I discuss, but my concern is with the terms in which they form a group. I argue that a significantly large number of generic signals in each of them indicates that they take a similar narrative stance, and that as a consequence of such generic similarity they not only illuminate one another but, together, force a reassessment of the traditional genre patterns of pastoral on which they call. The critics with whom I take issue are those who view these novels of simple life (which I am calling 'idyllic') as a mirror to social reality. Where they find the image inaccurate they assume a failure in the art or the artist. This is to ignore the role of art in forming as well as reflecting social attitudes, and to deny not fictionality *per se* so much as a particular kind of balance achieved in some novels between fiction and external reference. The structural elements of the novels pull apart, reflect on one another, complement or contradict one another in relation to the fictional rather than the social world. The resulting tensions, characteristically in these novels incompletely resolved, form the ground of a dialectic relationship between narrator and reader, in which their respective roles become temporarily interchangeable. For the brief duration of each novel, narrator and reader are assumed to share the problem of accommodating traditional patterns of thought and vocabulary to contemporary facts. External reference is not therefore achieved primarily through mimetic representation. Rather, the narrator persuades the reader to make a reconstruction of pastoral structures of feeling inside the constraints of a changing society, or, on the other hand, to enter on a tentative pastoral interpretation of the modern world.

My grateful thanks are due to John Goode of the University of Warwick. He is a teacher who remains consistently supportive while

offering rigorous and searching criticism. Inga-Stina Ewbank of
London University and Martin Price of Yale University read
substantial portions of the manuscript and gave valuable help. I
profited too from the readings and comments of Clive Bush, Joseph
Gordon, Mary Hunter and James Parakilas. Audrey Cooper of the
University Library at Warwick was interested and helpful beyond
the call of duty. I have been thankful for the tolerance and
encouragement of my children, Andrew and Ruth Hunter. My
greatest debt is to my husband, George Hunter. Inexhaustibly
generous with his time and his learning, he has made the project
possible and enjoyable too. The remaining faults have a stamp all
too familiar and undeniably my own.

S.H.

Introduction

This book is a study of one particular way in which simple, mainly rural people and ways of life are presented in nineteenth-century English fiction. The moral and political awareness that a common man is a worthy subject of art produced, of course, a simultaneous aesthetic demand for realism in his portraiture. Here, in part, is the story of the rise of the novel. But today we do not always immediately respond to Victorian pictures of rural life as, above everything else, 'real'. Indeed, novels like *Adam Bede* and *Under the Greenwood Tree* seem deliberately to flout the realistic conventions they just as deliberately invoke in the depiction of their fictional worlds. The paradox, however, does not lie in the means of presentation alone. It is inherent in the concept of such subject-matter at all. Simplicity, when it does not mean foolishness, is traditionally synonymous with certain kinds of spiritual wealth. Like goodness of any kind it is hard to portray. Allegiance to the devil's party is an immediately attractive narrative stance; activity and conflict are dramatic and subversive at once. But innocence is characterised by, and perhaps can only be preserved by, a stillness which precludes both mental questing and the movement towards change necessary to narrative. A novelist who wishes to show simple people engaged in a simple way of life is immediately confronted with the need to evoke what, in so many external respects, presents itself as an emptiness. He may map the area of the space with the rigorous economy and eye-on-the-object approach of Flaubert in *Un Cœur Simple* or with the profusion of detail and incident of Dostoevsky in *The Idiot*. But Félicité and Myshkyn alike are acted upon rather than active, and are defined by their relationships rather than by their psychology. What is needed for the presentation of innocence, it seems, is something approaching a flat canvas on which depth is suggested less by development or movement than by contiguity.

For one eminent critic of the whole pastoral tradition in which rural simplicities are value-laden, such a flat canvas is a mark of technical insufficiency. *Adam Bede*, for contemporary readers an exciting innovation and a revelation of the unfamiliar, is for Raymond Williams an uncompleted gesture in the direction of later achievement.[1] He sees the characters as lacking in depth and hampered in speech and action by the rigidities of a fixed relationship with the background:[2]

> What Adam or Dinah or Hetty say, when they are acting as individuals, is not particularly convincing. Into a novel still predicated on the analysis of individual conduct, the farmers and craftsmen can be included as 'country people' but much less significantly as the active bearers of personal experience. When Adam and Dinah and Hetty talk in what is supposed to be personal crisis . . . we are shifted to the level of generalised attitudes or of declamation. Another way of putting this would be to say that though George Eliot restores the real inhabitants of rural England to their places in what had been a socially selective landscape, she does not get much further than restoring them *as landscape*.

Adam Bede is unfortunate in being an early work by the author of *Middlemarch*. Judged by the standards of Leavis's 'Great Tradition', where the primacy of psychological observation and social realism in *Middlemarch* is the desirable norm, *Adam Bede* can be shown, as it is by Raymond Williams, to lack both technical virtuosity and moral insight. But as its inclusion in *The City and the Country*[3] indicates, it stands clearly in the pastoral tradition, that is in a tradition which, up to the nineteenth century, has been predominantly a poetic one. In modern criticism, to call a novel 'poetic' is usually taken to indicate a gap between the fictional world and the 'real' or external world. While the patently unrealistic but poetically suggestive Gothic strand in the nineteenth-century novel has found a critical vocabulary,[4] a 'poetic' version of the rural world is still commonly seen as selective to the point of untruth. A concentration on subject-matter as a defining quality suggests that a pastoral novel will be one which will describe country dancing rather than pig killing, though both are known to have occurred seasonally in nineteenth-century rural districts. To describe *Adam Bede* as a pastoral novel by intention rather than failure might seem perverse in the face of its self-declared allegiance to Realism as an artistic creed. This novel begins in identifiable if historic surroundings and with a meticulous description of the working conditions of its lowly protagonist. Alas for the real, the characters turn out to have more vigour as figures in a landscape than they have psychological motivation, and they and the narrator share a mode of discourse which, however clearly it may be differentiated inside the novel between educated and uneducated, is everywhere a mannered and obviously art-ful construction. Since contemporary readers received *Adam Bede* as a startlingly realistic picture of rural life, it is clear that to replicate anything like so holistic an acceptance of this novel we should have to modify our view of the conventions inside which it can give an appearance of reality.

Adam Bede belongs, I believe, to a class of Victorian works, some of them poems, some novels, which we may for the convenience of distinguishing them from older pastorals call 'idylls'.[5] The idyll as I shall attempt to define it is a distinctively Victorian transformation of the pastoral genre. Pastoral has not at this time wholly recovered from Samuel Johnson's characterisation of 'Lycidas' as 'easy, vulgar and therefore disgusting'. Indeed the word itself and the whole frame of reference it suggests are so familiar that pastoral can be used as a means of placing, of making, as Johnson's own remark does, a simultaneously aesthetic and moral judgement. Angus Easson points out, for example, how the pastoral characterisation of Dickens's John Chivery is in fact a judgement. We have no doubt that he is a good young man, but this cheerful swain is clearly both too simple and too grotesquely portrayed to be considered by the reader as a serious suitor for Little Dorrit.[6] Pastoral reference places the love-affair of George Eliot's Arthur and Hetty as born of the fateful 'ease' with which both of them allow the illusion to take them over. On the other hand Silas Marner's restoration to spiritual health and a right relation with other people is accomplished by an innocent soul, and in a country setting. *Silas Marner* is a novel with strong thematic pastoral overtones which carry the positive values of the work. Significantly the epigraph to this novel is from Wordsworth. Wordsworth is, of course, the most immediate nineteenth-century English inspiration behind the pastoralism of regeneration through a return to the sources of primal innocence. Elements of the pastoral are widespread in Victorian writing as in other periods as a signal. While its outworn conventions supply comedy or grounds for moral condemnation, its shepherds, flocks and *loci amoeni* attach with all the emotional resonance of tradition to contemporary equivalents. In this way the genre was absorbed and adapted. What I have called the 'transformation of the genre' is coterminous with these processes. It is, though, a more deeply radical process than absorption and adaptation. It is a renewal of the pastoral impulse itself. In the transformation of the pastoral into the Victorian idyll a contemporary scene is made accessible from a traditional standpoint, while, at the same time, the generic elements are shifted from their apparently central position under new pressures. The old impulse can be seen to remain alive in a structure of feeling independent of its ancient properties.

In modern criticism, where it is generally admired but not usually examined, the mid-century novel most often called 'idyllic' is Elizabeth Gaskell's *Cousin Phillis*. The characteristic effects of this short novel are of a delicacy which is hard to describe and of a kind not widely associated with the novel form. But 'Q' in 1925 did not feel obliged to apologise for the pastoral ancestry of *Cousin Phillis*:[7]

> I suppose its underlying sadness has kept it out of popular esteem . . . But it beats me to guess how any true critic can pass it over and neglect a thing with all that is best in Theocritus moving in rustic English hearts. And it is not *invented*. It has in all its movements the suggestion of things actually seen – of small things that could not have occurred to any mind save that of an eye-witness – of small *recognitions*, each in its turn a little flash of light upon the steady background of rural England. It is England and yet pure Virgil.

'Q' here sees the ancient structures of feeling not as confining contemporary social observation in a straitjacket of tradition but as liberating it into the appearance of a fresh truth. Thus the ancient tradition is itself the means by which its own tired conventions are stripped away. It allows the author of *Cousin Phillis* to fix her eye on the object and communicate her perception to the co-operative reader as an illumination of what he recognises. If a work operates by calling into play the reader's sense of the traditional and the real together in a new framework the effect, of course, is to modify his sense of both. As Gombrich has shown so convincingly in *Art and Illusion*[8] new art always involves the unpredictable interplay of stereotype and perception. Verbal art gives an illusion of describing a separable and independently real world, but the world of the novel is, of course, a construct, a fictional world. An author may keep looking at the same external circumstances and yet write about them in ways as distinct as those in which George Sand described the rural life of her native Berry. She wrote with journalistic vigour of class oppression and grinding poverty in the *Éclaireur de l'Indre*, and poetically of simple and innocent souls in instinctive communion with one another in the *romans-champêtres*.[9] Both these versions of the real are rhetorical in function – alternative ways of describing what is unfamiliar to an urban readership, and, in the case of this politically embattled author, of enlisting sympathy. No moment in the past is separable from the ways in which we learn about it. Its representation in paint and words is not only the way in which we know it, but also a part of the way in which contemporaries knew it too.[10] Unmediated contact with reality is possible only in the most limited way. A complete fictional world with a complicated story and numbers of characters has to be built up very largely from stereotypes, the new emerging from the rearrangement of the pieces.

In *Cousin Phillis* the generic is a window on to present realities, and this play of the timeless against the here and now is, I shall argue, typical of the Victorian idyll. The general structure of oppositions which underlies the pastoral[11] not only survives the nineteenth-century transformation but re-emerges with a new significance. A mode in which the past and the present are held together in a single frame is one particularly apt, obviously, for the description of social change. Hence this book derives from the paradox by which the ancient idyllic mode is used to depict a society under the pressure of hitherto unprecedented rapidity of change. Of the novels I discuss in detail in subsequent chapters, *Cranford, Cousin Phillis, Under the Greenwood Tree* and *The Woodlanders* are centrally novels of social change, while *Adam Bede* and *Far from the Madding Crowd* may be said to be more centrally concerned with ways of perceiving the rural world and of fiction-making about it. But, as pastoral always is, these novels are self-conscious of their own process. In the seminal *Some Versions of Pastoral* (1935) William Empson refers to pastoral as a *process*, 'the process of putting the complex into the simple', which explains with all the elegance of economical definition not only the fluidity of the exploratory processes which make up the novels in this study, but the muted nature of their final effect. This mutedness they share with pastoral poetry where, characteristically, the total effect is produced by a balance of opposite effects; loss may point to 'fresh woods and pastures new', or the knowledge of the brevity of human life to the bitter-sweet enjoyment of young love. These novels all lack a clear final resolution such as, by comparison, marks a tragedy. *Tess of the d'Urbervilles*, for example, however we may argue about the precise meaning of tragedy on the stage and in the novel, will, in the broad definition of the 'tragic' novel, be on the inside or on the edge of the category. *The Woodlanders*, on the other hand, is problematic, a failure as a tragedy, but clearly not a failure. It marks, I shall argue, the logical end of the idyllic method in its Victorian guise, but remains coherent as an 'idyll'. That is, it paints a picture of a remote and rural way of life in which the inherent oppositions of sophisticated and simple, and the historical layers of time present to the perception of such a world, are held for the last time in Hardy's work in final balance or irresolution.

The point of view from which the painting of such a picture, or in other words the perspective on it, is possible is here taken to determine the chief indications of genre. Genre in Rosalie Colie's definition is 'a set of "frames" or "fixes" on the world'.[12] The genre is construed by the reader from effects in the text itself.[13] Gombrich's definition of perspective in drawing provides a useful analogy. Perspective, he shows, requires the collaboration of the viewer to activate the image into a recognisable set of objects. It is not a convention so much as a relational model. To alter the position of the easel or point of view ever so slightly is to alter the relation of one object to another.[14] A pastoral perspective holds the oppositions which may be broadly grouped under the simple and the complex – sophisticated and unsophisticated, urban and rural, art and nature, present and past[15] – in a relation to one another which can best be described as a delicate balance. In literary terms the complex in the simple produces a density of texture which paradoxically presents itself as extreme simplicity. *Cranford*, *Cousin Phillis* and *Under the Greenwood Tree* all achieve this feat, while at the surface of *Adam Bede*, *Far from the Madding Crowd* and *The Woodlanders* the interest is as much in the process as in the final effect. The 'perspective' of these works is not in the first instance a philosophy or view of life. It may imply one, of course. A willingness, for instance, to hold in focus an ambiguous moment where opposed forces do not clash but briefly coexist is a conservative not a radical mode. But the perspective itself is simply a view from a fixed point and shows objects, scenes and people in a temporarily fixed relation to one another – a relation fixed, that is, for as long as the viewpoint is held. So restricted a focus is unlikely to be held beyond a few works at most.

Certainly the authors I discuss do not hold the focus I describe as idyllic beyond the works considered here. Further, and this is the root of much critical difficulty, it cannot be held without aesthetic distance. George Eliot, accused of patronising her simple characters,[16] is not, I shall argue, unsympathetically removed from them by the distance of her narrative stance. She is taking up a position at sufficient distance from the described world on the one hand and from the reader's world on the other for the two to be brought for the brief duration of the novel into continuously simultaneous focus. The creative co-operation demanded of the reader who must hold the oppositions in a corresponding balance, may achieve ease or calm as an end, but is in itself by no means easy. On the contrary, it is characterised by effort, and can thus hardly be sentimental – the pejorative which may well be the nearest equivalent in current use to Johnson's 'vulgar and therefore disgusting'.

Shepherds are incidental in this view of pastoral and subject-matter is not a defining factor. John F. Lynen in his book on Robert Frost, for instance, uses the many similarities between Frost and Wordsworth to define the peculiar individuality of Frost. The two poets, Lynen shows, share subject-matter but not their perspective on it, and it is Frost, writing from a distanced and reflective stance, and in the forms it dictates, who is the pastoral poet.[17] I could say of the idyllic authors I consider, as John Lynen says of Frost, that their 'meaning is in their manner, a way of viewing the world which is more fundamental than [they] may have recorded because of the condition of their perceiving'.[18] The fixed distance, or perspective, provides, as Gombrich says, a relational model. It follows from the analogy with drawing that a particular perspective will have its most marked effect in a work of verbal art on the structure, which provides, in a poem or a novel, the equivalent of spatial relations in a picture. But words have to exist in continuous time, and where the content is strung along a thread of narrative, movement in time, however handled, is a necessary condition. A multi-faceted view held in a single focus thus works against the natural flow of narrative. In a novel so focused it is not to be expected that every element will be developed to the extent of its potential. In fact the novels I call idylls are marked not only by a lack of final resolution but by a curtailment of the psychological probing of character. In *Adam Bede*, for instance, Adam and Dinah marry to the distress of many a critic. But there is as much loss as gain acknowledged in this ending and the marriage is an adjustment to the pattern of the fiction which has never raised questions of psychological depth and individuality except in the minds of readers applying standards which presuppose another kind of novel. Characteristically the idyllic novels I describe progress by combining devices which indicate movement with those which hold moments of stasis or simultaneity. As near as possible in the continuity of a novel they reach to the condition of a picture or flat canvas where appreciation of relationship can be ideally instantaneous.

One characteristically Victorian celebration of the simple is, of course, in painting itself. Genre pictures of humble and domestic scenes painted with elaborate skill for a sophisticated audience reached the height of their popularity around 1860. These pictures are, of their nature, entirely dependent on implied narrative to energise the pictorial moments and make meaningful the static relationships depicted. In my next chapter I seek to suggest the nature of the relation between genre painting and the Victorian idyll. But centrally in that chapter I look in the famous self-styled pastoral poems of the mid-century for a model for the structures which support a novelistic pastoral perspective. In so far as poetry does not raise the same expectations of development as the novel it lends itself more readily to the achievement of idyllic balance. But while Clough's *The Bothie of Tober-na-Vuolich* (subtitled 'A Long Vacation Pastoral') and Tennyson's English Idyls present an extraordinary range of innovative technique within the pastoral genre, the centrality of narrative to their method is most significant in my argument. *The Bothie* is in fact a narrative poem, and narrative is an essential, even when suppressed, element in all the English Idyls. For whatever reason the democratisation of the subject-matter in this period throws narrative into unprecedented prominence. At the same time critics of the novel like David Masson wrote as though the novel was only incidentally different from poetry,[19] and 'poetry' itself was a term which was applied to other arts in the sense of 'giving rise to reflection'.

While it has seemed to later critics that so close a connection with pastoral poetry renders the idyll unfit for the portrayal of the real, John Sterling hailed Tennyson, on the strength particularly of the English Idyls among the *Poems* of 1842, as the poet most likely to become the 'Poet of the Age'.[20] Sterling recognised in these poems both contemporary pressures and the pastoral tradition chosen to express a response to them. Tennyson's model in the idyls was, of course, Theocritus. So we are back to 'Q' on *Cousin Phillis*, where the progenitors of pastoral are seen to offer a vantage-point from which to survey a changing contemporary world. Placed in other company than that of 'the novel predicated on analysis of individual conduct'[21] the static and circular narrative patterns of the novels I call 'idyllic' and their pictorial and representative methods of characterisation take on a different significance. The contemporary chorus of pleasurable recognition of the 'real' in *Adam Bede* has something to tell us about the nature of the novel when it is compared with the similar reception of Tennyson's elaborately patterned Idyls. These 'idyllic' patterns are not neatly available for observation and summary in the novels I discuss since each work puts its own stamp on the structures of feeling. But an examination of the structures and self-conscious comment on the process of exploration provided by the poetic pastorals casts light on similar patterns underlying the novels. The poems and the novels are pastorals transformed by the pressures of new circumstances and new taste. Shepherds and their embarrassing surrogates are absent, but the structures of pastoral feeling remain. A complex network of oppositions holds together in the consciousness of the reader the urban and the rural, the sophisticated and the unsophisticated, the complex and the simple. But most particularly the past and its relevant modes of composition are held in continuous counterpoint with the present and its appropriately adjusted styles.

Certainly, whatever works we now attach to the phenomenon, a recrudescence of pastoral feeling during the social upheavals of the early nineteenth century was recognised at the time in both poetry and prose. R. H. Horne draws attention to it in *A New Spirit of the Age* in 1844. In his essay on William and Mary Howitt he charts the rise of a 'somewhat new class of writing' which has had 'great success, most fortunately for the public taste, as its influence is most healthy and sweet, most refreshing and soothing, most joyous, yet most innocent'. He calls this innovation 'the unaffected prose pastoral'. It has, he says, no ancestors in prose nearer than Sidney's *Arcadia* and Walton's *Compleat Angler*. He places the work of the Howitts in a revitalised tradition containing both poets and prose writers:[22]

the same feeling can hardly be said to have shown itself until the time of Lady Winchelsea; again some fifty years intervened and we had Burns, and soon afterwards Charlotte Smith, and then Wordsworth, and Keats in poetry, and Miss Mitford and Leigh

Hunt in prose. The numerous essays and delightful papers of Leigh Hunt, and one little work in particular, entitled 'The Months' – together with the pastoral sketches of 'Our Village', 'Belford Regis', and 'Country Stories', are known to all. These works of Miss Mitford, if read by snatches, come over the mind as the summer air and the sweet hum of rural sounds would float upon the senses through a tradition of fragrance and dew. It is hardly necessary to add, that her prose pastorals are all redolent of a cordial and cheerful spirit. They are the poetry of matter-of-fact nature, fresh and at first hand.

Among the works in this list the 'unaffected prose pastorals' have the least complex range of surface effects and have most obviously lost their charm. But Mary Mitford's sketches remained popular into this century as over a hundred years of reprints and selections show.[23] Her work becomes repetitive and formulaic, but among the early sketches in *Our Village* are some which under an appearance of direct handling of the rustic material reveal the complex structure of feeling which links the Victorian idyll with the pastoral tradition. Further the devices by which the structure of feeling is made manifest are those of narrative. In her best writing, self-consciously cheerful as the essays may be, the underlying unrest which calls for a restorative is held in a fine balance with the cordial itself. Some of the pieces are simple stories of the people in the neighbourhood, but those which purport to be first-hand reporting of natural scenes have the more interesting narrative techniques. The topography is real, but the devices by which the reader's contemplative reflections are incorporated in the text are the devices by which Elizabeth Gaskell creates Heathbridge or George Eliot Hayslope or those by which Thomas Hardy makes Mellstock out of his birthplace. By fictional means the simple descriptive surface is made to accommodate the ambivalence of the urban reader's relation to the countryside. At their best these simple prose sketches show the essential duality out of which a pastoral or idyllic balance is achieved. In the same way, *Cousin Phillis*, as melancholy as *Our Village* is cheerful, does not become a lament for a vanished past because by the complexity of the narrative technique the past is shown to endure in the present.

In the Victorian idyll the closely woven texture of the works is composed of the presented simplicities and concurrent reminders of conflicting claims on response. Simple subject-matter and a complex view of it combine to construct a convincing world. A fine balance is achieved between the enduring and the threatened, and the adjustments of the world to the inevitable passing of time are delicately drawn. The poise depends on complex structural patterns. We should not ask, I believe, whether elements of these works correspond to elements of an historical reality we happen to know about or can reconstruct from twentieth-century interpretations. Rather we should ask whether the means by which they seek to relate their separate elements present a convincing and self-explanatory world which we may take as one credible way of facing a contemporary reality.

Besides the pastorals of Clough and Tennyson and the analogical genre pictures of simple subjects, my next chapter examines a line of critical thought on the idyllic presentation of the simple from Wordsworth and Schiller to Arnold. In Chapter 2 I explore the paradox by which fictional techniques make Mary Mitford's prose sketches early narrative idylls and the prose exposition of political intent makes George Sand's *romans-champêtres* into tracts for the times. Chapter 3 distinguishes *Cranford* and *Cousin Phillis* as Elizabeth Gaskell's idylls, but finds strong evidence of idyllic methods in her two condition-of-England novels, *Mary Barton* and *North and South*. In Chapter 4 I show George Eliot in *Adam Bede*, her only idyll, teasing the reader into reassessing the stereotypes of his thinking about the presentation of the simple. Chapter 5 shows Hardy in *Under the Greenwood Tree*, *Far from the Madding Crowd* and *The Woodlanders* as the most varied of all nineteenth-century pastoral novelists. Chapter 6 considers the peculiar relation of the idyllic novel to social reality. The separate modifications of an ancient mode into authentic contemporary statements go side by side, of course, with newly emerging social perceptions. Literature has a place in this infinitely gradual process by engaging countless readers in small modifications of well-embedded stereotypes. This, my concluding chapter, offers a fleeting view of mid-nineteenth-century social change from an idyllic or pastoral perspective.

I The Victorian Idyll

Arthur Hugh Clough is doubly associated with pastoral, as the author of *The Bothie of Tober-na-Vuolich: A long Vacation Pastoral*,[1] and as the subject of 'Thyrsis', Arnold's Theocritan elegy. Arnold comments in a letter to J. C. Shairp:[2]

> 'Thyrsis' is a very quiet poem, but I think solid and sincere. It will not be popular, however. It had long been in my head to connect Clough with that Cumner country, and when I began I was carried irresistibly into this form; you say, truly, however, that there is much in Clough (the whole prophet side, in fact) which one cannot deal with in this way, and one has the feeling, if one reads the poem as a memorial poem, that not enough is said about Clough in it; I feel this so much that I do not send the poem to Mrs Clough. Still Clough *had* this idyllic side too; to deal with this suited my desire to deal again with that Cumner country: any way, only so could I treat the matter this time.

In this account of the creative process behind a nineteenth-century pastoral, the poet is shown 'irresistibly' fusing his central figure with the background. Arnold is conscious that in the process of identification of his friend with the countryside of their shared walks much of the real man had to be sacrificed, but the ideal of man and scene as one overrules other aspects of the friendship and respect which inspired the elegy and, moreover, has a poetic tradition behind it. Like the poet of Milton's 'Lycidas', the author remains alone at the end to continue what was begun in friendship. In 'Thyrsis' he continues the quest accompanied by the shade of the Scholar-Gipsy, lured over the rolling countryside by the signal elm in a highly poetic fusion this time of Nature and idea which continually invites and then defies allegorical interpretation. Clough's *Long Vacation Pastoral* is an expression of what Arnold called his 'idyllic side'. It shows him sensitive alike to natural beauty and the sterling worth of rustic character. But it shows him, too,

committed to the cultivated values of an Oxford education. The
poem speaks in a deeply pastoral, but also a new voice. How else but
in an original style, Kingsley asks in his review in *Fraser's Magazine*,
could Clough 'have drawn in the same picture' the 'sublime and the
ridiculous' which he found 'hand-in-hand'? Not, Kingsley says, in
any of the models which occur to him:[3]

> An Oxford colony in cockneyized Highlands! Conceive writing a
> pastoral thereon, after the manner of Theocritus, or Bion, or
> Virgil or anybody else! Would Catullus' *Atys* have done? or
> Apuleius? or Aristophanes with modifications? or the *Pastor Fido*?
> Or Sidney's *Arcadia*, perhaps? or *Comus*? or *Tristam Shandy*? or *Don
> Quixote*? or *The Vicar of Wakefield*? or Gray's *Elegy*? or Mr
> Wordsworth's *Ruth*? or Mr. Tennyson's *Gardener's Daughter*? or
> Goethe's *Hermann and Dorothea*? or perhaps Mr Gresley's *Bernard
> Leslie*?

The anonymous reviewer in the *Saturday Review*,[4] who wrote a
tribute on Clough's death, has an ambivalent view of pastoral.
Clough's gift were not really poetic, but, such as they were, they
were revealed 'by the chance of a very happy subject' – 'the life and
adventures of an Oxford reading party in a long vacation'. 'Perhaps
the English public would not care much for the poem',[5] but as the
reviewer himself points out the 'first edition was soon sold out, and
the poem . . . much admired in America'. A somewhat reluctant
admirer, he is nevertheless won over by the harmony of subject-
matter and style:

> It is full of the harmless slang in vogue at Oxford; it abounds in
> allusions to books and authors appointed for study at Oxford; and
> it is written in a very peculiar metre – in a kind of prosaic, halting,
> indistinct hexameter, in which no one but a classical scholar
> could see any metre at all, and which would at every third line
> oblige a classical scholar to read again and again the words before
> him, in order to discover how they were meant to run. These
> attributes do not tend to make a poem popular in England and it
> is a good thing that they do not. But still, this Pastoral, to those
> who can make up their minds to enjoy it, is a most delightful
> poem. It is in exact keeping with its subject. It is full of fun, of
> jokes bad and good, of discussions, of adventure, of lovemaking,
> of deep feeling. It embodies all that is ordinary and extraordinary

in the lives of a happy group of young men, in beautiful scenery, with perfect liberty allowed them, and yet with fixed tasks which they set themselves to do. . . . No Oxford men will forget the impression it made on them when they first read it. It offered them at once a glorification of their youthful happiness, and a serious though often playful examination of the deeper feelings of young men.

This is a familiar conception of pastoral – universally appealing feelings associated particularly with youth, against a background of harmonious nature. But it is its perfection or wholeness which the reviewer chiefly values in *The Bothie*. He is so much aware of this that when he comes to select a passage which will convey its quality to the reader who is unfamiliar with the poem, he finds the best ones 'too intimately connected with the thread of the story to be intelligible when standing by themselves'.

It would, of course, be equally unprofitable to try to convey the quality of the poem by telling the story. The material abstracted from the telling is slight to the point of commonplace. But the effect of the poem as it sets the scene of the reading party and then homes in on the story of one young man is extraordinarily complex. The poem is throughout and in individual parts both comic and serious. As vacations do, the reading party brings a number of worlds into uneasy contact, and the poem explores the intellectual discomforts and emotional rewards of the adjustments which make the story-line. The mock-heroic opening gives way to a serious love-story in which the hero puts into practice his radical views and the heroine challenges the stereotypes underlying them by revealing qualities of mind which equal his and a kind of beauty whose appreciation is not dependent on 'the charm of the labour'. Philip discovers reality by discarding notions of simplicity for simplicity itself. In this complicated and necessarily allusive process the controversial hexameters play an integral, indeed a central, part.

The hexameters may be peculiar, but they are also peculiarly successful.[6] At times necessitating reading out loud to make metrical sense of them, they reveal levels of comment on the ostensible material. At different stages of the poem they have different functions but always in some kind of counterpoint to the matter. At the opening where the Highland games are set against the games at Patroclus's funeral, both matter and manner are parodic. But double effects are common; in the lines on the postman, for instance:

For the postman made out he was heir to the earldom of Ilay
  (Being the younger son of the younger brother, the Colonel),
Treated him therefore with special respect; doffed bonnet, and ever,
  Called him His Honour . . .

the colloquial language and halting rhythm reflect both the speaker
and the scepticism of his hearers. In the following lines the flexibility
of the metre allows for the genuine appreciation of the tutor to be
conveyed along with the mock-gravity, and for the bathos of the
undergraduate comment:

Still more plain the Tutor, the grave man, nicknamed Adam,
White-tied, clerical, silent, with antique square-cut waistcoat
Formal, unchanged, of black cloth, but with sense and feeling
  beneath it;
Skilful in Ethics and Logic, in Pindar and Poets unrivalled;
Shady in Latin, said Lindsay, but *topping* in Plays and Aldrich.

Double effects are typical of the whole poem as they are of these
opening paragraphs. The suggestion of song, for instance, in the
repeated phrase about the 'charm of the labour' in Hewson's speech
in Section II, conveys, by the formality of the form within a form, the
lyricism of first sexual feeling, while the speech rhythms convey the
psychological reality of the uncertainty behind the young man's
self-examination. His conclusion, 'Better a cowslip with root than a
prize carnation without it', is funny in expression, but, with Adam,
we allow it philosophically. Rossetti said of the metre that it
'harmonises with the spirit of primitive simplicity in which the poem
is conceived; is itself a background, as much as are "Knoydart,
Goydart, Moydart, Morrer, and Ardnamurchan"; and gives a new
individuality to the passages of familiar narrative and everyday
conversation. It has intrinsic appropriateness. . . .'[7] This catches
the harmony which is undoubtedly there, but leaves out the creative
disharmony which allows the matter to say one thing and the metre
another.

By means of this shifting relationship between matter and manner
the mock-heroic, Highland frame of the action is shown to be also
truly Homeric in its rugged simplicities; it emerges as carrying the
true values of the poem against the embroidered waistcoats and
tinsel-decked castle balls of the society which is grafted on to this
remote place. At the same time, in the crucial conversations of
Philip and Elspie, which cut the most exquisite figures on the thin

ice over sentimentality, the metre adapts flexibly to English colloquial rhythms. It is in this way a running reminder of the everyday, earthy realities which the tender love-story is allowed to include along with its high-minded simplicities. The 'pastoral vacation', a withdrawal to a place of great beauty as a pause in ordinary life, is enjoyable in itself and also, for Philip, a spur to self-discovery. But in the nature of things an undergraduate reading party takes more than its books along with it; it takes all the notions associated with books and the cultivated life. The gilded social life of the kilted aristocracy playing Highland games provides in the opening a comic frame for the action; inside this frame is the 'epic debate' of the young men which culminates in the delightful absurdity of applying the classifications of architectural art-talk to women. Later, however, the real, live woman who is found in her unspoilt innocence in her cottage, uses her own fresh reading of books to support her sense of her own independence from the 'fancies' Philip supposes she unfortunately acquired in a year in England, and as a foundation for her fears that a social inequality made a perfectly proper division between them:

This is what comes of the year you spent in our foolish England.
You do not all of you feel these fancies.
                                        No, she answered.
And in her the spirit, the freedom and ancient joy was reviving.
No, she said, and uplifted herself, and looked for her knitting,
No, nor do *I*, dear Philip, I don't myself feel always
As I have felt, more sorrow for me, these four days lately,
Like the Peruvian Indians I read about last winter,
Out in America there, in somebody's life of Pizarro;
Who were as good as the Spaniards; only weaker;
And that the one big tree might spread its root and branches,
All the lesser about it must be felled and perish.
No, I feel much more as if I, as well as you, were,
Somewhere, a leaf on the one great tree, that, up from old time
Growing, contains in itself the whole of the virtue and life of
Bygone days, drawing now to itself all kindreds and nations
And must have for itself the whole world for its root and branches.
No, I belong to the tree, I shall not decay in the shadow;
Yes, and I feel the life-juices of all the world and the ages,
Coming to me as to you, more slowly no doubt and poorer:
You are more near, but then you will help to convey them to me.

When he says that he will not lend her a single volume, since men come to women, 'As to the woodland and water', she replies that then she will stay with her father and read as she has always done. The slight uncertainty of her formal rhetoric reflects only the informality of her education, not her spirit or her grasp of essentials.

Kingsley's appreciative review, besides stressing the originality of Clough's poem, offers, by implication, the reviewer's own interpretation of its claim to be 'pastoral'. Conflating the two traditions of epic and pastoral on which the poem draws into a generalised Greekness of spirit, Kingsley slightly distorts the total effect by omitting mention of the final return to the manner of the opening. Calling attention to the allusions to autumn at the end of the poem, 'each time with some fresh delicate addition to the charming miniature painting', he says,

> [they make] us recollect the stealing on of the swift, long, northern winter, and the breaking up of the party, with a sobered, and almost a saddened feeling, which harmonises, too, very artistically, with a more serious tone, both of thought and of verse, which takes gradually, towards the end of the poem, the place of the genial frolic of its commencement.

The end of the vacation is, as Kingsley suggests, most beautifully sad:

There in the bright October, the gorgeous bright October,
When the brackens are changed, and heather blooms are faded,
And amid russet of heather and fern green trees are bonnie,
Alders are green, and oaks, the rowan scarlet and yellow,
Heavy the aspen, and heavy with jewels of gold the birch-tree,
There, when the shearing had ended, and barley-stooks were
    garnered,
David gave Philip to wife his daughter, his darling Elspie;
Elspie the quiet, the brave, was wedded to Philip the poet.

The poem, however, has eight paragraphs still to go. To some extent, as the paragraph which introduces the conclusion shows, the end is a return to the mock-heroics of the opening:

So won Philip his bride. They are married and gone – But oh,
    Thou

Mighty one, Muse of great Epos, and Idyll the playful and tender,
Be it recounted in song, ere we part, and thou fly to thy Pindus,
(Pindus is it, O Muse, or Aetna, or even Ben-Nevis?)
Be it recounted in song, O Muse of the Epos and Idyll,
Who gave what at the wedding, the gifts and the fair gratulations.

This is also a reminder that Epos and Idyll have been simultaneously present throughout the story. The poet is setting a
distance between himself and his material as, in a restoration of his
dry, detached persona, he takes a last look at the whole party. Most
of the end is taken up by letters to Philip, from Hobbes at length,
and a brief one from Adam. By this means Philip is restored to his
place as one of the group. The narrator bows out of the narrative by
allowing the letters to tell most of the end of the story. His own
backward look is over the telling of the story, of the mingling of the
Epos and the Idyll. The heroic and the real mingle at this point in
the story too. Adam, comically cautious, rations the Piper's pre-
wedding visits to the Bothie, when he realises that Philip's friend is
in danger of supposing he can repeat Philip's success with Elspie
with her sister Bella, without being prepared for the heroic trials of
Philip's wooing. The heroism at the end is all mock-heroic, played
off against the real in a tone at once tender and wry. It is initiated
appropriately by the invocation to the Muse who is both 'playful
and tender'. Hobbes, 'the corpulent hero', has the last word on the
marriage in mock-scriptural grandeur:

> Go, as in Ephrath of old, in the gate of Bethlehem said they,
> One part heavenly-ideal, the other vulgar and earthy:

In being able to suggest both the heroic and the commonplace, the
romantic and the limited, the verse has throughout carried the hard
message of the last summary lines, which are the poet's not
Hobbes's:

> They are married and gone to New Zealand.
> Five hundred pounds in pocket, with books, and two or three
> pictures,
> Tool-box, plough, and the rest, they rounded the sphere to New
> Zealand.
> There he hewed and dug; subdued the earth and his spirit;
> There he built him a home; there Elspie bare him his children,

David and Bella; perhaps ere this too an Elspie or Adam;
There hath he farmstead and land, and fields of corn and flax
    fields;
And the Antipodes too have a Bothie of Tober-na-vuolich.

In these lines the poet has withdrawn from his characters; they are
reduced as if through the wrong end of a telescope, 'rounding the
sphere' with their reductively enumerated possessions. But the effect
of Philip subduing his spirit with an effort comparable to that of
breaking the land gives a resonance to the tidy, storybook final line
which reminds one what an exquisite balancing trick the whole
poem is. The tensions of the story continue into the future – there is
no real resolution. The withdrawal of the poet has a deprecatory
note about it, but is in no way coy or false as it establishes the
distance from which the reader can see the whole view.

  The whole view of this poem includes a consciousness of its
method; this way, we suppose as we read, is the only conceivable
way of presenting so complex a vision of qualified or mutually
mitigating truths. Such a vision together with an awareness of the
art by which we perceive it is characteristic, I shall argue, of the
Victorian idyll. *The Bothie* presents one way by which we are made
simultaneously aware of the seen and the seeing. Style in *The Bothie*
complicates our view of what we see. Different perceptions of life
form the substance of the story, but at each point in the narrative the
style can offer comment on them. The simple and sophisticated life-
styles are different not only in their contemporary aspects, but also
in their relation to the past. In this story a modern social solution is
wrung out of the rigidities of the ways of the past as a new style is
born out of engagement with the old. In *The Bothie* there is a balance
of loss and gain in the clash between ancient and modern in both
story and style. Reading the poem is a reflective exploration of the
relationships set up by the dialogue of matter and style and we
accept the idyllic ending of the story with a knowledge both of its
frailty and the heroic effort needed to sustain it. The twin inspiration
of *The Bothie* – the *Iliad* and Longfellow's *Evangeline*[8] – produces,
whatever one may think of the odds, a remarkable harmony of
matter and style, a rethinking of old modes which seems to run
continuously with the presentation of contemporary matter.

  The effect of Tennyson's English Idyls[9] is totally different. Not
the least of the differences is the most obvious one – the poems,
compared with *The Bothie*, are very short. The structure of Clough's

poem is determined by a straightforward response to the story's demand for continuity and progression. The stories in the English Idyls bear a different relation to what I shall show to be the overall idyllic pattern. Unlike the story of the vacation reading party and its far-reaching outcome, they are, for one thing, fully resolved. In 'Dora' the only one which is first and foremost a narrative, this resolution is a part of the poem. More characteristically the narrator looks back from the point of resolution, as in the summoned memories of 'Edwin Morris' or the more successful 'The Gardener's Daughter'. 'Morte d'Arthur' begins, paradoxically, *in medias res* by describing a death which, though the end of life, is the beginning of a legend. Typically, narrative in the Idyls is subsumed. It is, however, essential to an understanding of the poems to tease it out, as in 'Audley Court', for example.

In 'Audley Court' the picnic in the grounds of the great house acquires its golden glow from what we gather of the previous and subsequent lives of the two friends. The roving sailor, son of a rooted but impoverished farmer, and the poet with his 'wherewithal', who roams from restlessness not necessity, meet after a long time, have a picnic and walk home. The complex final effect is achieved by a fusion of the separate elements in the poem, which for the sake of analysis can be pulled apart to show how separate in origin they are. The realistic surface of scene, conversation, picnic and return, contains at a second level an economic survey of the district and enough hints to indicate partial biographies of the young men. The two songs with which they entertain each other, and which make up a large portion of the length of the poem, reach back into cultural history in a way which puts their obvious dramatic relevance in an historical frame. The sailor's song is a kind of ballad on a life with no attachments, the poet's an adaptation, with new names, of an old love-song in a book sold when 'Sir Robert's pride', his library, 'came to the hammer'. The poet, rootless ' in the fallow leisure of his life', and the sailor, driven to sea by bad times, are briefly reunited in this rural paradise with its home-baked bread and rich game-pie, picturesque house and beautiful landscape. They talk local gossip and related politics, 'split' on the Corn Laws, but regain some unanimity on the subject of the king's illness. The poem ends with a picture of the bay in the evening. The description is Tennyson at his pictorial best. The calm is vivid and unbroken and it resolves the tensions which have been shown to underlie the relationship of the two friends into a temporary acquiescence. The calm, though perfect, is frail; the threat to it is spelled out as a social one. Each single separable part of the poem repeats the same pattern of a way of life threatened with dissolution. The house with 'griffin-guarded gates' and sweeps of 'meadow smooth' will be let; the friendship is rooted and long-lasting, but both young men are moving away from the surroundings in which it is rooted; the songs are traditional, but have a dramatic poignance sung by these young men. The sailor's is the song of a man who has chosen a free life; the sailor leads one, but has not chosen it. The poet's is about going and returning to his sleeping love, but a 'rolling stone of here and everywhere' is unlikely to find his love peacefully asleep on every return. The effect of equally valuable but ultimately hardly compatible truths is not complete until the end of the poem when they are given their temporary resolution in the description of the evening walk home. This has about it the clear glow of a memory. The precariousness suggested by the social detail of the poem is reinforced by the knowledge that, at a naturalistic psychological level too, the glow given by the act of memory will not be recaptured except in the mind. But – the last 'but' in this particular analysis of an achieved idyllic balance but not the last in my argument – at the same time as we are following the poet home while he commits to memory an unrepeatable day of friendship and sunshine and beauty, the sophisticated memory in the reading is of the rural feasts and friendly song-contests of Theocritus's shepherds. The effect, of course, is to unite in one simultaneous comparison old and new ways of life and old and new ways of writing.

The particular way in which Tennyson's *Poems* of 1842, and notably among them the English Idyls, were received as a new and startlingly relevant way of writing is central to my argument in Chapter 6, the conclusion to this study. There is no need here to argue the relation of these poems to Theocritus's idylls. It is as clear as that of Pope's *Pastorals* to Virgil's *Eclogues* and Thomson's *The Seasons* to his *Georgics*.[10] Robert Pattison has argued that Tennyson's predominant mode is idyllic,[11] and there are ways in which the word can be legitimately extended beyond even Tennyson's complete *œuvre* into high Victorian poetry generally.[12] Further, in so far as genre painting, at the height of its popularity in the middle of the century, shares, as I argue below, a number of features with the Victorian idyll, the mode may well be seen to be a characteristically Victorian one, reflecting sensibilities which seem to distinguish the age from our own. But my concern here, as it is in the study as a

whole, is with the strategies of particular works in a distinguishable
and recurring Victorian mode of writing. This is a strain which can
be separated with some clarity from the wider reference of the term
'idyllic' into what might be thought of 'Victorian'. An extensive
study of Tennyson's English Idyls would have to take into account
the difficulty of deciding which poems Tennyson finally saw as
belonging to the group. Robert Pattison argues that the Idyls in
their final grouping may be considered as a mutually reflecting and
interdependent series.[13] This, if true, would add considerably to the
strength of my argument, which rests on an interdependence of
parts as an essential quality of an idyllic vision. But the length of
time Tennyson kept his poems by him before publication, his
extensive borrowings from himself and his continuing reordering
make it hard to establish just where these habits are particularly
significant in relation to these poems. I consider therefore only
single poems from Volume II of *Poems* of 1842. These, apart from
'The Epic', the frame for 'Morte d'Arthur', were first published in a
trial edition of 1842 with the title *Morte d'Arthur; Dora; and Other
Idyls*. What is clear in these poems, together and singly, is the
inspiration of Theocritus.

A critic who took this so much for granted that he used Tennyson
to elucidate Theocritus was J. W. Mackail. 'As Tennyson so
Theocritus', is the pattern of the account of Theocritus in Mackail's
Lectures on Greek Poetry in 1910.[14] His use of Tennyson in this way is
germane to my purpose because of its comparative closeness to
Tennyson's own world. For this reason it is interesting as much for
what it takes for granted as for what it says. It assumes a general and
unquestioning response to Tennyson's work which modern criticism
has to recover by more elaborate means, and since it seeks to use
Tennyson as a means of explication, indicates very clearly to us at
this distance of time how Tennyson was seen. Mackail is not
particularly interested in detailed correspondences between the
modern English and ancient Greek poems. He does not write of
Tennyson as an imitator, but sees the two poets, Alexandrian and
Londoner, as making very similar responses to very similar pressures
in the life of their times. To see the heavy framing of exquisitely
jewelled 'pictures' as what A. Dwight Culler calls Tennyson's
'means of responding to the call for relevance'[15] demands now an
abandonment of received assumptions about the 'sincerity' of a
work of art. But Mackail sees in Tennyson's response to the call for
relevance a mirror of Theocritus's. The English Idyls then, in this

view, are not stylistic exercises in an ancient mode, loosely attached
to modern circumstances, but an independent response to an
immediate situation with a perspective so similar to the ancient
poet's that it makes of him a natural source and inspiration.
Theocritus's originality (like any poet's) lay in his use of current
methods. A book of idylls was, Mackail says, 'simply a collection of
poems on a small scale, finely wrought and precious'. An analogy is
the pictorial 'idyllia':

> Idyllia are cabinet-pictures; small in size, highly finished,
> detachable, not imagined and executed as elements in any large
> constructive scheme of imaginative decoration, yet each holding
> its tiny convex mirror up to nature, each bringing art for a
> moment into relation with one facet or mood of life.   (219)

Mackail saw Theocritus's contribution to the history of Greek
poetry as the application of 'the idyllic method' (219) to the
material of all three kinds of poetry which criticism distinguished at
this point when Theocritus wrote – lyric, epic and dramatic.
Mackail's central concern is with Theocritus so he does not stress
what we can see clearly, that in reworking the ancient poet
Tennyson adds a further dimension of reference to his own poems.
The reworking itself becomes a part of the already heavy framing of
the Idylls. What Tennysonian idyllicism shares with Theocritan is
its origin in handling or method not in material; and it follows from
Mackail's assumptions, and is borne out by the evidence of
Tennyson's poems, that the only constraint on the choice of material
is that it must be suitable for portrayal on a small and quasi-pictorial
scale.

An exquisite artistry, sweetness of language, an 'almost mystical
passion for beauty' (225) is brought, Mackail thinks, by both poets
to common everyday scenes. 'The attempt is both cases is to give
new life to poetry by bringing the subjects of poetry into fresh touch
with the modern world.' (224). He gives examples of what he calls
'the specifically idyllic manner which we may call indifferently
Theocritan or Tennysonian' (226), and follows them with examples
of realism in Theocritus's poems, 'current phrases of the populace',
for example, 'so used and so reset . . . to bring out some vivid latent
colour . . . ' (221). The 'reaiism or modernism' of Theocritus, he
says, 'is sometimes most striking in poems where the poetic artifice,
the idyllic convention, is most strongly marked. His effort after

realism issued in a form of poetry which has become the very type of unreality' (227). Mackail's is a useful voice here since he spoke so near to Tennyson's own time, but what he has to say is only a restatement of what succeeding generations find out in different vocabulary about the pastoral genre. In its extreme artificiality it often seems the readiest way of conveying a sophisticated view of the simplest lives. Its artistry is not at odds with its material so much as in an abrasive relationship with it. This is paradoxical because, though the means are disjunctive, the final effect in the idyll is of smoothness and calm. Among the novels I consider it seems that sometimes the art, as in *Adam Bede* or *The Woodlanders*, is more evident than the simplicity, and sometimes, as in *Cousin Phillis* or Mary Mitford's sketches, that simplicity obscures the art. Either way, I shall argue, artistry and simplicity can be most interestingly seen in a new equal relationship. Meanwhile, as examples of this exquisite and elaborate art brought to bear on simple modern things, I shall look at two of Tennyson's English Idyls, 'The Gardener's Daughter' and 'Dora'. They are chosen to show an idyllic method applied to widely different material with final effects, predictably, equally different. Among those poems about which there is no doubt of their being intended as 'Idyls', 'The Gardener's Daughter' is the most elaborate, 'Dora' the simplest.

'The Gardener's Daughter' is elaborate both in style and structure. Structurally, the elaboration springs from what looks like puzzling treatment of a sequence of events which make up a story of friendship, love, courtship, marriage and old age. In not telling the story sequentially the poem is able to explore without any final resolution the relationships of life and art, memory and dream, dream and art and so full circle back to life. The centre of the poem, 'full and rich' as Tennyson said it should be,[16] is the verbal picture of Rose, the gardener's daughter, as the narrator, a painter, first saw her in his youth. It records the moment when the anticipation aroused by her reputation for beauty is overwhelmed by the reality, the moment immediately preceding, but, in the memory, fusing with the falling in love. The last words of the poem are an invitation to the un-named hearer of the narrator's story to draw the veil concealing a portrait, which we have not known about before, of Rose as she was at that high moment. The painted picture is all the painter has, now that 'the idol of my youth,/The darling of my manhood' is only 'the most blessed memory of mine age'. The story, which is the poem, is told, it turns out, in order to impart to the

hearer some of the memory's glow before he sees behind the veil to
the portrait, which is veiled because, 'what it holds / May not be
dwelt on by the light of common day'. Art is less than life, the poem
seems to say; but life itself, as this story is told, grows out of the
artistic imagination, dissolves into anticipatory dream in youth,
and, in age, into memory encapsulated by art. It is not until the end
when the portrait – the mirror, one might say, of the poem – is about
to be unveiled, that the narrator's relation to the story in time is
made clear. The seeming promise of a chronological story contained
in the first line, 'This morning is the morning of the day' is
immediately belied by the unexpected past tense of the continuation: 'When I and Eustace from the city went / To see the
Gardener's Daughter . . .' Only the description of Eustace and
Juliet his betrothed, with whom the narrator had once been lightly in
love, and the occasion of their setting out to see Rose are described
in an ordinary sequence of cause and effect. The visit to the naïve
beauty is a kind of artistic wager between three sophisticated
friends. It takes them to a *locus amœnus*, where Eustace and Juliet
disappear from the account and Rose herself makes only brief and
blushing conversation before withdrawing. The narrator disappears into his own dream which the banter of Eustace on the way
home identifies as love, love which will show itself in Art, 'in hues to
dim / The Titianic Flora'. The picture of the beloved is not unveiled
in the poem except in the last retrospective gesture which recalls the
first sight of Rose to the reader, as to the imagined listener. The story
does not tell if it was a painting of the narrator's old age from a long
and loving memory, or a painting of recognition and anticipation
painted on his first return from the cottage. The ambiguity allows
both the living moment and the living memory to seem realised in
Art. What the memory of love at first sight does in the poem, is to
unite in the experience of one night, an accurate anticipation of the
future with a sense of presence in the actual moment which is
conveyed by the sensuous language:

> So home I went, but could not sleep for joy,
> Reading her perfect features in the gloom,
> Kissing the rose she gave me o'er and o'er,
> And shaping faithful record of the glance
> That graced the giving – such a noise of life
> Swarmed in the golden present, such a voice
> Called to me from the years to come, and such

> A length of bright horizon rimmed the dark.
> And all that night I heard the watchman peal
> The sliding season: all that night I heard
> The heavy clocks knolling the drowsy hours.
> The drowsy hours, dispensers of all good,
> O'er the mute city stole with folded wings,
> Distilling odours on me as they went
> To greet their fairer sisters of the East.

A further time dimension is added by the fact that this is recall. At the heart of this poem is the narrator's sense that time, in so far as it is significant, is only properly measured by the moments when perceptions are fused by one colouring emotion. This emotion not only colours but shapes; it is at the heart at once of living and creating. So the sequential story of courtship and marriage resolves into a series of pictures and the poem presents a total effect of being composed in 'pictures within pictures within pictures'.[17] Even time itself is rendered in pictures. It is shown flowing as nearly a year passes:

> The daughters of the year,
> One after one, through that still garden passed;
> Each garlanded with her peculiar flower
> Danced into light, and died into the shade . . .

And it is shown freezing in a generic and timeless picture of lovers who seem as nameless as they are enduring:

> There sat we down upon a garden mound,
> Two mutually enfolded; Love, the third,
> Between us, in the circle of his arms
> Enwound us both; and over many a range
> Of waning lime the gray cathedral towers,
> Revealed their shining windows . . .

The narrator in his old age is haunted by the passing of time, but his 'real' time, even his sense of continuity, is in isolated moments of high intensity.

At high moments in 'The Gardener's Daughter' painting and poetry are fused. The evolution of the poem through extensive revision and abridgement is interesting in this connection. John

Dixon Hunt thinks that the poem becomes more 'painterly' with revision.[18] Since the verbal pictures of the early versions are considerably reduced in number and extent there is a sense in which that is not true at all. But the poem certainly gains in intensity for the reduction of the pictorial descriptions and the concentration by which the pictorial is absorbed into a total effect contributes, by definition, to the achieved idyllicism of the final version. One effect of the reduction of verbal picture is to tie more closely together what remains of the picture and the emotion the passage is ultimately intended to convey. For example the garden of the gardener's cottage is described by means of the sounds of the city which reach 'you' in the garden 'sitting muffled in dark leaves', with a distant view of the 'clanging minster clock' above the 'three arches of a bridge'. The passage continues:

> The fields between
> Are dewy-fresh, browsed by deep-uddered kine,
> And all about the large lime feathers low,
> The lime a summer home of murmurous wings.

The last two lines here replace nine manuscript lines which are minutely visual like the foreground of a Pre-Raphaelite picture. The manuscript lines are effective and give the impression of a man seeking accuracy in recall, much as Wordsworth corrects himself in the description of the pastoral landscape round Tintern Abbey, 'hardly hedgerows, little lines / Of sportive wood run wild'. But the lines of the final version, in ceasing to be purely visual, wonderfully suggest the absorption of the narrator into the remembered picture while he seems simply to describe. It is one of the underlying paradoxes of this poem that at the moments of most complete absorption into the remembered events the narrator is also at his greatest 'distance' from them. In the manuscript version the sense of a man looking from an actual spot is strong. In the final version the actuality of a single moment has gone. Psychological reality is maintained through the manipulations of the chronological sequence of the story – the narrator would 'really' at the point of telling in old age remember both the journey to the *locus amœnus* which was Rose's home and the detail and emotion which hindsight attaches to it. Thus the 'real' moment is the present in which the elderly painter talks to someone about to be shown the veiled portrait. Isolated and anthologised the lines describing the garden

would retain a langorous charm and a visual generality which
would bring to mind the peaceful outskirts of large cities, real and
pictured. Inside the chronological convolutions of the poem they
fuse dream and memory in a verbal picture which gives the illusion
of being transferable to canvas. Art is thus at this point inseparable
from reality; it is the means by which the real is realised. The
function of the submerged narrative in 'The Gardener's Daughter'
is to provide a present and a point from which the narrator
establishes his perspective on the past and on the separated
elements, simple and sophisticated, of his perception of reality.

The poem was originally more obviously framed by means of Art
than it is now. 'The Ante-Chamber', which was intended as a
prologue, begins and ends with a picture. As the narrator ushers his
hearer through the door in the last paragraph of the prologue he
promises to show the veiled picture with which the poem proper
ends. The ante-chamber is dominated by a large self-portrait of
Eustace, which is described, and which prompts a comparison of his
friend with the narrator himself. In 'The Gardener's Daughter' as
Tennyson published it the veiled picture is kept for the end, and the
portrait is reduced to, 'My Eustace might have sat for Hercules / So
muscular he spread, so broad of breast.' The poem proceeds in
Theocritan manner with the friendly artistic rivalry and the wager
between the two painters. The reduction provides the poem as
published with a double frame. The opening now refers to
Theocritus in the friendly contest; it also places the two painters in
an artistic tradition. A portrait of Eustace as Hercules would no
doubt have borne the same relation to tradition as Tennyson's
poetic version of Ulysses bears to Homer and Dante; in imitating it
would also have absorbed distance and difference. The poem
transforms the Theocritan mode most notably by incorporating a
much stronger narrative element. The present is an unexplained
given in a Theocritan idyll and his shepherds have no biographies.
But the artistic wager in 'The Gardener's Daughter' leads the
narrator to Rose and Rose becomes the lifelong centre of the
painter's life. The story is not an extra to the idyllicism, it is
the means by which the idyllic picture is held in focus; the present is
a fictional construction which allows the reader to see not only the
fictional past but the reality of the present.

The story of 'Dora' does not have to be uncovered. The poem
('Oh dear, yes') tells a story. One reason why it is appropriately
included among the Idyls is suggested by the title of the trial volume

of 1842, *Morte d'Arthur; Dora; and Other Idyls*. The two poems picked
out to characterise the volume exist at the two extremes; one is an
heroic English legend, the other a contemporary story of simple
English life, simply told. The style in each case suits the subject.
Such simplicity as the simplicity of 'Dora' is hard-won. Tennyson
said, ' "Dora" being the tale of a nobly simple country girl, had to
be told in the simplest possible language, and therefore was one of
the poems that gave most trouble.'[19] He is here describing the effort
to achieve what Arnold, in a comment to which I shall return later
in this chapter, calls 'a semblance of simplicity' or what, he says, in
the richer vocabulary of French criticism is called *'simplesse'*.[20]
Dwight Culler, in general a sympathetic critic of the English Idyls,
thinks 'Dora' a mistake, 'not for Arnold's reason that it sacrifices
simplicité to *simplesse*, but because its harsh Crabbean realism is at
variance with the sentiment it ought to inspire'.[21] What Arnold
says, however, implies that since simplicity could never be aimed at
it could not be sacrificed; it is the product of the natural genius who,
like Homer, 'presents his thought to you just as it wells from the
source of his mind'. Tennyson is too 'subtle' (Arnold's word) a
genius for this ever to happen; in his poetry 'it is all distilled thoughts
in distilled words'. The *simplesse* which can result from this process of
distillation is, Arnold thinks, 'often very beautiful and valuable'.
What Professor Culler sees as the 'harsh Crabbean realism' of 'Dora'
is plain and noble – simple in one sense of that word, not in itself
harsh. The 'beauty and value' which Arnold saw could attach to
simplesse are in this poem contained in the 'beauty'of simplicity as it
is 'valued' from a sophisticated point of view. This is another way of
saying it is an idyll. The idyllic method Tennyson applied to the
realistic story keeps the poem within the bounds of what is possible
in the idyll, even if the harshness takes it to the very edge. It is
interesting that the method is basically the same as Clough used in
The Bothie, also in any first definition a narrative poem. In both
cases the style draws attention to itself as separate from the story
content.

In 'Dora' the style has two interrelated functions beyond a simple
presentation of events: it is a framing device in itself and it provides
at the same time a running social commentary on the story. The
Biblical style is, of course, one way of relating the modern story to
old stories and suggesting, as the mock-heroic does, both continuity
and difference between ancient and modern modes and values. The
idyllic balance of 'Dora' is partly a balance between the continuity

with patriarchal Biblical ways and the difference from them indicated in Dora's actions, which are the centre of the story. The opening of the poem places the characters inside the patriarchal system which makes social sense of the old man's later wilfulness:

> With Farmer Allan at the farm abode
> William and Dora. William was his son,
> And she his niece. He often looked at them,
> And often thought, 'I'll make them man and wife.'

The Biblical phrasing by which the story leaps over the intervening time, 'then there came a day', 'Then when the bells were ringing', 'And days went on and there was born a boy', gives extraordinary authority to the narrative voice. It also continuously suggests the inevitability for Dora of the system in which, taken in by her uncle as conscience money for the failure of his relations with his brother, she becomes his property, which he may dispose of as he likes. Dora 'feels her uncle's will in all', all, that is, which concerns herself. The turning-point in the story comes when she acknowledges her acquiescence as a *sin*. At this point the relationship of style and content shifts. Dora has suffered the tyranny of the system passively and without speech. Driven to action she is also driven to speech. When she went to Mary,

> Dora came and said:

> 'I have obeyed my uncle until now,
> And I have sinned, for it was all through me
> This evil came on William at the first.

At the point of accepting the vocabulary of the system she repudiates its values, at least for others if not for herself. When she changes passive endurance for active initiative it is with the goal of rescuing the living family from the dead hand of the past and the self-defeating authoritarianism of the child's grandfather. Her effort and its success are conveyed in the only verbal pictures in the poem. Dora sits with the baby wreathed in poppies on the little mound in the middle of the wheat in the hope that her uncle will gather him up with the rest of the harvest and see that like the ripe corn he both symbolises and is the future. Her success is signified in a picture glimpsed by the two women through the open door when Mary has

insisted on returning to the house to reclaim the boy if he is to oust
Dora from her home:

> The door was off the latch: they peeped, and saw
> The boy set up betwixt his grandsire's knees,
> Who thrust him in the hollows of his arm,
> And clapt him on the hands and on the cheeks,
> Like one that loved him: and the lad stretched out
> And babbled for the golden seal, that hung
> From Allan's watch, and sparkled by the fire.

These pictorial episodes are remarkable inside the poem because,
without making an abrupt departure from the established style,
they do mark a change of method. To begin with they deal with
single moments at comparative length in a narrative characterised,
as I have said, by bold and summary leaps in time. Secondly they
portray scenes which are particularised and located in a way which
marks them off from the rest of the poem. Outside these scenes the
significant moments in the story are carried in dialogue, the quarrel
between William and his father, Dora's proposal to Mary, Dora's
pleading with the farmer and his refusal, Mary's decision to take the
boy back and rear him in kindly poverty rather than leave him in
hard-hearted affluence with his grandfather, and finally Mary's
pleading for Dora and the old man's burst of remorse. There is no
attempt at realism in these exchanges. The characters are seen like
speaking statues – their speech mere gestures inside a pattern of
relationships. The voices are identical:

> he and I
> Had once hard words, and parted, and he died
> In foreign lands; but for his sake I bred
> His daughter Dora: take her for your wife.

> 'O Sir, when William died, he died at peace
> With all men; for I asked him, and he said,
> He could not ever rue his marrying me –
> I had been a patient wife.

The first is authoritative, the second pleading, but the well-to-do
farmer and the labourer's daughter are not otherwise distinguished
in manner than their emotional roles in the narrative demand. In

matter the dialogue focuses with the most rigorous economy on the crux of the situation, without preliminaries or deflection. The characters are given meaning only by their relationships inside the patriarchal system established at the opening. They speak and gesture inside an empty space, without scenery. On the other hand Dora's assertion of particularly Victorian values – those attached to hearth and home, where women and small children are at the centre – is signified by the only pictorial descriptions in the poem. In the final sequence the two women join the old man and the child in the firelight and the reconciliation is effected. The two pictures hold the poem together as an idyll. Since there are only two, one becomes linked in the mind with the other so that hearth is linked with harvest, the values of home with those of the fruitful countryside. The end has the characteristic double idyllic effect. In spite of its glow it is sadder than *The Bothie* which does not have to achieve its partial resolution out of death. Pictorially the end is a happy picture of three generations of people whose centre is home, the old, the women and the very young, but the notable absence from the picture is of an able-bodied working male. In the picture as picture he might have been only awaited. The picture as resolution of the narrative forces our recognition of the loss at the heart of gain. Dora, who lives 'unmarried till her death', pays the price for breaking the moulds in which the past cast the living relationships of the family by being unable even to consider breaking them for herself. The love which Dora can persuade her uncle to submit to is, for her, what binds her faithful heart to what her uncle had originally meant for her.

'Dora' is particularly interesting in relation to the novels I am to consider because it seems to tell a straightforward story of rural life. As such it establishes characters who, inside the situation indicated for them, behave credibly enough for our interest in outcome to be maintained. But the imperfect resolution of their story, the partial mending of their broken lives, is told by means which play against the narrative as it has been set up. The pictures alter the pace of the narrative, but continue it in time. In the significant final episodes the characters are shown newly depicted in their background. The harvest field and the warm hearth carry whatever elements of the ending one might regard as positive or upbeat. They indicate the supremacy of the love which will allow these people to live out tolerable lives. The characters are depicted against them in frozen moments, as though they were, as Raymond Williams says of the characters of *Adam Bede*, a part of the landscape.[22] The relation of picture and narrative varies in the novels I discuss in the later chapters as it does in the English Idyls. But a particular kind of interplay between picture and narrative is, I shall argue, a defining characteristic of the Victorian idyll in prose as it is in verse. Idyllic pictures, or pictures which are used inside an idyllic method, are, like those in 'Dora', of relationships.[23] The pattern of the relationships between the figures, and between the figures and the background is too complicated to allow of identification with a single figure. The pictures freeze the narrative against its natural flow. Yet in bearing the continuing values of the story, as in 'Dora', they may become themselves indications of a dimension of time which is not contained inside the narrative proper.

J. W. Mackail thought the idyll had a general tendency to 'break its bounds', and singled out 'Dora' as an example (221). In the longer poems of Tennyson towards which it points, 'Enoch Arden' and 'Aylmer's Field', he says, 'the balance between subject and treatment is on the point of being lost'. Narrative, of course, with its demand for continuity and progress will always pull against balance. And the multiple perceptions and time-levels that we have seen in operation in these poetic idylls are hard to keep in any equilibrium. A final balance requires what Mackail is here speaking of, 'a balance of subject and treatment'. We must feel at any single time the pressure of other possibilities than the one we can immediately see. We need, for example, in following the simple and romantic story of *The Bothie*, the continuous reminder of other ways of feeling and telling provided by the curious hexameters; or to appreciate the lifelong devotion of a painter to a gardener's daughter, we need to experience the way in which, memory and art being indistinguishable for him, he has absorbed her simplicity into the highest reaches of his sophistication. We may here recall Empson. Clearly elaboration of style and structure is one way in which simple subject-matter can be held in the constant focus of a complex point of view. But equally clearly we can also begin to see the implications of Arnold's remarks on 'Dora' for a general conception of the idyll. Where 'subject and treatment' are balanced in this way the work will have moved from Arnold's 'simplicity' and will approach his '*simplesse*'. Simplicity as Arnold describes it arises from a much more direct handling of the simple material than is to be found in general in the idyll. *Simplesse* implies consideration or reflection on the subject, what Arnold calls 'distillation' of thoughts

and words. There is therefore a gap or distance between the
speaking voice of the idyllic poet or narrator and his material.
Arnold quotes the openings and endings of 'Michael' and 'Dora' to
illustrate simplicity and *simplesse*; to continue this comparison is to
define further the idyllic quality of 'Dora' as a narrative and so lead
towards a consideration of idyllic fiction.

Wordsworth greatly admired 'Dora'. 'I have been trying all my
life to write a pastoral like your "Dora" and have not succeeded', he
said.[24] This is a remark reported from a conversation and there is no
evidence of exactly what he meant, but it does support my effort to
define differences without going into questions of relative value.
Arnold makes the point that his distinction operates most clearly
and often in narrative or dramatic poetry, 'in which the poet has to
go out of himself and to create'.[25] The relation of the narrator, who
has to be created to tell the story, to the material of his story, is here
my concern. It will later be a central concern in my discussion of the
novels. The sophisticated mediator of a simple story, with well-
defined personality and circumstance which differentiates him
clearly from the author, is a figure who may, like John Galt's
minister, remain the most memorable feature of the work. In
comparison with such a figure, the narrators of 'Michael' and
'Dora' share a greater degree of anonymity and desire to tell their
stories as though they had a kind of inevitability quite apart from
the point of view of the teller. But as Arnold shows simply in
quotation there is a fundamental difference between the two. The
narrator of 'Michael' seeks to persuade the reader to his own single
view by its power to move. The narrator of 'Dora' leaves room for
the reader to see from potentially conflicting points of view. From
the initial description which echoes the rhythm of the rough walking
it takes to reach 'the straggling heap of unhewn stones', the narrator
of 'Michael' seems to speak directly to an imagined reader, as much
listener as reader, whom he, as it were, wills to see with his eyes by
means of the poem. The prologue to the story establishes the point of
view – this narrator is *parti-pris* and makes no pretence of neutrality.
The landscape, 'With a few sheep, with rocks and stones, and kites /
That overhead are sailing in the sky', moves him unutterably, so
that even as a boy he loved the shepherds who dwelt in the valleys
and worked the hills for 'the fields and hills / Where was their
occupation and abode.' He will tell the simple tale, he says, as a poet
for whom love of the rugged landscape has opened his imagination
to the rude lives of the men who live there. The 'simplicity' of

'Michael' in Arnold's sense of directness (or direct handling of the material) is a complete expression of the transforming and fusing power of the imagination. The landscape, the social condition in which these people live, the economic pressures on them and their simple hold on traditional values are fused inside the single vision of the story of one old man. The title and the prologue are one continuous polemic – this 'Pastoral Poem' is not a poem about an imaginary shepherd whose tale will, in spite of his calling, be of things 'you', the reader, know about and recognise behind the stage properties of crook and pipe; this is a tale about a life 'you' do not understand. 'My' telling will delight 'you', he seems to say; it will also teach future poets where to look for histories, 'homely and rude' but with the power to move 'a few natural hearts'. The effort, then, of this narrator is to make the unfamiliar real by the power of his imagination; his absorbed sympathy entirely excludes any world but the one he is describing and any point of view of Michael beyond his, the narrator's, own 'true' one. The tragic calm of the end involves an understanding of Michael inside the total circumstances of his story. The simple directness and measured pace of the style mirrors the story. It offers no comment on it and draws no attention to itself. The poetic imagination is the transparency through which the story is seen in all its stark but rich simplicity. The poem is framed by discussion of poetic intention, but the telling is designed to annihilate distance.

'Dora', on the other hand, acquires distance as it proceeds. The opening gives the impression of being told without a narrator, but the voice is a strange one in which to tell a modern story and it soon becomes apparent as we adjust to it that, by means of the Biblical echoes of this style, we are accepting the values it mirrors, not as our own even temporarily, but as part of the story. Stripped of ornament and any echoes of the speaking voice, the style is bare to the point of stiffness. At the point when it becomes noticeable it has entered the story as an element. The youth and natural feelings of William and Dora are seen as opposed to the authoritarianism of the father as they are inexplicable inside the world of this style. Paradoxically, while there seems to be no room for a narrator as any discernible kind of person and the characters remain distinguishable only as parts of a pattern of relationships, we have been made aware within the first forty lines of the conflict of points of view which is the substance of the story. Our sympathies are not directed towards a single point – William in his way is as wilful as his father and Dora's

devotion to him as much an unexplained given as her submission to
her uncle. The story can only be appreciated as a pattern of
relationships between the characters. Dora's simple actions alter the
pattern but without altering our focus on it.

'Michael' and 'Dora' both tell stories of heroic endurance in
simple people, against a background of social change. Comparison
of the different ways in which the social background is made a part
of the total effect of these two poems isolates the idyllic quality of
'Dora'. It will be shown later that the idyllic novels I consider may
be partly distinguished from other novels by the same authors in this
respect also. In 'Michael' the whole effort of the poem is to establish
a fully realised present moment. If we choose to recognise the
economic pressure on the smallholder as part of an historical process
we import the knowledge from outside the poem. The poem holds
up the assumptions, the modest and traditional aspirations and the
steadfast passion and frugality of Michael for us to understand and
admire. They are made explicit; we are not required to construct
them and we have no room to see the possibility of others. Luke's
defection is understandable in the merely human terms of human
weakness in the face of temptation. In the story it does not represent
the inevitable social future, only something with which Michael has
to contend in the story. The unfinished sheepfold is the loss of hope.
The end has the calm of tragic despair. These are the timeless terms
of Christian tragedy, translated into a vividly recreated background. The dimension of historical time outside the continuity of
events in the story has to be invented for 'Michael' if we wish it to be
there, and it remains external to the poem. A similar omission in
'Dora' is of psychological motivation in the characters whose actions
we have to accept without explanation. William and Luke both
break the pattern of patriarchal authority. But where the pattern in
'Michael' is the traditional one, its rupture is seen in the poem as a
betrayal of trust and love as well as authority and as one which can
only be endured, not in any way transcended. On the other hand
love triumphs in 'Dora' at least partially. In the poem its most
notable effect is in the shift of social values from patriarchal ways to
gentler ways in which women lead. The awareness of historical
change is as I have already noted established by means of style. It
might be said that while the story of 'Michael' is intensely realised
and engages our sympathies fully it lacks the dimension of historical
time. The narrator of 'Dora' on the other hand, at some sacrifice of
intensity, has incorporated historical time into his story as counter-

point to his narrative time. The calm in which the story of 'Dora' is left is not tragic like the noble stillness in which we leave Michael, nor, of course, has everything turned out all right after all. The calm is one of balance, held precariously against the flux of time, which is felt as strongly as the stillness.

The poetic idylls of the mid-century are characterised, it can be seen, by a balance within the elements of the story, and an interplay of different time-levels and perceptions of value. A firmly held narrative stance is required to hold them together in their mutual dependence and temporary balance. The narrator of 'Michael' has such a hold and it further involves the double consciousness of his simple subject and of himself as poet-observer which is a given for pastoral at all periods. But in telling the story of 'Michael' his effort is first to acknowledge and then to remove all distance between himself and his subject. In the true idylls the effort is to preserve it. The preservation of distance allows the elements to be held in perspective; they remain, in spite of the continuity of the narrative, in simultaneous focus so that their disparities are shown in mutually reflecting relationships. The final effect is the sum of these relationships. The art is one of paradoxes held in any single work in a fleeting glimpse of balance or suspension of opposing perceptions. It follows that the development of some elements of the ordinary sequence of cause and effect will have to be curtailed if such a balance is to be maintained. Characters, for instance, may have to be given rather than developed. In 'Michael' the central figure is representative and idealised rather than individualised, but the focus on him is so narrow and intense and the relation between his character and his social background and environment so subtly depicted that our sympathy gives the illusion of knowledge of him as an individual. In 'Dora' and *The Bothie* alike, our interest is directed to the changing pattern of relationships not to individuals. Both poems ultimately describe a radical adjustment of values through the change in the relationships. We are told only as much of the characters as will define their role in the pattern. The novels in the following chapters make comparable choices to achieve perspect-ive. Depth of characterisation and exploration of motive, for instance, do not characterise among those novels I call idyllic, *Cousin Phillis, Adam Bede* or *Far from the Madding Crowd*. The human centre of these books is a pattern of relationships. The narrative interest is in the shifting of the patterns in the course of the book, and the impression of depth proceeds not from the intensity of the focus on individuals, but from the interplay of perceptions of time and value which parallels the changing pattern of human relations. This allows us to participate in a mode of development dependent on the relation of parts rather than continuity of psychological development. These authors are all capable of an intense single focus as is evidenced by *Ruth*, *Romola* and *Jude the Obscure*. But these three latter novels, in removing the distance between the narrator and the central figure forgo the interplay of possibilities which distance allows and which is the strength of an idyll.

In choosing *The Bothie of Tober-na-Vuolich* and Tennyson's English Idyls to define a peculiarly Victorian 'version of pastoral I have drawn attention at the same time to the difficulties inherent in any such attempt. The poems are in so many ways immediately so unlike that mere listing indicates the difficulties. 'Michael' throws many characteristics of the other poems into relief by sharing so much with them and being in final effect so fundamentally different. The difference does not derive from elements the works contain. A discussion of the Victorian idyll as a version of pastoral cannot point to any single element which is not found used to quite other ends elsewhere. Our perception of the characters in *The Bothie*, in 'Dora' and in 'Michael', for example, is governed in all three poems by their relation to their rural background, but the use of it inside these three poems once again shows the likeness of *The Bothie* and 'Dora', and their difference from 'Michael'. 'Michael' is distinguished by the particularity of the description of the old man's way of life and the economic pressures on him; the detail serves in this poem, as I have suggested, to give the impression of individuality in an otherwise generalised figure. In *The Bothie* the natural beauty of Elspie's background is described, but in the pattern of the poem it is assumed, as one of the defining qualities of Elspie just as Oxford is of the undergraduates. Philip and Elspie can make the story by stepping out of their settings, because in the story's terms their initial relation to their backgrounds is assumed not explored. In 'Dora' the farm is visualised only at the point of the harvest to mark the first change in the pattern of relationships. Comparison reveals endless paradoxes. 'Dora', for instance, while retaining its idyllic quality by distancing the reader from the story, lacks the most obvious distancing device of all – a frame which separates the narrator from what he tells us.

A further complexity is that not only can single devices be used to different ends, some idyllic, some unidyllic, in different contexts, but no one element in these works can by itself indicate an idyllic perspective. 'Michael', for instance, unidyllic by reason of its single focus and some didacticism, is framed in a way which elsewhere establishes idyllic distance. The narrator of 'Michael' uses his double consciousness of himself in relation to his story as we have seen to set up the situation from which he will bring his reader to his own position of unequivocal absorption in Michael's story. The imaginative act by which he disappears in presenting the story directly to us is itself a lesson to future poets in how to see from this documented account the potential for grandeur in humble circumstances. In Wordsworth's definition of the *idyllium*, which I shall look at shortly, an intention to teach removes a poem from the range of the idyll. While the narrator of 'Dora' plunges into his story directly without introductory frame, the Biblical style of the telling has exactly the same function as an introductory verse or 'frame'. Among the English Idyls Tennyson uses such a frame for 'Godiva', and 'The Epic', which introduces and concludes 'Morte d'Arthur'. Both devices, continuous style and proem, are used to the same end, to bring the past into the same focus as the present of the poem. The time-relation is thus presented as part of the total effect, or one aspect of the sum of parts the end must take account of. To be able to keep the time-levels held in relation to one another, to make the continuous comparison which the method invites, the reader cannot become totally absorbed in the present of the poem. This is only another way of saying that the poet must establish and maintain the distance from which we are expected to see.

'Distance', of course, presents a considerable critical problem in often being taken to imply an unacceptable degree of emotional detachment. Since in pastoral the subject-matter is always simple, the lack of involvement is often taken to be condescension or, at best, social awkwardness in face of the unfamiliar or different. It would seem clear, for instance, that at the beginning of 'Godiva' Tennyson is establishing his distance from the scene of the ancient legend for the purpose of keeping the past and present in simultaneous view:

> I waited for the train at Coventry;
> I hung with grooms and porters on the bridge,
> To watch the three tall spires; and there I shaped
> The city's ancient legend into this: –
>
> Not only we, the latest seed of Time,
> New men, that in the flying of a wheel
> Cry down the past, not only we, that prate

Of rights and wrongs, have loved the people well,
And loathed to see them overtaxed; but she
Did more, and underwent, and overcame,
The woman of a thousand summers back,
Godiva, wife to that grim Earl, who ruled
In Coventry:

Leigh Hunt, however, thought the framing devices by which the ancient legends of 'Godiva', and 'Morte d'Arthur' too, are brought into relation with the present had a 'boyishness' which he would be 'happy to see Mr Tennyson, who is no longer a boy, outgrow'.[26] Hunt thought the 'exordiums' to these two poems, 'little better than the rhyming fine-ladyism of Miss Seward, who said she used to translate an ode of Horace "while her hair was curling".' His radical susceptibility was aroused by the singling out of grooms and porters for mention 'with contempt and nonchalance' in the four lines prefixed to 'Godiva'. 'The Epic', Hunt thought, was intended to 'excuse' the 'Homeric echoes' which could properly be included in a modern poem only with some 'self-banter'. In confusing the narrator with the poet Hunt fails to appreciate the difference made to the total effect when the recreation of old legends is seen explicitly in reference to the present. 'Self-banter' as a continuing focus on the material of the poem assumes the poet is always, *qua* poet, diminished by poetic echoes of the past. But the separated frame of these two poems enables Tennyson to make a statement of a different kind about the relation of the present to the past in art and life. The 'poet' who thinks of Godiva as he waits for the train is not Tennyson congratulating himself for rubbing shoulders with grooms and porters, but a figure in the narrative remarking that the business of life goes on in one age as in another with the everyday work the age demands. The train for which he waits is a modern phenomenon on the same territory as a legendary act of a woman who identified herself with the poor and starving among her own kind, 'the others who brought / Their children, clamouring, "If we pay, we starve!"'

The importance of the 'presentation' of the legend of Godiva as an indication of idyllic method is twofold. Firstly the relation between past and present is presented as one of style; the quatrain is humble in style, the retold legend lofty. The idyllic is conscious of and explicit about its own artistry, and makes its statements frequently by drawing attention to the presentation. Secondly, the relation is presented without explicit judgement; the introduction and the legend together remark on the neutral fact of continuity, and the nature of the relation is left for construction by the reader, who is invited simply to look at the two temporarily in the same frame. The reader may, like Hunt, refuse the invitation but one of the paradoxes of the idyllic method is that while the narrator distances the material, he at the same time exploits the reader's compulsion to fill gaps by persuading him to connect separate entities by means of the context the artist provides. I shall argue that in the richest and most complex of the idyllic novels I consider, *Adam Bede* and *The Woodlanders*, the relation of narrator and reader is the closest. It may be that this is why a tendency to confuse narrator and author leads readers to see a patronising George Eliot in *Adam Bede*, and an intolerably pessimistic Thomas Hardy in *The Woodlanders*. We may again compare 'Michael' which deliberately sets out to remove distance. One of the reasons why we give in so readily to Wordsworth's portrait of Michael is that we recognise the poet's voice in the introduction which thus authenticates what we are going to see. In 'Michael' there is no invitation to the reader to see for himself; in the story proper there is no gap between reader, poet and story. The reader's task is to absorb the poet's vision as the poet has absorbed the reality. This is not an idyllic method. But since any single element of the idyllic method may be used, as we have seen, with quite different effects in different contexts, it will be as well now to look at two further nineteenth century descriptions of the idyllic to distinguish more clearly the final effect which justifies calling a work an idyll.

I have already used Matthew Arnold's distinction between simplicity and *simplesse*, and I have enlarged on his comparison of 'Michael' and 'Dora' to show the way in which the *simplesse* of 'Dora' may be said to constitute the essential quality of its idyllicism.[27] The 'distillation' of thought and expression which Arnold notes in comparison with the directness of 'Michael' means that the simple story of 'Dora' is presented side by side with the poet's reflection on it. What Tennyson finally conveys is a picture of a simple life and, at the same time, his distinctly contemporary perception of it in relation to the historical past. In the poem the feelings and values are juxtaposed against the values of the narrator's present. Arnold's sense that for all its starkness 'Dora' is characterised by its reflective quality is not, in the nineteenth century, an isolated perception of how simple lives can be presented. It was convenient to quote it first because it attaches the idea to two important nineteenth-century poems. But although his opposition of 'Dora' and 'Michael' in this way has an elegant and seminal simplicity, it is not explicitly related to the idyll. What he says, however, can be supported, elaborated and given further particularity as an implied description of what I am calling the idyllic by two earlier nineteenth-century views. These are both explicit descriptions of the idyll, one brief, the other extended. Wordsworth's own definition of the idyll occurs in the 1815 Preface. Even earlier, in 'Naive and Sentimental Poetry' (1795–6), Schiller describes the idyll as one 'sentimental' or reflective mode. The three views derive from independent standpoints. Together they offer different ways of expressing the artistic possibility of presenting simple subject-matter simultaneously with comment or reflection on it, and of achieving by such apparently opposing means a single harmonious effect. From Schiller to Arnold in 1860 they span two-thirds of the century and show the pervasiveness of this thinking through the period covered by the novels I consider. Only *The Woodlanders* lies well outside the time covered by these comments.

Wordsworth himself defines the *idyllium* by a list of examples more remarkable at first glance for their differences than their similarities. The poems he lists are united by subject-matter – nature or simple life – but more deeply by the authorial intention which determines the 'mould in which they are cast'. The *idyllium* is the fourth of the six categories into which he divides all poetry:[28]

> 4thly, The Idyllium, – descriptive chiefly either of the processes and appearances of external nature, as the 'Seasons' of Thomson; or of characters, manners, and sentiments, as are Shenstone's 'Schoolmistress', 'The Cotter's Saturday Night' of Burns, 'the Twa Dogs' of the same author; or of these in conjunction with the appearances of Nature, as most of the pieces of Theocritus, the 'Allegro' and 'Penseroso' of Milton, Beatties 'Minstrel', Goldsmith's 'Deserted Village', The Epitaph, the Inscription, the Sonnet, most of the epistles of poets writing in their own persons, and all loco-descriptive poetry, belong to this class.

These examples suggest not only the elaboration of means which may be employed in 'description', but the specific comparisons through which the simple is realised. Rural family life in 'The Cotter's Saturday Night', for instance, is directly presented in dialect and reflected on in standard poetic diction. Strangely the

final effect of the poem is of smoothness. The harmony is achieved by
the uniformity of the stanza form on the one hand, and an unbroken
sympathy on the other. The narrator passes from recorded observation to celebratory comment giving the illusion, despite the
difference in the language employed, that they are the same thing –
to see in this poem is to admire. But the sophistication is informed
and authenticated; the interaction of the dialect stanzas and those in
conventional diction places the frugal virtues and open-heartedness
of the family in the contexts of history as well as of a varied national
social pattern. Beattie and Shenstone in Wordsworth's list both
paint contemporary portraits with borrowings from ancient styles
which place or frame their subjects in historical continuity and in a
comparative scale of values which ensures that neither the present
nor the humble is diminished. The doubt which exists about
whether Shenstone saw his poem as a burlesque or not adds an
interesting ambiguity. Wordsworth thought that the 'absurd prose
commentary' indicating his lack of seriousness, which Shenstone
added and then subsequently dropped, was just a symptom of
Shenstone's timidity.[29] The Spenserian style for Wordsworth was a
means of revitalising a language which would be capable of
conveying accurately a particular perception of present reality. In
fact all the long descriptive poems Wordsworth names here describe
by means of comparison and oppositions. *The Deserted Village*, for
example, paints the decaying village by keeping a vision of what it
was constantly before the reader and by describing the departure of
the dispossessed villagers to the hostile city and far parts of the world.
The continuity of art as a means of encapsulating the ever-changing
present is here suggested by a glimpse into the future rather than a
reference to the past. Poetry herself finally departs with the
emigrants to continue to record and support the enduring virtue of
the simple, 'self-dependent' poor. Wordsworth's final poetic kinds
are the didactic and the satiric. The descriptive *idyllium* is very near
to both, so near that the three, he says, can be joined in 'a composite
order, of which Young's "Night Thoughts" and Cowper's "Task"
are excellent examples'. Clearly between these two kinds with their
explicit object of influencing the reader directly the 'descriptive'
idyll is a balancing act of some dexterity.

There are senses in which the greater the precariousness of the
balance the more 'idyllic', in this nineteenth-century sense, a work
may be thought to be. This is a paradox illuminated by Schiller's
'Naïve and Sentimental Poetry',[30] in which the idyll, one of the

three 'sentimental' modes, is characterised by balance. Writing earlier than Arnold or Wordsworth, Schiller is the connection between them in my argument.[31] Arnold's distinction between simplicity and *simplesse* is clearly related to the general distinction between the 'naïve' and the 'sentimental'. His view of Homer in 'On Translating Homer' is very like Schiller's, as is his conception of Shakespeare in the sonnet, 'Others abide our question. Thou art free.'[32] Arnold's essay has a specific literary task in mind and, while the implications of what he has to say go beyond the immediate problem of translating the ancient poem, the substance of the essay is critical and the illustrations are all literary. The range of Schiller's essay is, of course, philosophical; in so far as it is part of the history of the Romantic imagination it pushes towards transcendance or 'ideality' in the sense of pure thought. But his concern with modes of perception (*Empfindungsweise*) implicit in the text and determining the response of the reader, justifies consideration of Arnold's *simplesse* as an instance in Schiller's wider conception of the 'sentimental' mode.

While it is Schiller's view of the idyll as a moment of balance or equilibrium which is really my concern here, some aspects of the general view of which it is a part provide a background not only to the nineteenth-century depiction of the simple life, but to the general questions of the transformation of ancient modes and the relative nature of definition which underlie my study. The sentimental or reflective mode is necessarily a product of civilisation, though civilisation does not rule out the naïve experience. 'The poet . . . either *is* nature or he will seek her' (110). No longer in touch with Nature as an actual experience the poet seeks it as an idea:

> The correspondence between his feeling and thought which in the first condition *actually* took place, exists now only *ideally*; it is no longer within him, but outside of him, as an idea still to be realised, no longer as a fact in his life. (111)

> Die Übereinstimmung zwischen seinem Empfinden und Denken, die in dem ersten Zustande wirklich stattfand, existiert jetzt bloss idealisch; sie ist nicht mehr in ihm, sondern ausser ihm, als ein Gedanke, der erst realisiert werden soll, nicht mehr als Tatsache seines Lebens. (22–3)

Schiller is at pains in this portion of his essay to make clear that he is not comparing ancient times with modern, but, as Arnold does, types of poetic temperament in both ancient and modern poetry. Thus, while to use an ancient mode in modern times is necessarily to reflect on it and also necessarily to produce something 'very new' (147n), any mode of perception may exist at any time. The idyll is the third, and least attainable of the sentimental modes Schiller describes. The 'universal concept' of the idyll is, Schiller says, that it is the poetic representation of 'innocent and contented mankind'. Such a state seems at odds with civilisation, but the usually removed scene of an idyll is only incidental to its main purpose, which is simply the depiction of man 'in a state of innocence, i.e. in a condition of harmony and peace with his environment' (146–7). There is throughout Schiller's essay, and nowhere more crucially than on this issue, a puzzle about where, if anywhere, the line is to be drawn between the 'idea of' and the 'ideal' in its common and emotive sense. I take it that, as in the sentence just quoted where the 'ideal' is *explained as* an 'idea', the word 'ideal' in this section of the essay is not specifically value-laden. It thus seems admissible to relate the gap between the actual and the 'ideal', as described by Schiller, with Arnold's conception of the reflection on, or 'distillation' of thoughts about, simplicity as it is conveyed in *simplesse*. Schiller in fact says that the sentimental poet '*reflects* upon the impression objects make upon him, and only in that reflection is the emotion grounded which he himself experiences and which he excites in us' (116). [Diefer reflektiert über den Eindruck, den die Gegenstände auf ihn machen, und nur auf jene Reflexion ist die Rührung gegründet, in die er selbst versetzt wird und uns versetzt (26).] The naïve and the sentimental are ways of perceiving the same reality but they transform it differently into art. The idyll is not a naïve mode since naïve poetry conveys the 'state of innocence' and the conditions in which it is found as one. Sentimental poetry 'refers actual conditions [den wirklichen Zustand], at which [naïve poetry] halts, to ideas, and applies ideas to actuality' (146n). Meaning in all three sentimental modes thus resides in the relation of the 'idea' to the 'actual conditions' in which it is embodied. The names he gives to the modes, 'satiric', 'elegiac', 'idyllic', refer not to generic forms (such as the novel or tragedy), but to the 'mood into which the poetic species known by these names place the mind' (146n). Where idea and actuality are seen to contradict one another the mode of perception is satiric; where there is a sense of separation so strong as to amount to loss the mode is elegiac. The idyllic perception, in Schiller's view, is the least attainable of the three. Grounded no less than the other two in a sense of a separation between the ideas of innocence (its characteristic subject-matter) and the conditions in which such innocence may be found, it depicts the momentary, harmonious coexistence of idea and actuality as a cause of joy. The moment is one of 'dynamic calm' (energische Ruhe), the 'calm of perfection, not of inertia . . . accompanied by a feeling of infinite capacity' (153).

This moment of stillness containing the potential for movement, this moment of equilibrium or balance, is not easy to sustain. Certainly the idyllic is not a mode any of the authors I discuss stay in throughout their total work. The idyllic vision comes, characteristically, early in their writing careers. Since achievement, and initial perception too, of the idyllic moment requires what Mackail calls 'a balance of subject and treatment', it comes early, it could be argued, because this is a stage when a writer is most conscious of his art as art – none of it has been internalised as in some way natural to him. In his section on the idyll (short because he intended to write more on the subject later, though he never did) Schiller illustrates an inherent difficulty in the mode. His example is from Gessner,[33] probably the first Romantic pastoralist. It is particularly telling in relation to idyllic narrative since it concerns the creation of convincing character:

> One of Gessner's shepherds . . . cannot delight us as nature by the fidelity of the imitation, since he is too ideal a being; he can as little satisfy us by infinitude of thought since for this he is much too inadequate a creature. (151)

The thought (or reflection) in the sentimental mode, which has 'the unconditional freedom of the faculty of ideas' (156) is the poet's, not the subject's. The attendant problem is to give a convincing reality to the character's field of action. A great deal of authorial tact is required to achieve just the right mixture of individuality and generality, and Schiller thinks Gessner did not succeed. I shall argue that if the novels I discuss are considered in their total unity, that is without abstracting separate elements so as to measure them against an external reality, they can be seen, each in its own individual way, to deal with this problem. They direct attention away from a central figure and create a harmony between him and his field of action. They elicit the reader's creative response to the limited circumstances of a fictional world and call its limitations to mind by reminders in the story-telling of other ways of telling. Their deliberate restriction of range and scale, their minute attention to the actuality of a small world tends away from the transcendence of 'idealism', but the existence of the 'ideal' remains as a function of the precarious harmony achieved.[34] Such harmony, between a convincingly real world and the potentialities within it, which can be activated by the reader, is largely suggested by the variety of alternatives in the means of presentation. The reader is alerted to the continuing presence of alternative modes of seeing because they are indicated as possibilities in the text. The range of the reader's thoughts, or, in Schiller's words, his sense of 'capacity', if not 'infinite', reaches at least to the very edges of the world he has entered, and his sense of mastery is lodged in his creative activity. There still remains, however, the problem which is at once the difficulty and the supreme achievement of the novels in my later chapters. Centrally concerned as they all are with social change, they share the inherent difficulty of the bucolic idylls Schiller describes. These, Schiller says, set the scene of innocence in a Golden Age, but innocence is a continuing human potential and the idylls set out so to picture it: '*Theoretically*, then, they lead us backwards, while *practically* they lead us forward and ennoble us' (149). An idyll in verse or prose is successful not only to the extent to which it can temporarily fuse a particular reality and a representative idea, but also to the extent to which, at the level of emotional response, it can balance loss and hope.

It will be seen that the idyllic balance is a balance at all three levels of perception and response, emotional, intellectual and aesthetic. It is made, as equilibrium always is, out of the potential for movement. Between the didactic and the satiric in Wordsworth's categories, and the satiric and elegiac in Schiller's, the idyllic presents a more static vision than either mode to which it is close. But to put it in this way is to emphasise stasis at the expense of the inherent or potential movement which characterises the idyll. In Schiller's view the expression of this particular kind of motion is the central difficulty of the idyll:

for the very reason that all resistance vanishes it will then be incomparably more difficult than in the two former types of poetry to represent *motion*, without which, however, no poetic effect whatsoever can be conceived. (153-4)

Aber eben darum, weil aller Widerstand hinwegfällt, so wird es hier ungleich schwieriger als in den zwei vorigen Dichtungsarten, die Bewegung hervorzubringen, ohne welche doch überall keine poetische Wirkung sich denken lässt. (55)

Schiller's vocabulary nowhere clearly differentiates between the psychology of response and the aesthetic problems of presentation. Here as he draws to the close of his brief, incomplete section on the idyll, he refers, apparently, to presentation. In coming to characteristic nineteenth-century expressions of the idyllic mode of perception we may here recall a related modern view of pastoral art as the expression of unresolved oppositions.[35] Any art which presses towards resolution works against the idyllic perception. One kind of resolution is the intellectual judgement in favour of one or other opposed side; this pushes a work towards the didactic or satiric in Wordsworth's terms, towards the satiric in Schiller's. Schiller's conception of the elegiac, the other mode close to the idyllic, is characterised by emotional movement, an oscillation between loss and hope. The idyllic is an art to which the reader is meant to respond with a suspension of completed judgement and a recognition of potentially conflicting emotion. In the analyses of the idyllic poems of Clough and Tennyson above I emphasised methods of achieving simultaneity in the relation of parts. But the idyllic representation is often a temporary reconciliation of means which in themselves tend in different directions. The realistic novel accentuates the element of movement in the idyllic equilibrium since it both requires time in the reading before it can be perceived as a whole, and, in itself, represents a continuity of time. Stories tend to resolution, the depiction of character to development, the depiction of circumstances to explanation of cause and exploration of effect. The idyllic novel must seek ways to halt progress in order to show permanent or potential relationships from a static point of view. There must be, as it were, an anti-novel inside the novel, a picture inside the story.

The word 'picture' here is not just an analogy. Picture and story are, it seems, inseparable in the nineteenth-century depiction of the 'characters, manners and sentiments' of simple people in a rural or natural setting. To look back on 'The Cotter's Saturday Night', for

instance, from the point of view of the reader of Clough or
Tennyson, is to see the opportunity for narrative which Burns, as it
were avoided. The introduction of Jenny's sweetheart is rendered
with as little sense of the before and after of the occasion as is
consistent with the aim of describing the manners and sentiments of
the family. In the frame of the narrator's comment the present
moment of the 'Saturday Night' is sufficient. Similarly framed (in
Spenserian style and less direct comment than Burns's family),
Shenstone's schoolmistress is shown in a series of quite formal
vignettes which do not tempt inquiry of before and after. By
contrast, Southey's English Eclogues of 1801, the first English
poems written in imitation of Gessner's *Idyllen* (not themselves
narratives), are all narratives. In each eclogue the frame is an
established poetic present in which, characteristically, a traveller
questions a native about some event. The answer is a 'history' which
forms the main substance of the poem. The tendency to idyllic
narrative continues through the century. *The Bothie* approaches the
length of a verse novel, and the English Idyls have a central
narrative element. In the new-fashioned 'unaffected prose pastoral'
of Mary Mitford narrative and description mingle as a means of
evoking a picture of rural life. Nineteenth-century paintings of
common life parallel the compulsion to narrative in literary
representation. Titles such as 'Waggoner with Horses', or 'Rustics
at a Cottage Door', which characterise the works of Gainsborough,
Morland or Francis Wheatley, for instance, give way to such
nineteenth-century evocations of story as 'A Hopeless Dawn', 'An
Intercepted Letter', or 'Where's Grandpa?' These later pictures are
not complete without the continuous narrative the viewer reads into
the frozen moment. The eighteenth century generalised by means of
a lack of particularity. The nineteenth century generalises its more
particular depiction of scene and its greater interest in individuality
by means of story. Realism, it seems, creates a need for narrative – as
explanation and development.

In many Victorian genre paintings the static relationships
portrayed in the picture are given the meaning which allows us to
see them as representative by the sense of before and after they
contain. The Victorian idyllic novel, which depicts at length the
'characters, manners and sentiments' of simple people, relies on this
potential for generalisation in the relation of story and picture. In
some senses each novel reaches for the static condition of a picture in
which all the relationships can be seen at once. The immediate

expectation raised by narrative, is, however, very different. The reader's task may be compared with that of the viewer in front of a genre painting in that each will achieve a complete response by a correction of expectation – the one by imagining a continuity of event when all he can see is a single charged moment, the other by resting in simultaneous relationships when he is being carried along in a continuity of time. The novels discussed in later chapters seek a single focus on disparate elements. They do not necessarily reach a fully resolved ending and they leave sufficient space, or distance, for the reader to experience briefly a moment of delicate equilibrium in contemplating the relationships depicted. In the sub-title of *Under the Greenwood Tree*, 'A Rural Painting of the Dutch School', Hardy makes explicit the comparison with a painting. In this novel an ambiguous ending directs the attention back to the relation of parts in the absence of final resolution. *The Woodlanders*, I shall argue, achieves coherence as a picture in an Impressionist mode. But the earlier idyllic novels are, like *Under the Greenwood Tree*, more usefully compared with the contemporary realist mode of genre, the descendent of the Dutch pictures. While the main effects of pictorial stasis on narrative show in the structure of the story, in final ambiguity, for instance, or curtailed development, particularly in character, it is clear that painters and novelists share a view of their simple subject-matter as at once worthy of artistic treatment and intrinsically resistant to it. They are challenged by the gap between the consciousness of the observer and the obliviousness of the observed to find means of making the simple significant without falsification, and at the same time of retaining an honest perception of difference. The function of Hardy's sub-title, as of George Eliot's famous discussion of Dutch paintings of common life in chapter XVII of *Adam Bede*, is to declare the subject-matter 'low', and at the same time to cite authority for its worth as a representation of permanent values. In this sense both authors are proclaiming their membership of a 'realist' school.

The realism of the novels, as of the paintings, is designed to assert the values underlying their subject-matter – geniality and openness, delicacy and domesticity. This is not so much to deny the values of public life as to seek to incorporate public glamour and possibility into a picture of admirable private life. Pater describes the process and assumes its connection with the novel in his 'Imaginary Portrait' of Sebastian Storck. The artists who gathered in the prosperous house of Burgomaster Van Storck are the manufacturers of products for the leisured class. They brought, as well as landscapes designed to reinforce their patron's conception of Holland's individual beauty,[36]

> innumerable genre pieces – conversation, music, play – [which] were in truth the equivalent of novel-reading for that day; its own actual life, in its own proper circumstances, reflected in various degrees of idealisation, with no diminution of the sense of reality (that is to say) but with more and more purged and perfected delightfulness of interest. Themselves illustrating, as every student of their history knows, the good-fellowship of family life, it was the ideal of that life which these artists depicted; the ideal of home in a country where the preponderant interest of life, after all, could not well be out of doors.

The realism allows what is genuinely 'common' to hold the attention of the idealising mind. Max J. Friedländer, defining genre painting by what it is not, not religious, not Biblical, not historical, sees generalisation as the quality which distinguishes genre from historical painting:[37]

> Everything that man's activity offers to the physical eye is so much grist to the genre painter, material in which he can discern the typical, whatever is peculiar to this or that kind of man. Anybody observing the battle of Waterloo as a truth-loving eye-witness, like Stendhal, sees nothing but genre. The painter can turn the battle-picture into an historical picture if, looking back from his knowledge of the decisive significance and results of the event, he sets about it with hero-worshipping imagination. Without the 'pathos of distance' (in time) the historical picture cannot thrive. Observed with the unspoken thought: 'This is how it always is', the event becomes a genre picture; observed with the knowledge that 'it was like that at one particular time and place', it becomes an historical picture. Strictly speaking, nothing is *in itself* genre-like or historical, only thinking makes it so.

Such 'thinking' means that as genre grew in popularity through the early years of the century it defined itself in relation to the older and recently popular historical painting. The significance of the common can really only be perceived in terms of the singular. In 1866 in their chapter on genre painting in *A Century of British Painters*

Samuel and Richard Redgrave show how the art of the most famous
early genre painters evolved out of initial attempts at history
painting. David Wilkie, who first showed 'how Dutch art might be
nationalised and story and sentiment added to scenes of common
life',[38] like Mulready after him, only took to invented subjects after
'emerging from historic art'. Leslie too 'passed from the "grand
historic period" as a student to the illustration of incidents in the
work of the poets and classic writers'.[39] The 'emergence' was not
necessarily complete as is shown by the history of Wilkie's 'British
Soldiers Regaling at Chelsea', which, commissioned by Wellington
after Waterloo, 'eventually became almost historical, although not
undertaken with that idea'.[40]

The reception of such pictures too included a sense of their
relationship to a grander and more usual conception of significance.
Thackeray welcomed the new mode and the deposition of the
heroic. As 'M. A. Titmarsh' he wrote to 'Sanders McGilp, Esq' on
the Academy Exhibition of May 1843:[41]

> The heroic, and peace be with it! has been deposed; and our
> artists, in place, cultivate the pathetic and the familiar. But a few,
> very few, worshippers of the old gods remain. There are only two
> or three specimens in the present exhibition of the grand historic
> style. . . . The younger painters are content to exercise their art
> on subjects far less exalted: a gentle sentiment, an agreeable,
> quiet incident, a tea-table tragedy, or a bread-and-butter idyl,
> suffices for the most part their gentle powers. Nor surely ought
> one to quarrel at all with this prevalent mode. It is at least
> natural, which the heroic was not.

Naturalism, restraint, quietness of appeal, lack of exaggeration are
prized along with finish and skill in the painting. If along with these
virtues the selected moment contains within itself an overt narrative, then the result is near perfection:

> Mr Stone's 'Last Appeal' is beautiful. It is evidently the finish
> of the history of the two young people who are to be seen in the
> Water-Colour Exhibition. There the girl is smiling and pleased,
> and there is some hope yet for the pale, earnest young man who
> loves her with all his might. But between the two pictures,
> between Pall Mall and the Trafalgar Column, sad changes have
> occurred. The young woman has met a big life-guardsman,

probably, who has quite changed her view of things; and you see
that the last appeal is made without any hope for the appellant.
The girl hides away her pretty face, and we see that all is over. She
likes the poor fellow well enough, but it is only as a brother; her
heart is with the life-guardsman, who is strutting down the lane at
this moment, with his laced cap on one ear, cutting the
buttercups' heads off with his rattan cane. The whole story is told,
without, alas! the possibility of a mistake, and the young fellow in
the grey stockings has nothing to do but jump down the well, at
the side of which he has been making his appeal.

  The painting of the picture is excellent; the amateur will not
fail to appreciate the beauty of the drawing, the care, and at the
same time freedom, of the execution, and a number of ex-
cellencies of method which are difficult to describe in print,
except in certain technical terms that are quite unsatisfactory to
the general reader.

Thackeray's reception of this picture is essentially pastoral or idyllic
in its point of view. It can only deal with simplicity in full
consciousness of its relation to sophistication. The combination of
sweetness and humour, sentiment and playfulness which he distils
from this one exhibition is repeated in innumerable art reviews of
the period. Thackeray's are better written than most and interesting
for the explicit statement of criteria. The tone of his reviews is
mocking, but is intended to provoke a readjustment of view and a
serious reappraisal of the nature of the simple. Such a use of some
version of the mock-heroic characterises *Our Village, Cranford, Adam
Bede* and *Under the Greenwood Tree* among the works I consider. In
others something else performs the same function of stimulating a
simultaneous consciousness of the observed and the manner of
observing. In *Cousin Phillis* the attitude of the narrator to his own
youth, both wry and tender, at once understates and enhances the
remembered past. In *Far from the Madding Crowd* and *The
Woodlanders* the implied comparison of the traditional interpretation of the heroic and the simple is continuous but not humorous.

  The deprecation with which the nineteenth century depicts the
simple is, of course, accompanied by compensatory means of
enhancing the apparent significance of a subject which has no
singularity or intrinsic heroism. As might be expected in an art
which is not itself contemplative, but which invites its reader to
contemplate, the idyllic novel is strongly visual. Pictorial techniques

are not, of course, unique to the idyllic novel and do not in themselves imply a structure of idyllic or pastoral feeling. But where they can be shown to reveal another dimension of significant time, to illustrate another set of values, to halt the flow of the narrative to induce contemplation of relationships of characters or perceptions, where, in short, they are used as they are in the English Idyls, then they are being used to an idyllic end. A list of the most memorable narrative 'pictures' from the idylls in this study might include Mr Burge's workshop, Dinah preaching under the tree, Farmer Allan's grandchild grasping for the shining seal, Holdsworth showing the theodolite to Phillis and her father as the storm gathers, the tranter's cottage and its outbuildings. More than anything in these pictures the evocation of light is indispensable. It marks the objects with meaning and temporarily isolates the moment of imaginative grasp of what the mind's eye conjures up. It indicates how we should interpret the relationships in the 'pictures'. A late nineteenth-century defence of genre painting sees the use of light as a distinguishing feature of the best in genre painting. Frederick Wedmore saw the great genre painters, De Hooch, Van der Neer and Maes, as 'poets of light'.[42] They transform the ordinary into satisfying objects of contemplation by the power of light to create significant relationships. George Eliot is talking about the same power in chapter XVII of *Adam Bede*. Describing a typical Dutch picture, she refers to the 'noonday light, softened perhaps by a screen of leaves', which falls on the old woman's mob-cap, 'and just touches the rim of her spinning wheel, and her stone jug, and all those cheap common things which are the necessaries of life to her'. There is in these pictures a particular harmony between the figures, between objects and between both and the background or setting.

This elusive sense of harmonious relationships between parts of a picture is well caught in two quite different contexts by Hazlitt. Like Thackeray's, Hazlitt's art criticism is remarkable for the writing and will therefore best illustrate what many contemporaries could also provide less well. Comparing David Wilkie and Hogarth, Hazlitt quotes a letter of Archbishop Henry 'written during a tour in Wales'.[43] On a walk over rough country the travellers come to an inn 'in a place of most frightful solitude', where they are entertained by a harper, 'who soon drew about us a group of figures that Hogarth would give any price for'. Hazlitt says that Hogarth 'would not have meddled with them at all', but that the group would have made a 'very delightful companion' picture to Wilkie's 'Blind

Fiddler', the bishop's picture 'clearly' having 'the *poetry* on its side'
(my italics):

> The harper was in his true place and attitude; a man and a
> woman stood before him, singing to his instrument wildly, but not
> disagreeably; a little dirty child was playing with the bottom of
> the harp; a woman, in a sick night-cap, hanging over the stairs; a
> boy with crutches, fixed in a staring attention, and a girl carding
> wool in the chimney and rocking a cradle with her naked feet,
> interrupted in her business by the charms of the music; all ragged
> and dirty, and all silently attentive.

Something of the same removed intentness of the figure and
harmony of figure and background haunted Hazlitt in a picture of
Gainsborough's, of which he had seen only an 'indifferent copy in a
broker's shop'. Nevertheless,[44]

> the unconscious simplicity of the boy's expression, looking up
> with his hands folded, and with timid wonder, the noisy
> chattering of a magpye perched above him, and the rustling of
> the coming storm in the branches of the trees, produced a
> romantic pastoral impression, which we have often recalled with
> no little pleasure since that time.

These verbal pictures indicate clearly how the emotion of the viewer
casts a unifying and, in both cases, equalising harmony over the
scenes. In the Archbishop's picture, the 'wild solitude', the strange
ethnic music and the ragged figures make one impression. Hazlitt is
surely right in supposing it most unlike Hogarth's characteristic
satiric or comic modes, but he values the picture as a piece of genre,
a vivid piece of actuality shaped by emotion. In the picture as it
might have been painted by Wilkie, there is no judgement; there is a
recorded observation and emotional colour, but no sympathetic
identification on the one hand or criticism on the other. In Hazlitt's
memory of an actual picture the impression of connection between
elements has been so strong that he has named them in the '*timid
wonder*', the '*noisy* magpye [*sic*]', 'the rustling of the coming storm'.
These cannot in their nature have existed in the picture; Hazlitt
describes them joined in one 'romantic pastoral impression'.
    At times in pictures of the period the 'one romantic pastoral
impression', or, to go back to Schiller, the perception of a moment of

perfect or dynamic calm, encompasses a narrative as these two
'pictures' from Hazlitt do not. The analogy with the Victorian idyll
is then at its closest, and its most illuminating as a comparison with
the idyllic novel. Francis Danby's 'Disappointed Love', for instance, tells a sad story against a natural background of great
beauty. The point of the picture, however, is not to draw attention
to the enduring beauties of nature and the fleeting sorrows of
mankind. It joins the disappointed girl and the bushes and flowers of
the bank in what one might call 'one romantic pastoral impression',
'Danby sought', in Redgrave's words, 'to treat his picture as a poem,
to give ideal interest to his works'.[45] The landscape in this picture as
in others by Danby, 'carries the poetic message',[46] partly by its
symbolism, partly by its actuality. The girl is generalised by
anonymity; we cannot see her face and her figure is thin and
youthful but unremarkable. Redgrave refers to her as 'the girl who
is going to drown herself'. In fact, of course, the picture does not
press this conclusion to the story. It paints the moment at which
various possibilities are still equally active. What it sets out to do is to
'tell' the story not, in Friedländer's words, as 'how it always is', but
certainly as 'how it may very well be'. To this end the realism of the
painting of the background and the simplicity of the figure carry
the 'poetry', that is they are at once the reason why we look and the
invitation to reflection. The terms in which Danby's picture
presents the total story by means of the relation of the figure and the
background may remind us of Raymond Williams's criticism of
George Eliot, who in *Adam Bede* only got as far as presenting the
characters 'as landscape'. There are ways, this study suggests, of
accepting his point and turning it to description of kind rather than
of a falling short in some other aim.

Danby's picture is as much an illustration of the limitations as of
the relevance of genre painting when seen as an analogy to the
idyllic novel. By reason of its length and the simple fact that the final
impression can only be accumulated over time, a novel, even a short
one, will never approach the immediate effect of harmony and
beauty given by a picture. But, of course, its greater explicitness can
be turned to all kinds of advantage. The key to these advantages is
the figure of the narrator. Virtually absent from a painting, his
function curtailed by the compression of style and form in a poem,
he emerges as the centre of an idyllic novel. It is the narrator's
continuous presence which makes possible in a novel the harmonious balance which is the hallmark of the Victorian idyll. In

whatever guise he appears inside an individual novel, he speaks in all of them as a sophisticated observer of a simpler life; as one who understands, if he does not share, the assumed views of an assumed reader, and at the same time as one who understands but *cannot* share the life he depicts. From his in many ways uncomfortable position he lays no claim to omniscience, but he does lay claim, implicitly, to being in possession of a vantage-point from which comparisons can be made. His art is made up of these comparisons. Rival claims to sympathy inside the story are balanced in a generalised understanding of the way things are. The narrator knows that the story is about people whose lives and values are not the same as his or as those of his reader, and that, from some points of view often taken up in literature, they are outstanding only in unimportance; he knows too that while sophistication imported into these lives would endanger innocence, sophisticated people feel the need of some means of contact with the values overlaid by sophistication and represented by the rural or otherwise remote. The narrator knows that standing between two worlds he will lose credibility if he sentimentalises one or lectures the other.[47] He knows, and knows his readers know, that his story could be told in other ways and that similar stories have been so told; he defines his story partly by referring to other ways of telling. This is one way in which he can describe with sympathy without sacrificing distance; he enhances his subject by recalling traditional handling of it; he implies the intrinsic historical worth of his material while he brings it into contemporary focus with realistic detail. He is aware at this contemporary moment that the world is changing rapidly around him and his readers; his sense of the timeless nature of the values he celebrates is equalled only by his sense of the threat to them. He knows too, since the present moment is hard to compass in description, so rapid is the rate of change, that in the story as he presents it he is making a statement in the very act of describing.

The narrator in all the novels I discuss is a constructed persona. His stance has to be identified by the reader as the story proceeds. Consideration of the novels is thus an examination of the closely woven expressive narrative texture which results from the demand made on the reader to, in James's phrase, 'make up' his point of view. The texture is often more dense than the pellucid overall effect would suggest. The harmonious balance of an idyll is achieved ultimately by structure, by the ways in which the separable elements are shown to relate to one another. The particular task of the idyllic narrator is to maintain a sympathetic distance from his subject and continuous contact with his reader. Entry into the fictional world of these novels is usually direct, as in, 'To dwellers in a wood almost every species of tree has its voice as well as its feature.' But sooner or later, like the narrator of *Adam Bede* who compares himself to an Egyptian sorcerer, the narrator emerges as separate from the world he is describing, and conscious of his role as presenter. The reflective nature of his consciousness is taken over by the reader, as is the narrator's role in most kinds of fiction. The reader of a Victorian idyll is asked to contemplate the precarious existence of the ideal in a 'real' world of social change, and to bring into simultaneous focus the enduring and the shifting. The maintenance of distance, or, in other words, of a balance between his sympathy and whatever it is (time or sophistication) which removes him from the fictional world, is crucial to the success of the idyllic narrator. Such distance, it must be stressed, is entirely without irony. Pastoral feeling always attaches to a life simpler, closer to the 'natural', than that of the supposed reader, and involves an acknowledgement or consciousness of a complex response to the comparative simplicity. In the final pastoral picture the values of the simple life and the stance of the sophisticated observer coexist in a precarious and temporary balance. Distance allows this and undermines neither the complex nor the simple.

2 George Sand and Mary Mitford: Politics and Poetry

To throw into relief the qualities of the nineteenth-century English idyllic novels which are obscured by considering them exclusively with other novels by the same authors or with other novels in the realist tradition, this chapter looks briefly at a French novelist and an English essayist. George Sand's prefaces to her *romans-champêtres* shed pertinent light on the stance of the narrator of rural stories for sophisticated readers. The extreme simplicity of Mary Mitford's early sketches in *Our Village* proves on examination to be a complex structure similar to that underlying longer works which present the simple to those whose ideas about it have stronger roots than their experience of it.

In life and work these two authors are separated by more than a generation and the English Channel. One was a free-living political revolutionary, the other a political innocent whose personal life was governed by her parents, the only known object of her passions. George Sand, a born story-teller, converted into fiction one after another of the emotionally charged issues which she and her circle aired in socialist periodicals. Mary Mitford's political acquaintance was limited to her father's conservative circle, where she was early acclaimed as a literary prodigy, but which she was neither invited nor tempted to join as an equal.[1] She was first a poet, secondly a poetic dramatist, lastly a prose-writer and never a good story-teller. Her first public literary effort was in the strenuous commercial world of the theatre, where she struggled with quarrels, receipts and acclaim as best she could from her disadvantageous position as a woman. Her subjects were remote and romantic like that of her two tragedies, *Foscari* and *Rienzi*.[2] With her initial inspiration exhausted, she searched Froissart for material sufficiently 'high' without needing the 'learning' demanded by Greek and Roman subjects.

She settled on 'a grand historical tragedy on the greatest subject in the English story – Charles and Cromwell', but never completed 'the boldest attempt ever made by woman'.[3] The pastoral mode, to which both George Sand and Mary Mitford in time turned, occupies a very different position in their total *œuvres* and in their reputations. Leslie Stephen considered George Sand's 'country stories . . . perfect',[4] but they make only an interlude in a long career and she was better known in England for novels like *Lélia*, which Matthew Arnold looked back on as marking a crucial emotional point in his formative years.[5] Her capacity to shock is not a natural part of any pastoral effect. Mary Mitford's hundred-year reputation, on the other hand, rests deservedly on the mode which once found she did not leave and whose most successful expression is in the sketches of *Our Village*. They struck the right note at the right time, as R. H. Horne pointed out in *A New Spirit of the Age*, and though they created a fashion they were not, as 'unaffected prose pastorals', ever surpassed.

It is at the point where these two writers turn from other kinds of writing to the pastoral that their work has most to tell about the nature of the pastoral impulse in the nineteenth century. It might seem in both cases that the pastoral presented itself as a refuge. From *Jeanne* in 1844 to *Les Maîtres Sonneurs* in 1853 George Sand's *romans-champêtres* cover the years of her greatest political disillusion. The first appearance in *The Ladies' Magazine* of the sketches which were the germ of *Our Village* marks for Mary Mitford not only a retreat from the hurly-burly of the London theatre but a desperate point in the family fortunes, when she was required to earn the money to keep her parents and minister to them physically in reduced and confined circumstances. A natural resource was to look around her from the cottage they had taken near Reading and use the material to hand. But in both cases the willing confinement to pastoral restriction is only partially a retreat. George Sand wrote her country stories not to turn her back on politics but to make the same political statement from another point of view and by a different means. As Mary Mitford's early sketches succeeded one another through the first two volumes she developed a vein from which not only she but readers in touch with more far-reaching problems than a loss of fortune and a deplorable father took a renewal of hope. In fact the works which mark the nineteenth-century recrudescence of pastoral feeling are stamped with the pressures with which they and their readers are attempting to deal. And the appeal they make to the reader is to recreate imaginatively the place of innocence inside the complexities of their own ongoing concerns.

George Sand is interesting for the explicit expression given to her purpose and attitudes in the prefaces to the *romans-champêtres*. These novels, five in all, are an interlude in her total work. They can be seen as a series[6] in which the pastoral oppositions of urban and rural, simple and sophisticated, folkways and learning are first, in *Jeanne* (1844), embodied in the story in characters from different walks of life, and, as it were, adjudicated by an omnipresent narrator. Then in the following three novels, *La Mare au Diable* (1845), *François le Champi* (1847), *La Petite Fadette* (1848), the stories are told as directly and simply as possible without explicit reference to the sophisticated world. They are, however, set in the frame of sophisticated concerns by prefatory remarks from the author to the reader. *François le Champi* and *La Petite Fadette* have long prefaces, rhetorical exercises in which the complicity of the reader is sought. The two prefaces are linked and make a continuous conversation in which George Sand discusses with a friend the importance and difficulty of making rural life real for an urban audience. The much shorter preface to *Les Maîtres Sonneurs* (1853) clearly regards the theoretical issues as more or less exhausted as a topic, and comment is confined to the narrator's language. In this novel comment or reflection on simple life and ways is restored to the text of the story, where it began in *Jeanne*. Unlike *Jeanne*, however, *Les Maîtres Sonneurs* presents a fusion of theme and narrative comment. The tension between art and life, and between the artist and society, is here absorbed into the texture of the novel in a way that probably justifies Leslie Stephen's high claims for George Sand's 'country stories'. *Les Maîtres Sonneurs* is, in one of its aspects, the successful end of her experiments in the presentation of simple people in their own language.[7] The last three novels in the series are increasingly assured in the handling of the dialect which is most pervasive in *Les Maîtres Sonneurs*. As in *Cousin Phillis*, differences in language can be drawn to the reader's attention and accepted as a natural result of the narrator's awareness of change over the time which has lapsed between the occurrence and the telling of the story. In *Jeanne* the gap between folk and sophisticated language is part of the complexity of the story-line. The point at which George Sand is particularly interesting in relation to my argument is where, in *La Mare au Diable* she rejects the methods which had produced in *Jeanne* 'un roman de contrastes',[8] and set about the problem of achieving an effect of

harmony with direct presentation. The story of *La Mare au Diable* is
itself very short and composed largely of dialogue between the two
central characters. There is no dialect and no effort to reproduce
peasant speech. Germain and Marie are revealed as unsophisticated
in the sense of speaking directly from felt experience. They are so
artlessly open with one another, so self-forgetful and so mutually
concerned for Germain's child, that they appear to be talking
straight from the heart. The inevitability of the wedding bells with
which the story ends does not seem sentimental, only a sign, in
Marian Evans's words, of George Sand's power 'to delineate human
passion and its results'.[9] The framing or presentation, however, of
this jewel-like story is heavy and elaborate. There is more to be said
about George Sand's mediation of her home in the Vallée Noire for
her Parisian audience, but I shall here let the method of *La Mare au
Diable* make my point. The declaration of purpose, although it
relates to French political and social circumstances, describes, and is
aware of so doing, the common situation of the modern pastoral
narrator.

La Mare au Diable was introduced by an address to the reader
from which extracts called 'Préface d'un roman inédit: Fragments'
were published before the novel in *La Revue Sociale*, December 1845.
'L'Auteur au Lecteur'[10] argues that the times require an idealistic
not a realistic art. It begins with the epigraph to an engraving in
Holbein's 'Dance of Death':

> A la sueur de ton visaige
> Tu gaigneras ta pauvre vie,
> Après long travail et usaige,
> Voicy la *mort* qui te convie   (6)

The description of the engraving which follows dwells on the grim
message of the picture – the peasant, 'vieux, trapu, couvert des
haillons', drives a plough in a vast landscape at sunset, attended
by death performing his 'dance macabre'. Holbein's thought, 'la
pensée stoïcienne du christianisme demi-païen de la Renaissance',
was, 'l'auteur' supposes, appropriate in the society he was painting.
But now in another time consolation should be looked for in life not
in death, and the artist should assume quite another role. Some
contemporary artists, nearer to Holbein's mood than she herself
would wish to be, have dwelt on 'l'abjection de la misère'; they have
faithfully shown the ills of society and the threat to the rich from the

desperation of the poor. But this like Holbein's is the art of terror for which this author would substitute the art of love:

> Nous croyons que la mission de l'art est une mission de sentiment et d'amour, que le roman d'aujourd'hui devrait remplacer la parabole et l'apologue des temps naïfs, et que l'artiste a une tâche plus large et plus poétique que celle de proposer quelques mesures de prudence et de conciliation pour atténuer l'effroi qu'inspirent ses peintures. (12)

This 'poetic' task is to look beyond externals to an inner truth: 'L'art n'est pas une étude de la réalité positive; c'est une recherche de la vérité idéale.' After this she makes the traditional pastoral apology for the lowliness of the subject-matter and the slightness of the form. Her 'historiette' is only about a labourer, but her hero and his small child have their story, 'tout le monde a la sienne'. It concerns the imperative demand for marriage in a traditional community, and begins in chapter II with Germain's father-in-law advising him to remarry. The story, though, is further framed by a continuation of the author's remarks in chapter I, and an appended anthropological description of 'les noces de campagne'.

Chapter I, 'Le Labour', takes up the Holbein rendering of the poor peasant to whom the macabre figure of death offers imminent relief from rags and toil. The author is walking in the fields with the engraving fresh in her mind and is struck by the sight of two men, one old and one young, ploughing at opposite ends of a field. Against Holbein's grim *memento mori* she presents a picture, idyllic in Schiller's terms, of the condition of innocence in which man exists in a state of harmony with his environment. Her hero, young and vigorous, is seen driving a team of splendid oxen, and attended not by death but by a beautiful child. The picture is a study in relationships; the old man ploughs in a further corner with professional concentration; the young man and the child exchange glances of mutual affection and pride in the work. The man sings a traditional ploughing song which soothes the toiling oxen under the yoke and the earth yields to their mutual effort:

> Tout cela était beau de force ou de grâce: le paysage, l'homme, l'enfant, les taureaux sous le joug; et, malgré cette lutte puissante, où la terre était vaincue, il y avait un sentiment de douceur et de calme profond qui planait sur toutes choses. (20)

The message of the picture is of hope, an humanitarian faith based
on a sense of the repetition of enduring patterns from the human
past. As an observer of the rural scene the artist alone can convey
what it has to say and speak what the peasant cannot say for himself.
The landowner, the only other urban dweller habitually in contact
with the country, is parasitic; the land supports his leisure and he
goes to the country for 'un peu d'air et de santé', returning to the
town to spend 'le fruit du travail de ses vassaux'. George Sand, with
some anachronism, invokes Virgil in support of her aesthetic and
political faith:

> Et le rêve d'une existence douce, libre, poétique, laborieuse et
> simple pour l'homme des champs, n'est pas si difficile à concevoir
> qu'on doive le reléguer parmi les chimères. Le mot triste et doux
> de Virgile: 'O heureux l'homme des champs, s'il connaissait son
> bonheur!' est un regret; mais, comme tous les regrets, c'est aussi
> une prédiction. Un jour viendra où le laboureur pourra être aussi
> un artiste, sinon pour exprimer (ce qui importera assez peu alors),
> du moins pour sentir le beau. Croit-on que cette mystérieuse
> intuition de la poésie ne soit pas en lui déjà a l'état d'instinct et de
> vague rêverie?   (15)

Where George Sand's peasant lacks self-awareness which he could
and would cultivate if he were not ground down by hard work,
Virgil's lacks only the means of comparison which the poet has from
his knowledge of the wider world. George Sand's sense that history
will alter the basic situation is, of course, not to be found in Virgil.
She closes the circle of observers of the rural scene by including the
reader, whom she scolds for upholding the social code in which the
peasant has no leisure to become his own 'artist' and express 'le
sentiment' of his simple life in natural surroundings. Chapter 1 ends
with a return to the ploughing figure in a metaphor which
poetically unites the visual recall of the initial 'picture' with its
meaning:

> L'année prochaine, ce sillon sera comblé et couvert par un
> sillon nouveau. Ainsi s'imprime et disparaît la trace de la plupart
> des hommes dans le champ de l'humanité. Un peu de terre
> l'efface, et les sillons que nous avons creusés se succèdent les uns
> aux autres comme les tombes dans le cimetière. Le sillon du
> laboureur ne vaut-il pas celui de l'oisif, qui a pourtant un nom, un

nom qui restera, si, par une singularité ou une absurdité quelconque, il fait du bruit dans le monde? (25)

George Sand then tells the story, with a narrator as absent as possible and in what Elizabeth Gaskell had called 'a seeing-beauty spirit'.[11] The story ends with an avowal of love after some mutual misunderstanding. After this the author returns *in propria persona* to describe the subsequent wedding of Germain and Marie as an example of 'les noces de campagne'. Up to now she has exhorted sophisticated attention for this story by an appeal to the reader's sense of moral justice and an assumption of some superiority on her own part, not over the subject but over the reader. After the story itself she takes up a position at a distance from both reader and peasant subject. She becomes a kind of social scientist who explains the folk-ways to an audience who are unaware of their significance not through moral blindness but simply from lack of experience. She now includes, with parenthetical explanations, some peasant vocabulary, absent in the story, and she signals her own return as story-teller to the urban fold by the light touch of the mock-heroic in the description of character and action.

In the 1851 'Notice' attached to this book for a popular edition of her work George Sand disclaims 'aucune prétention révolution-naire en littérature' which the critics might have imputed to her since since its publication. She sees herself as writing in a tradition of 'roman[s] de mœurs rustiques', which have been written 'sous toutes les formes, tantôt pompeuses, tantôt maniérées, tantôt naïves', and says she has done nothing new 'en suivant la pente qui ramène l'homme civilisé aux charmes de la vie primitive'. But, of course, apart from the successive attempts to convey a simple life which reveal on their own account an experimental hand, there is the evidence of the two 'Avant Propos' to *François le Champi* and *La Petite Fadette* to prove how exercised she was about the right way to do it for readers of her own time. Her consciousness of her readers, or 'vous autres', as she calls them, is paramount; it is not possible, she says, to depict simplicity and natural beauty exactly as one has seen it, but it is possible to persuade 'ceux qui ont des yeux à regarder aussi'. Amongst the English idyllic novels discussed in the following chapters, *Adam Bede* is the one in which this dialogue between narrator and reader is most explicit, but as George Sand's *romans-champêtres* and their prefaces make clear, it can be implicit in the most pellucid and apparently unrhetorical little story. A social bias

in modern criticism frequently leads critics to underrate or ignore
the dialogue implicit in nineteenth-century pastoral and so to
distort the nature of the works. R. Godwin-Jones, for example,
regards the novels as sentimentalising for a particular purpose. He
contrasts George Sand's novelistic representation of rural life with
two of the contributions she made in 1844 to the *Eclaireur de l'Indre*.[12]
In both 'La Lettre d'un paysan de la Vallée Noire' and 'Le Père Va-
Tout-Seul' she assumes the point of view of a peasant and writes,
with accuracy supported by all historical evidence, of grinding
poverty. In the novels George Sand proposes the solutions of
'utopian socialist thought from the Saint-Simonians to Pierre
Leroux', and what Mr Godwin-Jones calls 'economic verisimili-
tude' gives way to poetry and the picturesque. Their 'softening
methods' were chosen, he thinks, for their greater effectiveness as
social propaganda than 'brutal realism'. 'Softening', as so often in
modern criticism, is related to a distanced point of view. He quotes
the entry of Marcelle into the poor but spotlessly clean home of a
peasant woman in *Le Meunier d'Angibault*. Marcelle is touched by the
woman's struggle to conceal her poverty by scrupulous cleanliness
and an imposition of order on her pitifully meagre possessions. Mr
Godwin-Jones comments: 'It is clear that poverty here is being
sentimentalised right out of existence. The emphasis in the passage
is on the way in which the woman's poverty touches the observer's
heart, not on the kind of deprivation and despair it engenders.'
Presumably Mr Godwin-Jones knows that many poor houses are
and have always been clean. Perhaps the reason why he finds the
despair imputed to the peasant in the first person narrative of 'La
Lettre' convincing, but the sympathy with which an observer
discovers the possibility of self-respect in adversity mere sentimentality, is revealed in his handling of an extract from one of George
Sand's letters. In it she explains:

> Les romans parlent au cœur et à l'imagination et quand on vit
> dans une époque d'égoisme et d'endurcissement on peut, sous
> cette forme, frapper fort pour réveiller les consciences et les
> cœurs.

His comment on this passage omits any mention of the word George
Sand couples here so significantly with 'le cœur' – 'l'imagination'.
His judgement confuses her art with her solutions: 'To a world
familiar with Karl Marx's more logically consistent program and

the more drastic measures it advocated Sand and her fellow romantics appear hopelessly naive.' Beside the complications of the imagination the application of logical consistency to human affairs may appear equally naïve, but what should be clear to anyone is that the sophisticated writer portraying simple life cannot assume any point of view, either the subject's or an observer's, without art, and the art necessarily employed in the portrayal of degradation besides being as selective as that devoted to showing dignity, works through the imagination.

George Sand goes on in the prefaces to the two rural novels which follow *La Mare au Diable* to explore the means by which the imagination of the reader may be stimulated to construct a sufficiently 'real' picture of an unfamiliar mode of life. The interest here of the framing material of *La Mare au Diable* is that it demonstrates clearly the elements which make up the narrative stance of the pastoral writer who knows equally well the worlds of subject and reader. It plots the relationship of the rural and sophisticated worlds, selectively directing the reader's attention to the relative degrees of awareness rather than to the economic relativity of poverty and wealth. The primary consequence of this selection is that by it the artist's role on the map of social consciousness is clearly defined. The next two prefaces go further in defining George Sand's conception of this role in practical detail, but the implications of the position are clear here. The peasant lacks the language which will allow him to speak for himself across barriers of culture. But he is fully integrated into a traditional culture where moral and emotional choice is offered in a restricted pattern of communal and familial bonds, and his language is as rich as his personal life inside the referential pattern of his culture. The artist can speak for him if a 'translation' can be made which renders his meaning intelligible to the sophisticated reader. Such a constructed language is one concern of the next two prefaces. The peasant's meaning or the inner truth (the 'vérité idéale') of his life does not lend itself to abstractions, so that the artist must create a credible world for her characters to move in. The reader must be made to see his own likeness to the peasant, but he can only be made to see affinity through a perception of difference. He must, that is, understand the peasant's world before he can hear the peasant speaking. The nineteenth-century pastoral artist does not take equality and brotherhood for granted, he seeks to re-establish the moral and psychological grounds of such indubitable human fellowship. The aesthetic position is a radical one in which both world and character must be created at once. But a strange world can only be created from familiar material and the rural or otherwise simple world has always been familiar to the sophisticated world in the artistic constructions by which people define themselves by simultaneous perception of sameness and difference. Hence the assurance with which, in the introductory chapters of *La Mare au Diable*, the Holbein engraving is set against the idyllic landscape with figures, opens the way for George Sand to signal a reassessment of the current relation of religion and politics by recalling Virgil, who himself described the rooted peasant in a world of wars and displacement. In this way art – that is, the persuasive means by which the imagination is engaged – is put to work in a political cause which is moral before it is economic. If suffering were not morally offensive economic inequalities could be accepted with equanimity. There is a sentimentality of grimness as there is of prettiness. The failure of both is the failure of the art fully to engage the imagination. While art should not seek to anaesthetise, it cannot either be effectively directed to solutions. The reader must re-create, not simply consume. The inevitable distance of the sophisticated artist from the described world of pastoral art is compensated for by his consciousness of a double focus. Maintaining the difficult stance from which simplicity can be seen in its relation to complexity is the end to which the imaginative effort of narrator and reader must be directed.

This process is nowhere clearer than in *Our Village*, of which the purpose and effect are so simple, but of which the means on examination prove so subtle. Henry Chorley, introducing his selection of Mary Russell Mitford's unpublished letters in 1872 politely forbore to 'name the copyists', who, following in her footsteps, went 'before the public on the strong and safe ground of observation truthfully recorded . . . since neither pleasure nor duty is performed in depreciating by comparison'.[13] At this distance in time it is possible to distinguish the 'safe ground of observation truthfully recorded' in a work like Mary Howitt's *Wood Leighton: Or a Year in the Country* from the 'prose pastoral' of *Our Village*. Mary Howitt is a good writer, but her direct expression of nostalgia for her early home and her 'observed' and carefully composed landscapes would never have created the fashion they followed. Her serviceable prose may be illustrated briefly from the introduction to the scene of a story in *Wood Leighton* called 'The Sinner's Grave:'[14]

One of our first rambles was to the picturesque village of Henningly, about three miles from Wood Leighton, lying on the other side of the river, and, indeed, on its banks. . . . No more perfect pictures of rural happiness can ever be presented than may be found every day upon this green, or under this tree. Three things I could not fail remarking in this village: the neatness and general aspect of comfort of these cottages; the affection that seemed to subsist between the labouring men and their families; and the universal taste for gardening which reigns throughout it.

The preface to the first edition of *Our Village*, on the other hand, is some indication at least of the indirection and play of implicit dialogue with the reader which did instigate the fashion for prose description of the countryside:

The following pages contain an attempt to delineate country scenery and country manners, as they exist in a small village in the south of England. The writer may at least claim the merit of a hearty love of her subject, and of that local and personal familiarity, which only a long residence in one neighbourhood could have enabled her to attain. Her descriptions have always been written on the spot and at the moment, and in nearly every instance with the closest and most resolute fidelity to the place and the people. If she be accused of having given a brighter aspect to her villagers than is usually met with in books, she cannot help it, and would not if she could. She has painted, as they appeared to her, their little frailties and their many virtues, under an intense and thankful conviction, that in every condition of life goodness and happiness may be found by those who seek them, and never more surely than in the fresh air, the shade, and the sunshine of nature.

This is clearly a writer who sees the necessity of constructing for herself the frame of mind of her potential reader if her 'delineation' is to be effective.

The freshness with which the reader perceives the scenes of *Our Village* can be accounted for by the indirection of the narration, by the success of this author in persuading 'ceux qui ont des yeux à regarder aussi'. She learnt the art of holding an audience in two hard schools, the theatre and financial necessity. Her move to prose for the depiction of rural realities after the poetic dramas cost her much labour. 'You would laugh if you saw me puzzling over my prose', she told Sir William Elford, her most frequent correspondent through her early life. Her style, she thought, had been spoilt by 'a certain careless sauciness, a fluent incorrectness' brought on by overmuch letter-writing. 'So I ponder over every phrase [and] disjoint every sentence . . .'[15] This is like the trouble Tennyson had with 'Dora'; the problem is to match the simplicity of the subject-matter with an appropriate style which condescends to neither the subject nor the reader. Elizabeth Browning thought she succeeded:[16]

> my own opinion is that she stands higher as the authoress of Our Village than of Rienzi and writes prose better than poetry, and transcends rather in Dutch minuteness than in Italian ideality and passion.

The interest of her success in a study of the Victorian idyll lies in the way in which her communication of material close and familiar to her, but largely unfamiliar at first-hand to her presumed reader depends on a combination of distance and fictionalisation. The life she describes in a small village some thirty miles from London was not, of course, a separate peasant culture like that of the Vallée Noire; some of her sketches indicate that it is already within sight of the outer edge of urban sprawl. Nevertheless the gap between urban and rural perceptions was felt to be a large one, which could only be bridged by attention to fine linguistic and stylistic distinctions. A modern reader has to re-construct a world in which a generally appreciative reviewer of the first volume took exception to such reminders of ordinary life as 'a roly-poly child' or a 'scrap dinner'.[17] The fictions are the means by which she bridged this gap and made the described world 'real' for her reader. The best are found in the 'Walks in the Country', the backbone of the miscellany of stories, character-sketches and descriptive pieces which make up each volume. Some of the little stories are appealing (Tennyson's 'Dora' was based on 'Dora Cresswell' in volume III), the character-sketches are lively but not innovative in method; her original work is in the 'Walks'. Those in the first volume are nearest the cottage, those in the second are slightly further afield and the people she meets are observed with less affection and more attention to what they may signify as representative figures. Three-Mile Cross is the same kind of starting-point for Mary Mitford as Bockhampton for Hardy. But as Hardy's work progressed he entered imaginatively further and further into the fictional world, while Mary Mitford's imagination was most vivid the nearer to the 'real' she was working. Her later volumes repeat the success of the early ones, but the initial inspiration was new. She refound a way of describing the rural real in such a way as to keep it constantly accessible to and in interchange with sophisticated patterns of thought. She fictionalises her experience and uses for her own purposes other art which has mediated the country for the town. Each in its different way is a distancing device, but the effect is of freshness and immediacy.

The narrative voice which is consistent from sketch to sketch and volume to volume is established in the 'Walks'. No doubt the walks were taken by the author herself, but the narrator is not the author either observing in order to write or telling directly about the experience. She is a 'character' in the neighbourhood, though she bears a strong resemblance to the Mary Mitford who emerges from the letters. She is a stout, deprecatory lady, with a homely acquaintance with practicalities, an unselfconscious acceptance of muddy boots as the end of a country walk, bookish tastes and a tendency to reflection which she purports to have to 'shake off' when it threatens melancholy. An underlying melancholy, a recognition of the frailty of any joy, is present along with the determination to see the best in everything. The sunny glow is thus revealed as a kind of stoicism – a statement about the capacity for hope. The walks become, in a modest, understated way, a demonstration of the source of such hope in simple lives and natural beauty. In 'Violeting' in volume I the narrator describes her own spiritual recuperation from the 'fever' of London on a brief solitary walk to a place where she knows there will be violets to pick. In 'The Tenants of Beechgrove' in volume II the need for healing is transferred to 'a strange lady' whom the narrator meets on one of her walks. She belongs to the rootless suburban society which is encroaching on the countryside in rented villas. Haunted by a past sorrow, discreetly unstated but not too difficult to imagine, she finds temporary relief in quietly observing the life of a poor but happy family in a clearing in the wood, where a healthy baby is minded by older children. Transference is in fact a characteristic device of the sketches. Its source lies in the kind of tact she describes in a letter to Elford:[18]

If I was ever guided by any other motive than the feeling of the moment in writing to you, I certainly should not have chosen this time to send you a specimen of my rural enthusiasm, which you will receive in an atmosphere where enthusiasm cannot breathe – in the gay bustle of St. James's Street.

It is well for me that I can plead privilege (the privilege of gentle poesy) for my madness; or you might, perhaps, out of friendship for papa, send down Dr. Willis and a strait waistcoat, or exert yourself to gain me admission to St. Luke's.

In the sketches, particularly the 'Walks in the Country', she found a way of mediating in prose the 'madness of gentle poesy' without obtruding the personal on the reader. She could delineate while persuading the reader that the 'seeing-beauty' eye was his own. For the most part the narrator has a surrogate for her 'enthusiasm' in child, dog or young visitor. These companions on her walks go where she would not, touch whatever excites their curiosity, exclaim and otherwise respond with spontaneous physical delight to flowers, hidden places, and tiny creatures. The countryside is thus associated with innocence and the springs of feeling. The narrator's tucked-up skirts and muddy boots are explained away by indulgence of her young friends and of May, 'the exquisite greyhound', and are even made to seem a little staid. A prey to the child ('Her Mother is right, I do spoil that child!'), and fussy in an 'old shawl' and changing everything wet straight away, the narrator makes sure that for much of the time we cannot identify completely with her any more than with the innocents. In so far as the narrator's 'poesy' or 'enthusiasm' becomes the reader's own it is depersonalised. The distance thus achieved is used to place his own experience, which is not so much of the countryside, but of a literary tradition in which the country has acquired its associations. He is invited to see it freshly in this delicately drawn but indubitably 'real' modern context. In 'The Cowslip Ball' in volume I, in which the narrator walks with both dog and child, her depression (thoughts of poverty and disappointment, real in the author's life) is generalised enough for anyone's anxieties to be attached to it. It is lifted by a stoical surrender of the self. Not only does she amiably agree to the walk and make a cowslip ball twice (since Lizzie broke the stems too short the first time), but she focuses her eye steadily on the water, the banks and flowered dells, and that part of her mind not occupied with her charges moves through a series of literary recollections:

Robinson Crusoe on his lonely island and Isaac Walton, who 'would have loved our brook and our quiet meadows', occur to her; 'Shakespeare's Song of Spring bursts irrepressibly from our lips', and, the ball finished and Lizzie off to enjoy it on her own, 'pleasant thoughts, delightful associations, awoke' as the narrator listened to the nightingales, and the whole of 'the beautiful story of the Lutist and the Nightingale from Ford's Lovers Melancholy' ran through her head.

While Lizzie and the dog define the experience of nature as perennially accessible to innocence, the literary references link it to a tradition. The sketch at one level is about permanence. But in the apparently gossipy naturalness of her manner she recalls the threat which is at the heart of pastoral art. The scene is only preserved through the stability and unspoken communal values of the neighbourhood. The background of more ambitious pastorals like *Adam Bede, Cranford, Cousin Phillis* and *Under the Greenwood Tree* is an extended version in each case of what is lightly suggested here:

> They [the meadows] belong to a number of small proprietors, who allow each other access through their respective grounds, from pure kindness and neighbourly feeling, a privilege never abused; and the fields on the other side of the water are reached by a rough plank, or a tree thrown across, or some such homely bridge. We ourselves possess one of the most beautiful; so that the strange pleasure of property, that instinct which makes Lizzy delight in her broken doll, and May in the bare bone which she has pilfered from the kennel of her recreant admirer of Newfoundland, is added to the other charms of this enchanting scenery; a strange pleasure it is, when one so poor as I can feel it!

The very lightness here distances in a way which allows for a perception of serious issues to be a part of the precarious psychological balance of the narrator's calm of mind. The balance is also an aesthetic one between, on the one hand, the exclamatory exchanges between the narrator and the child and the rhythmic uncertainty dictated by the pace of a walk with a dog and a child, and, on the other, the steady focus of minute observation which develops into the fluency of recall. A perception of style as a mode of perception underlies the best of these sketches. In 'The Hard Summer' (volume 1), for example, the mock-heroic opening is the preparation for an account of a walk on a rare sunny afternoon in a

wet summer on which expectations are shown to be as ready for
reversal by experience as the narrator's enjoyable pause to contemplate rough village boys playing an orderly game of cricket.
Style and stereotypes are unobtrusively aligned with an immediate
'reality' of a simple and accessible kind. In 'The Dell' (volume II)
the walk, realistically continuous with pauses only for the dog to
root in the undergrowth or the narrator to catch her breath, resolves
into a series, seven in all, of 'pictures', examples of popular images
familiar to a cultivated Londoner from exhibitions.

'The Dell' begins with a little genre 'painting' of blind Robert
and his small helper, the significance of which becomes plain at the
end of the sketch; a comprehensive view from the gate follows,
cornfield in the foreground, river, mill and farm with 'picturesque
outbuildings' in the middle ground, and the 'range of woody hills
beyond' in the background. The dell itself, an 'irregular piece of
broken ground', picturesquely 'owes its singular character of
wildness and variety' to the 'labyrinthine intricacy' of the high
banks which enclose it; this is a particularly detailed piece of
description in the language of the picturesque. 'One or two old
pollards', for example, 'almost conceal the winding road that leads
down the descent, by the side of which a spring as bright as crystal
runs gurgling along.' An occasional turn affords a 'peep at an
adjoining meadow where the sheep are lying, dappling its sloping
surface like the small clouds on the summer heaven'. 'Another
turning of the dell' affords the wildest and darkest picture of all – the
dark coppice in the background, a marshy, rushy pool in the
foreground. Here, as often in the sketches, when the narrator is
enclosed by banks, trees or darkness, she takes to 'guessing', always
making clear where sight ends and reverie takes over. And here, as
in other sketches, the wildest picture, the most secluded spot
reached by the roughest terrain leads into the clearing where the
figures in that landscape reveal the human meaning at the centre of
the sketch. When the narrator 'emerges suddenly' from the dell she
faces the 'small homestead of our good neighbour Farmer Allen'.
The elderly Allens are a part of rural history; they have resisted the
social forces which might have swept them away by clinging to
'industry' and 'frugality', and now since their 'admirable son',
unlike Wordsworth's Luke, has made good and used the wealth of
the city to support the values of the country, they can 'keep their
little property undivided'. Mrs Allen, seated in the orchard with her
grandchildren round her feeding the poultry makes the final

picture, in which there is a strong suggestion of contemporary perspective staging. This is picked up by a comparison of her aging beauty with that of Mrs Siddons, with a decision in favour of Mrs Allen, since her splendour has emerged from the struggles of her life and is not the simulated heroism of the imagination.

'The Hard Summer' and 'The Dell' both end in a moment of contemplation, in which the range of perceptions touched on in the 'Walk' are resolved in a moment of harmony. After the cricket match (and another encounter with a pair of representative country-dwellers) the narrator finds glow-worms in the gathering darkness and reflects on their frail beauty, and (in the last reversal of expectation, that set up by her own previous appreciation) is thankful they are safe from the boys, who are 'at best thoughtless creatures'. 'The Dell' ends in what at first glance might look like a piece of 'rural enthusiasm': 'What a sunset! how golden! how beautiful!', but it is turned into a thanksgiving, more like public prayer than personal emotion:

> My heart swells and fills as I write of it, and think of the immeasurable majesty of nature, and the unspeakable goodness of God, who has spread an enjoyment so pure, so peaceful, and so intense before the meanest and lowliest of His creatures.

Old blind Robert, helped by the loving boy, we now see is one of the lowly creatures in God's sunshine, and the narrator has created a total picture out of many familiar ones.

Unlikely as their conjunction might seem in most respects, George Sand and Mary Mitford make a joint appeal to 'ceux qui ont les yeux' to use them to look freshly at simple things. They want change – George Sand in the lot of the rural poor, Mary Mitford in the fevered hearts of the urban rich. George Sand is explicit about her relation with her audience. Mary Mitford, like the English idyllic novelists in the following pages, is inexplicit in that her dialogue with the reader can only be inferred from the text. The world each creates, though, is similarly made out of multiple perceptions, held in a brief stasis and interaction. The strong political impulse behind the pastoral interlude in George Sand's work, and the extraordinary acclaim accorded to Mary Mitford's slender pieces are not altogether strange or paradoxical at a time when social change was so profound and so steadily disrupting of familiar configurations. In the chapters which follow I hope to show

how, from the distance implied in the double focus of pastoral art, multiple perceptions are held in a balanced relation to one another over the length of longer pastorals than *La Mare au Diable* or *Our Village*. The works I discuss differ from one another as much as the work of George Sand and Mary Mitford, and they differ from other works by the same authors. They are alike, however, in a careful accuracy about the narrator's position between two worlds, and in an assumption that ways of perceiving are a significant part of what is seen.

3 Elizabeth Gaskell: History and Fiction

Elizabeth Gaskell's total work is more varied and more variously accomplished than could be assumed from what is written about her. She has been most widely valued in this century as a recorder of social change. *Mary Barton* and *North and South*, for instance, appear along with *Hard Times*, *Sybil*, *Alton Locke* and *Felix Holt* in the chapter called 'The Industrial Novels' in Raymond Williams's *Culture and Society 1780–1950*,[1] and her work occupies two chapters in John Lucas's *The Literature of Change: Studies in the Nineteenth Century Novel*.[2] She is also known to have, or is perhaps hampered with, 'charm', which John Gross rightly calls a 'dubious asset' for a serious literary reputation.[3] But whether, as in John Lucas's earlier consideration of her contribution to our knowledge of nineteenth-century society,[4] she is taken to task for middle-class evasiveness in the face of the social implications of her observations, or whether, as in John Gross's more fair-minded and appreciative study of her literary virtues, she is credited with a 'cool head', description of her approach to the material of her novels tends to be expressed in terms which relate to her character or to her circumstances or to both. A full-length study of Elizabeth Gaskell will eventually, I am sure, redress this curiously biographical bias by a study, for instance, of all the literary modes with which she experiments in the short stories. The stories are of many kinds, among them ghost stories ('The Poor Clare', 'The Old Nurse's Story'), children's Sunday school stories ('Bessy's Troubles at Home'), historical stories ('Lois the Witch', 'My Lady Ludlow'), and Crabbean tales of stern morality ('John Middleton', 'The Doom of the Griffiths'). In all the variety of kind, of which this is only a sample, there is also experimental variety in the methods of telling. She is, for example, particularly skilful in establishing a narrative position from which to make the most economical use of the material. There is the cool but engaged narration of 'The Moorland Cottage', the assumption of the point of view of the central character in the third person narration of 'The Old Nurse's Story', the employment of John Middleton to tell his own story in his own characterising language, or the combination of memory and historical reconstruction in the double narrative of 'My Lady Ludlow'. All kinds of patterns of cross-reference, repetition and development could emerge from a study of this versatility. My own intention here is limited to one strain in her work. It is a significant one because it serves to link the topical in her work with what has been called 'charming' in a single distinctive vision, reflective in its nature, observant and conscious in its choice of and reference to mediating means.

The pattern I am concerned with is apparent at the tentative start of her career in the planned series of poetic 'Sketches among the Poor', which she and her husband were to write together. The only completed one of these scenes from Manchester life is a character-sketch of Mary,[5] who like Alice Wilson in *Mary Barton*, carries the memory of the trees and clear skies of her childhood home as a resource among the ills of the town, and retreats into it in final illness. The sketches were to be *'rather* in the manner of Crabbe . . . but in a more seeing-beauty spirit'.[6] William Gaskell dropped out of the project and Elizabeth Gaskell's work developed into a continuous exploration of modes. The line I am going to trace retains a strong central perception observable in this early sketch. The poem describes a precarious state of innocence preserved in threatening circumstances. The 'poetry' of Mary's life survives in the 'prose' of her circumstances:

> To some she might prosaic seem, but me
> She always charmed with daily poesy.

The currency of these critical concepts is partly the subject of Chapter 6 below. Here I am concerned with the practical application inside Elizabeth Gaskell's work. The 'prosaic' attaches to externalities, contingent circumstances. The 'poetic' is an inner reality, perceivable with insight and reflection, and describable only by indirect means. Here the 'reality' is the compassion and dignity, which, unaffected by circumstance and unlimited by a restricted language, redeems 'daily' ordinariness. Clearly, while this is the response of a social commentator, the commentary will be of a particular kind. History will be mediated by the art which will suggest what cannot be seen.

The central perception in this early sketch is of two kinds of reality, outer and inner, social and personal, seen in a necessary and fixed relationship. The necessity is social and aesthetic; it is unalterable by the characters because they are powerless, and by the observer because it is 'true'. The relationship between the 'realities' is the subject of the poem. The double focus might be described as two-dimensional, and it is no accident that many of Elizabeth Gaskell's most characteristic social observations have a strong pictorial, even emblematic quality. The 'origin' of *Mary Barton*, as she described it in the preface to the first edition, occurred in a brief perception of people driven to dumb desperation, 'the lips compressed for curses, and the hands clinched and ready to smite' (lxxiii–iv). The picture comes to life and begins to move into a story. As she told Mrs Greg, wife of a Manchester employer,[7] while the tale 'was forming itself and impressing [her] with the force of a reality', she thought herself into the position of an 'ignorant man, full of rude, illogical thought, and full of sympathy for suffering which appealed to him through his senses', until she could see how it could lead to 'a course of action, violating the eternal law of God'. I shall return later in this chapter to the position of violence and extreme expression in *Mary Barton*, but want at the moment to stay with the structural pattern of this initial perception. In this structural pattern lies the link between Elizabeth Gaskell's topical observation and the recollections of an earlier and simpler time which constitute the 'charm' of *Cranford* and *Cousin Phillis*.

The correlative for inner peace and human worth in the story of Mary in the single 'Sketch' is, of course, the long pictorial memory of the countryside. Elizabeth Gaskell was a shrewd and compulsive observer of the social scene at a moment in history when significant change had touched most lives, when even the most peaceful countryside was not far from the noise of a recent railway, when even the oldest towns had a huge proportion of inhabitants whose roots were in the country. This complex historical moment has the basic pastoral opposition built in to the social realities of living. In seeking to describe, Elizabeth Gaskell is part historian, part celebrant of the enduring virtues in individual, often simple, lives. Historical necessity is the unalterable force behind the changes in the social scene; the characters must adjust to circumstances which they cannot control or alter. The precarious equilibrium of any achieved peace in their lives is matched by the balance of interest in each narrator's observation between setting and story. Figure and background share the focus of attention and are interdependent in all the novels which take a panoramic view of the historical moment. Miss Matty and Margaret Hale are 'heroines' of a different stamp, but they are alike in sharing the centre of their stories with the social scene. In a sense what happens to Miss Matty happens to the town, and Margaret Hale's story is a story of what looks like a choice between two worlds becoming the sketch of a new country which contains both. Elizabeth Gaskell's social awareness was pre-eminently a sense of the opposing pressures on individual lives of long-established values and contemporary movement and economics, of the continuing but fading presence of the past in the present. She sought for fictional methods of representing the complexities of the cross-currents and oppositions she perceived.

The pattern of tension between historical observation and fictional rendering is nowhere better illustrated than in the successive versions of her own early memories of Knutsford. The first is an historical record, an article called 'The Last Generation in England'.[8] It arose from disappointment at discovering that Robert Southey 'had proposed to himself to write a "history of English domestic life"' but had never completed the plan:

> This quarter of an hour's chance reading has created a wish in me to put upon record some of the details of country town life, either observed by myself, or handed down to me by older relations; for even in small towns, scarcely removed from villages, the phases of society are rapidly changing; and much will appear strange, which yet occurred only in the generation preceding ours.

The article is interpretative history not simply a record. The personal recollections are used as illustrations to an historical view of a disappearing way of life. Oddities of character and behaviour are shown to develop freely and to be cherished in a society where the codes both of social life and duty are more rigidly prescribed than they came to be in the author's adult life. The second 'version' of this community is Duncombe in 'Mr Harrison's Confessions',[9] a delightful story in which a young medical student arrives from the town, and after an initial restiveness under the restrictions put on his lax and comfortable student habits, is totally absorbed into the community by a combination of professional involvement and, of course, love. In two ways this story looks forward to *Cousin Phillis* rather than to *Cranford*, the next version of the same community. The narrator is Mr Harrison himself, who, like Paul in *Cousin Phillis*, looks back on his own youth. And as in *Cousin Phillis* the values embodied in the community are given their peculiar attractiveness in verbal pictures of vivid stillness:

'Here's Mr Morgan, Sophy,' said she, opening the door into an inner room, to which we descended by a step, as I remember well; for I was nearly falling down it, I was so caught by the picture within. It was like a picture – at least, seen through the door-frame. A sort of mixture of crimson and sea-green in the room, and a sunny garden beyond; a very low casement window, open to the amber air; clusters of white roses peeping in; and Sophy sitting on a cushion on the ground, the light coming from above her head, and a little sturdy round-eyed brother kneeling by her, to whom she was teaching the alphabet. It was a mighty relief to him when we came in, as I could see; and I am much mistaken if he was easily caught again to say his lesson, when he was once sent off to find papa. Sophy rose quietly; and of course we were just introduced, and that was all, before she took Mr Morgan upstairs to see her sick servant. I was left to myself in the room. It looked so like a home that it at once made me know the full charm of the word. There were books and work about, and tokens of employment; there was a child's plaything on the floor, and against the sea-green walls there hung a likeness or two, done in water-colours; one, I was sure, was that of Sophy's mother. The chairs and sofa were covered with chintz, the same as the curtains – a little pretty red rose on a white ground. I don't know where the crimson came from, but I am sure there was crimson somewhere; perhaps in the carpet. There was a glass door besides the window, and you went up a step into the garden. This was, first, a grass plot, just under the windows, and, beyond that, straight gravel walks, with box-borders and narrow flower-beds on each side, most brilliant and gay at the end of August, as it was then; and behind the flower-borders were fruit-trees trained over woodwork; so as to shut out the beds of kitchen-garden within. (III 417–18)

The glow of such memories in *Cousin Phillis* is to prove transient. But in the unironic voice of this elderly narrator they are fully endorsed as permanent in his own life and unmitigated by any subsequent or opposing set of values. *Cranford* has no such glow and the narrative voice is predominantly ironic except where it is fanciful, and it is

nearly always playful. By the end of the same year (1851) Knutsford
has become Cranford, in 'Our Society at Cranford', published in
Household Words in December. Here and in the novel which evolved
from this single paper,[10] history and fiction are played off against
one another in a way which accommodates the values which attach
to the past and those which come inevitably in the train of change.
The end of the game is a draw in which all parties, values, modes
and characters alike, can be said both to win and to lose. *Cranford*, in
its final form, the fourth working over of the material from Elizabeth
Gaskell's personal past, is, within my terms, idyllic. The memory is
recalled with a sense of history; it is seen as both particular and
representative; it is given a form in which the rendering itself
contributes to the continuous consciousness of permanence and
change in the same frame or focus. The end effect is of a balance or
equilibrium, since as in *Cousin Phillis* but not 'Mr Harrison's
Confessions', change is seen as inevitable and the values of the past,
though appreciated, are not endorsed at the expense of those which
come with accommodating to change. *Cranford* and *Cousin Phillis* are
Elizabeth Gaskell's achieved 'idylls'. They are distinguished
amongst her other works by the particular way in which the
elements, not in themselves peculiar to these novels, are put
together. The narrators' interest in social change and individual
lives, the viewpoints of historian and fiction-maker are held in
balance inside the unresolved stories.

On her own much-quoted evidence,[11] Elizabeth Gaskell 'never
meant to write more' than one paper in *Household Words*, chs I and II
of *Cranford* as we now have it. The growth of the novel from this
beginning is no doubt a small portion of the history of serialisation as
it affected the Victorian novel. My concern is with the finished
book, which I take to be a novel, in which one of the discernible
structural patterns is repetition. The first paper in *Household Words*
provides the model in a number of ways. The material is part story,
part history. The unity is in the style. The centre of fictional interest
is the characters, but since there are too many of them to lead us to
suppose they can all develop as individuals, the interest will
presumably lie in their relation to one another. As in 'The Last
Generation in England', the relationship is social. Although the
part contains a brief story and two deaths, it is called 'Our Society at
Cranford'. The first paragraphs suggest the nature of the world. In
ways equally vital to the single part and to the novel it is a frail
world. It is threatened like the rural world of *Cousin Phillis*, but its

virtues, like those of Heathbridge, lie in individual integrity and social cohesion. Predominantly feminine, it is drained of its men by the wider world – by the armed services which could send them anywhere or by 'the great neighbouring commercial town of Drumble, distant only twenty miles on a railroad'. By its femininity and its poverty it is a world turned in on itself; 'questions of literature and politics' can be settled without 'unnecessary reasons and arguments', and attention, not required on wider concerns, can be given to the trimness of gardens and the unwritten laws of social life. These laws themselves help to keep the wider world at bay – in paying calls the Cranford ladies were far too occupied in keeping track of inner time in order to keep the calls to the prescribed length ever to touch on any 'absorbing subject'. Poverty is restricting and if, as in Cranford, it is tacitly agreed that as far as possible it will be concealed, it absorbs energy and drives the small society further in on itself behind its 'smiling front'. But in times of trouble the strength of this society lies precisely in this inwardness; concerted humanitarian action is possible only in a small society. In Miss Jessie's unenviable position, who would prefer Drumble to Cranford?

The mock-heroic which, throughout the story, carries the ambiguity of the narrative point of view, is established in the opening paragraphs with the lightest of touches. In 'The Last Generation', explaining the lack of gentlemen at card parties, the author says, 'if ever there was an Amazonian town in England it was—'. In the descriptive and historical essay the form of this remark is itself descriptive; in the novel simile is condensed by the narrator to metaphor: 'In the first place, Cranford is in possession of the Amazons; all the holders of houses above a certain rent are women.' Powerful by virtue of their class, the ladies are active warriors. As the whole part shows they can be a beneficent and healing force. Stylistically the remark has become truly mock-heroic which in its first form it was not. It is supported by two more mock-heroic touches in these opening paragraphs. The 'rules and regulations for visiting and calls' were 'announced to any young people who might be staying in the town with all the solemnity with which the old Manx laws were read once a year on Zinwald Mount'. And, on the question of poverty, the 'gentlefolks of Cranford' were 'like the Spartans, and concealed their smart under a smiling face'. The mock-heroic conveys what is developed in the whole novel, the mingled comedy and near-heroism of these socially restricted lives.

It mirrors the substance of the original part in showing Cranford society as comic against larger considerations, but heroic if you adjust your scale accordingly and see the magnitude of the individual adjustments to passing time and death. Cranford absorbs Captain Brown, is glad of him as a man and coughs politely at his crass announcement of his poverty. When the real sham he has been conducting is revealed by his death Cranford bands together in true compassion to ease Miss Brown's passage from this world and her sister's continued life in it. The story ends in a little tableau of Miss Jessie's eldest child by then sufficiently advanced in years to read to the ageing Miss Jenkyns.

Apparently simple, as so often in Mrs Gaskell, the function and method of this last paragraph of part I are complex. The tableau not only sums up the themes of the two introductory chapters, but, whether a further part was originally intended or not, implies continuation so clearly that it must have been easy to pick up. Further it makes its own comment on story-telling. The leap of years has been made in the convincing memory of the narrator; under this naturalistic cover all kinds of comment can be made. Miss Jenkyns has not relinquished her quarrel with the long-dead Captain but the old ladies' kindness to Miss Jessie has extended over the years and now includes her growing child. The quarrel itself over the relative merits of Dr Johnson and Dickens is partly a quarrel over the old and the new, partly one over style. The child patiently stumbles through pages of the *Rambler* but seizes the opportunity while Miss Jenkyns 'babbles on' to take 'a good long spell at the "Christmas Carol" ', which is available to her because Miss Matty has left it on the table. Miss Matty then is already ranged with the child, clearly if unobtrusively on the side of the new rather than the old, of the heart rather than the head. The themes are picked up immediately in the following story of the early stifling of Miss Matty's heart in social forms and in the third part (chapters v and vi) with the alienation of Peter's by the rigidity of his father. Along with loss of Peter is told the story of the Rector's loss of capacity to express feeling as the style of the old letters hardens off into Latinate phrases. Expression and behaviour are one. In the same way the mock-heroic in the author's own style not only makes the thematic comparison of the large with the small, the important with the trivial, but implies a comparison of ancient and grander methods of legendary story-telling with her own modest little real-life story of the near past.

The serial version of *Cranford* was published in eight parts. The first part contains one statement within one short story of all the themes of the book and a picture of the world in which they are worked out. It is written as from the present, but the past is shown to be living; the style is comic, the matter not always so. But however repetitious the design may be shown to be, readers have felt much more involved in the novel as a whole than can be accounted for merely by unity of the theme-and-variations kind. Ward quotes John Forster as saying before the conclusion, 'I hope if Peter is to die in India, he'll leave Matty really well off, after all her troubles', and Ruskin as wanting more and more:[12]

> I do not know when I have read a more finished little piece of study of human nature (a very great and good thing when it is not spoiled). Nor was I ever more sorry to come to a book's end. I can't think why you left it off! You might have killed Miss Matty since you're fond of killing nice people, and then gone on with Jessie's children, or made yourself an old lady – in time – it would have been lovely.

No one claims strength for the plot; the root of the reader's involvement and the sense of progression must lie elsewhere. John Forster was, I think, suggesting part of the explanation in his response to the very first paper:

> I can hardly tell you, with how much pleasure I could quarrel with you for killing the poor Captain; but that the scene of the daughter's death could not have been written without it.

This has an optimistic sense of rightness or inevitability. Captain Brown's death is a tragic accident, but it enables the tortured life of his daughter to end in unlooked for peace and hopefulness. As in other idylls, 'but' is crucial to the structure of *Cranford*. The standards of gentility may seem inflexible, *but* they will give before the claims of good sense and humanity; Miss Matty's taste in caps may be ridiculous, *but* her dignity as she offers her sovereigns to the man in the Bank or serves tea in her shop cannot be faulted. The oppositions are not simple-mindedly weighted on one side – Miss Pole thinks that a generous and forgiving response should be made to Mrs Jamieson's tardy invitation to tea with Lady Glenmire, *but* that is largely because she has bought a new cap. Down to the smallest things the pattern of the narrative is consistent, as, for instance, Miss Barker's vulgarly plentiful refreshments which all disappear. Oppositions held in a fine balance and presented with affection and distance, these are the staple of pastoral art. And yet the early reactions to the book, which I have taken because they are sophisticated in the sense of being those of sophisticated readers, but unsophisticated in being contemporary and so unaffected by the layers of criticism which later overlay response – these comments by Forster and Ruskin stress progress and continuity. Ruskin suggests that the pattern through the generations would be as absorbing as in its first statement, Forster that, while this may not be the best of all possible worlds, compensating good can come out of bad and will be seen to do so in this novel. However hard it may be to imagine a reader thumbing through *Cranford* to see how it ends, the pleasure of reading on for Forster was a sophisticated version of 'What happens next?' – that is, 'Are my expectations going to be fulfilled?'

The creative reading which involvement in any fiction demands is, in *Cranford*, used to a reflective or contemplative end. The gaps between the narrator and her material are the realistically conceived ones of generation and place. They are paralleled by the distance between the reader and the fiction which not only allows space for such reading but in the smallest details requires it. In the elements of style most frequently commented on the reader is involved in a very complicated activity. Take, for instance, one of the narrator's direct questions to the reader, 'Have you any red silk umbrellas in London?' The answer presumably is 'no', but it can hardly stop there. In its context the question appears to be about fashion:

> The materials of their clothes are, in general, good and plain, and most of them are nearly as scrupulous as Miss Tyler, of cleanly memory; but I will answer for it, the last gigot, the last tight and scanty petticoat in wear in England, was seen in Cranford – and seen without a smile. (1 2)

Assuming the complicity of sophistication we smile and continue to do so, to begin with, at the 'little spinster' pattering to church under the flamboyant and unsuitable umbrella. But as the last survivor of a large family she is not simply amusing. When the 'strong father' held it over 'a troop of little ones' it had presumably been chosen, like Cranford's clothes in general, for its practicality; it would have had its fashionable time in London long before it reached Cranford, where it would originally have been a survival. Now, this single example of red silk umbrellas is itself a survival of what had once caused a stir in Cranford and shelters a lonely, elderly lady, herself the surviver of a 'troop of little ones'. This is not simply that Cranford is compared with London; the question becomes the centre of the reader's consciousness of the process of time. No less than three time-scales are shown here – town, country and family time. Add to this realisation the fact that the reader may as easily live in Manchester or Birmingham as London and another dimension of relativity is uncovered in which the reader is placed in space as well as in the flux of time. If an illustration were needed for the cover of a new edition, the little lady under the huge umbrella could well serve as an emblem of the whole book. At once pathetic and comic, frail and tough, she stands for surviving courage in a world of fluctuating values. The narrator's question leads the reader to the depth of the vignette's significance; at least it directs him, only his answer can go all the way.

Any transference of the attention away from this active relationship between narrator and reader distorts the total effect of the book. A recent television musical version of *Cranford* used the obvious film flashback technique to recall Miss Matty as the sweet girl who became the still sweet but eccentric spinster. A ball in the Assembly Rooms was shown, Miss Matty in an Empire gown with a fan and curls. The whole lengthy dance down the couples was enclosed in dimmed edges to show us that we were inside her memories. The origin of this episode in the book is very different:

We went into the cloak-room adjoining the Assembly Room; Miss Matty gave a sigh or two to her departed youth, and the remembrance of the last time she had been there, as she adjusted her pretty new cap before the strange, quaint old mirror in the cloak-room. The Assembly Room had been added to the inn, about a hundred years before, by the different county families, who met together there once a month during the winter to dance and play at cards. Many a county beauty had first swung through the minuet that she afterwards danced before Queen Charlotte in this very room. It was said that one of the Gunnings had graced the apartment with her beauty; it was certain that a rich and beautiful widow, Lady Williams, had here been smitten with the noble figure of a young artist, who was staying with some

family in the neighbourhood for professional purposes, and
accompanied his patrons to Cranford Assembly. And a pretty
bargain poor Lady Williams had of her handsome husband, if all
tales were true. Now no beauty blushed and dimpled along the
sides of the Cranford Assembly Room; no handsome artist won
hearts by his bow, *chapeau bras* in hand; the old room was dingy;
the salmon-coloured paint had faded into a drab; great pieces of
plaster had chipped off from the white wreaths and festoons on its
walls; but still a mouldy odour of aristocracy lingered about the
place, and a dusty recollection of the days that were gone made
Miss Matty and Mrs. Forrester bridle up as they entered, and
walk mincingly up the room, as if there were a number of genteel
observers, instead of two little boys with a stick of toffy between
them with which to beguile the time.   (IX 102–3)

Here Miss Matty gives only 'a sigh or two to her departed youth'
and the memories are unspecific. The glimpse we are given into the
past is hardly of the past at all, it is only the legends that have lived
on. They are introduced with 'it was said' and 'it was certain', the
'said' casting a doubt on the 'certain'. In fact the whole paragraph is
emphatically about the present – the peeling plaster and the
lingering legends are part of Cranford now. However, the past is not
just a legend; it lingers in a very real way in instinctive behaviour. It
is the indelible stamp of the past which stops the ladies' party 'short
of the second front row'; their adjustment to the altered present is
inside the patterns of the past:

> We stopped short at the second front row; I could hardly
> understand why, until I heard Miss Pole ask a stray waiter if any
> of the county families were expected; and when he shook his head,
> and believed not, Mrs. Forrester and Miss Matty moved
> forwards, and our party represented a conversational square. The
> front row was soon augmented and enriched by Lady Glenmire
> and Mrs. Jamieson. We six occupied the two front rows, and our
> aristocratic seclusion was respected by the groups of shopkeepers
> who strayed in from time to time and huddled together on the
> back benches.   (IX 103)

The narrator apparently identifies herself with the social
stereotypes, but 'augmented and enriched' and 'huddled' are a
verbal joke with the reader. She becomes herself increasingly

constrained by the effort not to turn round and the boredom of aristocratic seclusion is so great as to send Mrs Jamieson, of all people, to sleep. The whole ridiculous scene is watched from behind the 'obstinate green curtain' by 'two odd eyes, seen through holes, as in the old tapestry story'. The division of the audience into aristocracy and merry peasants is as unreal as the 'aristocracy' is precarious, and the merry togetherness of the shopkeepers a matter of conjecture since it was 'not the thing' to turn round to see if the truth bore any relation to the stereotype. The reader comes 'independently', as it were, to the conclusion that it bears no such relation, indeed that such relation in fact belongs to the world of story where it had its own appropriate vocabulary. I hope to show later that the mystification of the conjuring act is central to the structure of *Cranford*. Meanwhile these examples illustrate the close involvement of the reader in the construction of a sense of passing time. This is not simply an historical awareness, though that is involved, but an emotional awareness of the past as part of the living present both as a source of strength and, in its hardened vocabulary, an emotional straitjacket.

In a sense the end of the book releases the reader from this straitjacket. The effort of reconstruction I have described is a backward movement as the reader grasps what once was in its relation to what now is. This is paralleled, of course, by the similar effort made by the narrator, who is in only intermittent contact with Cranford and is herself younger than the characters she describes. The overall forward movement of the book, felt so strongly by Forster and Ruskin, is one of emotional effect and works on a larger scale over larger portions of the book than the indications of time. The novel moves from dark to light. Death and loss are confined to the first three of the eight parts. There is the death of Captain Brown in Part i, the death of Miss Jenkyns which leaves Miss Matty alone and the death of Mr Holbrook in Part ii, and the disappearance of Peter in Part iii. Each of these parts moves in the general direction of the whole book, towards lightness. Part i ends with Flora, Part ii with Miss Matty submitting to Love and Fate at the news that Martha has Jem Hearn just waiting to step into the role of allowed follower, and Part iii with Love and Fate putting Miss Matty to a further proof of resolution as Martha and Jem kiss goodnight on the doorstep. Each of the parts begins comically, encloses the sadness, and ends comically again with a look to the future. The end of the book follows the pattern of these endings. After the extremity of Miss

Matty's difficulties, and the concerted community effort which has received them, Peter bends his energies to the comic resolution of an essentially unserious quarrel in which ruffled feelings and some social unease are all that is at stake. The rout of Mrs Jamieson by Peter's 'tricks' restores her to Cranford and: 'Ever since that day there has been the old friendly sociability in Cranford society.' The narrator is 'thankful', as now Miss Matty can end her days in peace. Margaret Tarratt[13] sees Miss Matty as an active force and the movement of the book as showing the good effect of Miss Matty on Cranford. I do not think Miss Matty is active as a character in this way. Her heroism is of the kind that endures rather than acts. The good in Cranford has been active since Part 1; she calls it out but no more actively than Miss Jessie in Part 1, who, like Miss Matty later, is prepared to endure and look around for methods of self-help.

Many a critic has seen the return of Peter as a forced happy ending, an easy way out of ending on too stern a note. I think this is a mis-reading of the book. There are, in fact, two happy endings in *Cranford*, one 'historical', one fictional. The happy ending in the social dimension of the book is, it is true, independent of Peter's return. It is prepared for in the long chapter, 'Friends in Need', which is a part on its own in the serial version. The part is divided in two halves, the ineffectual, followed by the effective action. It begins with the touching comedy of Martha's pudding and a sadly truthful if comic indictment of Miss Matty's education, which renders her quite unfit to teach – an occupation she could have followed with no loss of gentility. In the second half Cranford is shown as effective in its own way. Martha and Jem settle in with Miss Matty, Miss Matty makes the ultimate sacrifice of the past, arranging 'a little in order as to their pecuniary estimation' such things as 'her mother's wedding-ring, the strange, uncooth brooch with which her father had disfigured his shirt-frill, &c,' and the narrator's father arrives from Drumble to settle things in his own gruff way. And in a wonderfully caught parody of the ways of the world, the ladies arrange a 'movement' with a board meeting and a secret ballot, in which Mrs Forrester's contribution of a twentieth of her entire income would bear 'a different value in another account-book that I have heard of'. Cranford is thus identified by its place between the living Christianity of the small community and the efficiency of the business world. As a representative of the larger world the narrator's father feels he has his limitations:

Confound it! I could make a good lesson out of it if I were a parson; but, as it is, I can't get a tail to my sentences – only I'm sure you feel what I want to say. (XIV 169)

The parson's rhetoric would make a lesson out of it but the fact would be unaltered. Peter's return makes a 'story', it is fun and delightful, but the book makes the specific point that 'plot' is at one level, 'character' at another. All the additions to the facts that Peter makes are 'extras', but in Miss Matty's heart he is not an extra but the living past. In 'A Happy Return', all the themes of the book are resolved in a series of vignettes and economically dramatised episodes. With Lady Glenmire married, Martha's baby on the way and welcomed by Miss Matty, Miss Matty herself sharing Mr Johnson's tea custom in her whitewashed shop with a little piece of oilcloth for customers to stand on, then Peter can return. He has sold everything and made the journey back as impulsively as he left. He closes the shop, which was doing perfectly well, in a shower of gifts, and justifies his return by making Miss Matty happy, and most memorably, by the comic rout of Mrs Jamieson.

Peter's return brings the tragic and the comic aspects of the book full circle. Peter links Miss Matty with her past; the real denouement for her comes when they link hands and speak of their mother long dead. He has the unwitting aid of the Gordons in the reconciliation of Mrs Jamieson with Mrs Hoggins, and we are reminded lightly that Jessie Brown and her family were our glimpse into the future at the end of Part 1. The comic element of Cranford resolves into the retrospective defeat of Deborah Jenkyns as well as the return of Mrs Jamieson to social life. This return is, in fact, a rather qualified happy ending since who can suppose that a continuous effort of social tact and good will would not be needed to stop the gap from opening again? Nevertheless, in the frail way in which the values of Cranford can be sustained, this feat is a triumph. Peter accomplishes it by applying the 'strong stimulants' Mrs Jamieson needed to 'excite her to come out of her apathy'. These stimulants are the absurd tales of his travels, in which the Himalayas get higher and higher, reaching eventually so near to Heaven that Peter shot a 'cherubim' as game. Meanwhile Mrs Jamieson has been persuaded to patronise the performance by Brunoni arranged by Peter. The ladies' consternation at Peter's apparent wooing of Mrs Jamieson turns out to be as unnecessary as their panic over the robberies and violence they had previously connected with the conjuror's presence in Cranford. Peter turns his own legend into an exaggerated absurdity, and the conjuror's magic is likewise confined to the theatrical. But Brunoni leads to Peter and Peter heals wounds both small and large in Cranford. The living power of the past is unexpectedly revealed everywhere in this book, as individual stoicism and community feeling show the peeling plaster and outmoded fashions of this sleepy town to be its least significant characteristics.

When Peter is forgotten in the story the East is present in the person of Signor Brunoni. He is, in a way, central to the pattern of doubling and reflection in the book since he provides the link with Peter in the Providential remark of his wife, which causes the idea to 'flash' through the narrator's head that Peter might be the Aga Jenkyns:

> True, he was reported by many to be dead. But, equally true, some had said that he had arrived at the dignity of Great Lama of Thibet. Miss Matty thought he was alive. I would make further inquiry. , (XI 133)

The letter the narrator sends 'on its race to the strange wild countries beyond the Ganges' as a consequence of this remark, has its comic counterpart in the advertisement for fake marvels, to which 'only the name of the town where he would next display them was wanting'. Signor Brunoni and his wife are occupied with this when the narrator goes to them for the address for her letter. The conjuror had appeared in Cranford a mysterious and sinister figure, but has turned out to be a poor struggling family man, sick and greatly in need of all the help Cranford can give, even bread jelly. The story of little Phoebe's survival is stranger than the tricks at the conjuror's command. It is a story of effort, endurance and Providence. In such a story, that of the other Browns, the book begins, and it is Miss Matty's story too. While Peter, in this pattern of romance and reality is a romantic legend which materialises, he puts his charm to constructive use at the end and links the social and personal dimensions of the book inside a light-hearted fairy-tale mode. Much of the delight of *Cranford* is in the pleasure of repeated patterns and the link between the conjuror and the lost brother takes them in a particular narrative mode as far as the absurd exaggerations with which Peter charms Mrs Jamieson. His return out of the past and the restoration of social harmony in Cranford is like the last and most heavily ornamented repeat in an eighteenth-century aria – it pleases by the daring of its fanciful treatment of the expected. But, of course, there is a sense in which this flight of fancy is a part of what the book ultimately says, that the survival of what is enduring in Cranford is, under the circumstances, truly marvellous.

In *Cranford* history and fiction move in counterpoint to show the present in a continuous relation with the past. The permanent values of the story are suggested by the repetitive patterns and comment by juxtaposition which make up the structure. Beneath a placid surface *Cranford* is, in fact, a book of exaggerated contrasts held in skilful blance. The mock-heroic, for instance, which could reduce this world to a collection of cardboard comic characters, is here made truly effective by an underlying sympathy for individuals. The sympathy is held in check well this side of sentimentality, not only by the comedy of the mock-heroic, but by the perspective from which the narrator makes conscious patterns of the material. As parodic suggestions of the marvellous act to make the confined circumstances of the story that much more solid and real, exaggerated or obvious fictionalising turns into 'story' the 'truths' of social observation.

The achieved idyllic balance of *Cousin Phillis*, on the other hand, contains the underlying contrasts inside its own world. There is no observer to measure scale and no self-reflecting reference to narrative modes. A late work, it conceals its artistry behind an appearance of complete naturalness. This is not simplicity but, in Arnold's sense, *simplesse*, even though there is no obvious sign, as there is in *Cranford*, of an invitation to the reader actually to consider the handling as part of his response. The varied pace, the alternating elisions and elongations of time-span, the evanescent recall of speech and the settled composition of visual recall – these structural features of the book are accurately mimetic of the working of memory. Paul as middle-aged narrator speaks from a standpoint at once distant and intimate. The mingled detachment and concern which makes a slightly puzzling figure of the narrator of *The Woodlanders*, for instance, is here completely unproblematic; the *naïveté* of his point of view at the time of the events, as onlooker and participant, is allowed by the reader and the mature narrator to be a part of youth. Paul is an attractive narrator because of his tolerant but unbemused view of his youthful self. The harmonious beauty of *Cousin Phillis* resides in this naturalistic use of the narrator. At a prosaic level of probability the work satisfies. A complete world at a brief moment of time is, it seems, fully recalled. Because the central hold on the material is so firm, so ordinary and so natural, the richness of what is in fact shown arouses no comment; each new detail as it surfaces in the process of narrative recall adds first of all to credibility, to the solidity of the fictional world.

The formal division of *Cousin Phillis* into four parts marks the structured phases of the story, and, like other devices used in this tale, conceals its art by an apparent naturalism. The parts, two expository, one climactic, one the denouement, mirror the varied pace of recall. The first part establishes the fictional world in all its variety, and the relation of narrator and reader. It has the relaxed discursiveness of settling down to tell a memory and takes the story to the point where all the characters have met. In Part II the characters and the worlds they represent begin their interaction; Paul is removed from the centre of the stage, but after his farewell to the idea of 'my dear Cousin Phillis as the possessor of my heart and life', his disinterested credibility is established. Part III, the shortest by some pages, contains nearly all the high moments of the love-story for Phillis, and, with the departure of Holdsworth for Canada, Paul's acceptance of the change in his world. Part IV is elegiac. Phillis's secret and illusory happiness is destroyed. The family, chastened as much by the cause of her illness as by her approach to death, reunite in closer knowledge of one another, the work of the farm continues, Holman is softened and, above all, the community strengthened by the concern for the Minister's family and his renewed commitment to them. The narrator, caught up in the effects of the story, becomes less and less a factor in it. In *Cousin Phillis* what Mackail calls 'the balance of subject and treatment' is so complete that an effort to describe it runs into the difficulty encountered by the reviewer of Clough's *The Bothie*, who was unable to find any extractable part. It seems to achieve its balance by means so particular to this story of these people at this time that they are unrepeatable. But the celebration of community, albeit in a minor key, at the end of *Cousin Phillis* is found not only in *Cranford* as well, but in *Adam Bede, Under the Greenwood Tree* and *Far from the Madding Crowd*. In *Cousin Phillis* and *Adam Bede* the celebration includes a sense of loss, in *Cranford* and *Under the Greenwood Tree* a sense of continuing adjustments in individual life beyond the end of the story, in *Far from the Madding Crowd* a little of both. In all these idyllic novels we see a world touched by experience regather its forces at the end for a precarious survival into the future.

The elements of the fictional world of *Cousin Phillis*, in spite of the single focus of the title, can be presented as a set of oppositions like the railroad and the farm, technology and books, travel and roots, movement and stability. But the essence of the story does not lie in their conflict, but in their temporary mingling at a precise moment of apparent permanence in a process of historical change. At every level of organisation the story avoids schematisation so that the achieved balance always seems to be simple observation. It is, for instance, in Paul's ruffled feelings on his first evening at Hope Farm that we first encounter the friction between the worlds of mechanical invention and the dead languages. Feeling at a disadvantage in the strange world which is soon to be so rudely shaken by his own familiar world of work, he indicates that he too knows something worth knowing:

'. . . You've a good clear head of your own, my lad – choose how you came by it.'
'From my father,' said I proudly. 'Have you not heard of his discovery of a new method of shunting? It was in the *Gazette*. It was patented. I thought everyone had heard of Manning's patent winch.'
'We don't know who invented the alphabet,' said he, half-smiling, and taking up his pipe.
'No, I dare say not, sir,' replied I, half-offended; 'that's so long ago.' (I 20)

The Minister makes amends by asking Paul's help with the technical words he has come across in a book of 'stiff mathematics' he acquired by accident. Having acquired it he has read it. He enjoys conversations with Paul's father as well as with Holdsworth; Paul says of him, 'he could have been an engineer', and on his farm the Minister has a good grasp on physical fact and a practical sense of what to do:

'Ned Hall, there ought to be a water-furrow across this land: it's a nasty, stiff, clayey, dauby bit of ground and thou and I must fall to, come next Monday.' (I 15)

Holman is stiff-backed and inflexible in some respects, blind to his daughter's approaching womanhood, but, conversant as he is with the dead languages his mind is open, dangerously open he feels:

'Yes' (once more hesitating), 'I like him, and I think he is an upright man; there is a want of seriousness in his talk at times, but, at the same time, it is wonderful to listen to him! He makes Horace and Virgil living, instead of dead, by the stories he tells me of his sojourn in the very countries where they lived, and where to this day, he says – But it is like dram-drinking. I listen to him, till I forget my duties and am carried off my feet. Last Sabbath-evening, he led us away into talk on profane subjects ill-befitting the day.' (II 53)

If the lines of opposition are blurred in themselves in this way, they are also complicated – or made more real, it amounts to the same thing – by the workings of time. Holman and Paul's father, Minister and mechanic, are alike, for instance, in their affectionate misunderstanding of their children. But in this story the generations meet with the same openness to one another and mutual respect as do the various worlds the characters represent:

Towards Christmas, my dear father came to see me, and to consult Mr. Holdsworth about the improvement which has since been known as 'Manning's driving-wheel'. Mr. Holdsworth, as I think I have before said, had a very great regard for my father, who had been employed in the same great machine-shop in which Mr. Holdsworth had served his apprenticeship; and he and my father had many mutual jokes about one of these gentlemen-apprentices who used to set about his smith's work in white wash-leather gloves, for fear of spoiling his hands. Mr. Holdsworth often spoke to me about my father as having the same kind of genius for mechanical invention as that of George Stephenson; and my father had come over now to consult him about several improvements, as well as an offer of partnership. It was a great pleasure to me to see the mutual regard of these two men: Mr. Holdsworth, young, handsome, keen, well-dressed, an object of admiration to all the youth of Eltham; my father, in his decent but unfashionable Sunday clothes, his plain, sensible face full of hard lines, the marks of toil and thought, – his hands blackened, beyond the power of soap and water, by years of labour in the foundry; speaking a strong Northern dialect, while Mr. Holdsworth had a long, soft drawl in his voice, as many of the Southerners have, and was reckoned in Eltham to give himself airs. (II 32)

This last passage is typical of the method of *Cousin Phillis*. The tone is conversational, but the metonymic use of detail is powerfully evocative because so economical. The 'hands blackened, beyond the power of soap and water', stand for a whole way of life. With the shared joke about the gentleman-apprentice in 'white wash-leather gloves' the passage is unified by the notion of hands. Detail here both particularises at a naturalistic level of recall and generalises inside the underlying pattern of the book. Similarly the light suggestion of the varied speech patterns indicates the social inclusiveness of new work-patterns. In this short paragraph there is technical shorthand – 'Manning's driving-wheel', the class-based joke, Manning's 'strong Northern dialect', Holdsworth's drawl and Eltham's gossip which 'reckoned' Holdsworth gave 'himself airs'. A warm, work-based relationship which crosses social barriers is the idealised subject of this paragraph. This too is conveyed by tone of voice; Paul's affectionate pride, 'it was a great pleasure to me to see the mutual regard of these two men', makes the memory of Holdsworth's appreciation of Manning's inventive genius glow with a felt intensity. Paul has a sharp aural memory and the prose of *Cousin Phillis* is shot through with echoes of the spoken voice. The sharpness of the detail always supports the idyllic balance of oppositions and the warmth of the narrator's feelings gives the harmonious idyllic glow. His boyish hero-worship of Holdsworth is fleetingly recalled, for instance, when he seems to catch a turn of speech that would come more naturally to Holdsworth than to Paul; the portrait of this 'fine fellow' tells the reader as much about the probable folly inside the terms of the tale, of relying on Holdsworth's dependability as it does of the impression he made on Paul:

The afternoon work was more uncertain than the morning's; it might be the same, or it might be that I had to accompany Mr. Holdsworth, the managing engineer, to some point on the line between Eltham and Hornby. This I always enjoyed, because of the variety, and because of the country we traversed (which was very wild and pretty), and because I was thrown into companion-ship with Mr. Holdsworth, who held the position of hero in my boyish mind. He was a young man of five-and-twenty or so, and was in a station above mine, both by birth and education; and he had travelled on the Continent, and wore mustachios and whiskers of a somewhat foreign fashion. I was proud of being seen with him. He was really a fine fellow, in a good number of ways, and I might have fallen into much worse hands. (1 3)

The recall of such detail brings vividly before us what 'Q' called the 'the steady background of rural England'. The detail is both vivid and socially telling, of course, because it attached to people and how they felt. However, we know comparatively little about the characters except in the terms in which they interact. We know their world rather than them. Phillis, who is the centre of the pattern of relationships and gives her name to the book, is known by the impression she makes rather than as a character. She is the centre of Paul's recollections, but he has never been close to her. While the world of work, the pattern of social relationships attached to class, is summoned in vivid observations of individual details, separate but with an accumulative effect, Phillis herself and the countryside around the farm are described in a series of static, composed verbal pictures. The countryside is the setting for Phillis. We have seen how, among Tennyson's English Idyls, in 'Dora', 'Audley Court' and 'The Gardener's Daughter', static pictures and a sense of moving time are complementary in the Victorian idyllic vision. So they are in *Cousin Phillis*. The pictures have a timeless glow and yet in the telling the narrative is obsessed with time. Again this is a part of the naturalistic method of the book; the strongest emotional memories are frequently pictorial and accurate recall involves an effort to reproduce the sequence of events which memory often obscures. Paul himself links the initial memory and the effort to impose an order on it:

> The remembrance of many a happy day, and of several little scenes, comes back upon me as I think of that summer. They rise like pictures to my memory, and in this way I can date their succession; for I know that corn-harvest must have come after hay-making, apple-gathering after corn-harvest. (III 54)

The strength of the 'poetic' feeling in these pictures, as Paul recalls them, no doubt arises from his knowledge of what is to follow this momentary calm. Paul's sense of approaching climax conveys itself, however, in more generalised terms to the reader to whom it is clear that the different social worlds have in fact come too close, so close that the balance is endangered.

This central part of the story is introduced in two pictures; they are Paul's impressions as he comes on the scene, but they give the sense of a world caught on the point of vanishing. The first is the hay-making scene – a rural landscape with figures, a generic picture of the Holmans' world:

> I went off . . . through the farm-yard, past the cattle-pond, into the ash-field, beyond into the higher field, with two holly-bushes in the middle. I arrived there: there was Betty with all the farming men, and a cleared field, and a heavily-laden cart; one man at the top of the great pile, ready to catch the fragrant hay which the others threw up to him with their pitchforks; a little heap of cast-off clothes in a corner of the field (for the heat, even at seven o'clock, was insufferable), a few cans and baskets, and Rover lying by them, panting and keeping watch. Plenty of loud, hearty, cheerful talking. . . . (III 55)

The second is a Romantic landscape in which the figures are in a very different relation to the background:

> So 'out yonder' I went; out on to a broad upland common, full of red sand-banks, and sweeps and hollows; bordered by dark firs, purple in the coming shadows, but near at hand all ablaze with flowering gorse, or, as we call it in the south, furze-bushes, which, seen against the belt of distant trees, appeared brilliantly golden. On this heath, a little way from the field-gate, I saw the three. I counted their heads, joined together in an eager group over Holdsworth's theodolite. He was teaching the minister the practical art of surveying and taking a level. I was wanted to assist, and was quickly set to work to hold the chain. Phillis was as intent as her father; she had hardly time to greet me, so desirous was she to hear the answer to her father's question.
>
> So we went on, the dark clouds still gathering, for perhaps five minutes after my arrival. Then came the blinding lightning and the rumble and quick-following rattling peal of thunder, right over our heads. (III 55–6)

The dark contrasts of this 'picture' relate only to the coming thunderstorm. The absorbed attention of the group of figures is unrelated to the background, but their activity is unproductively theoretical – almost as far removed from the work of the farm as they would have been if reading Virgil – and we may, if we wish, read the darkness as the threat of emotional storm, which is absent from the harmonious sunshine of the hay-making scene. The

progress of the six months from this moment to Christmas is marked
by two more 'pictures', both high moments in Phillis's emotional
life, pointed by the precision and beauty of the description of the
setting. She offers the nosegay to Holdsworth in the autumn garden
and is given her illusion of happiness in her childhood 'hermitage'
in the snow-covered wood-pile. These static or timeless moments
have a double function in this most concentrated of the parts.
Ironically they not only mark the timeless quality of the feelings
in them, but the inexorable progress of time as the year seems to rush
through high summer to Christmas. Distance of space as well as time
isolates the events. Holdsworth departs for Canada; his vision of
himself returning in two years' time like a prince to waken his
sleeping beauty has a touch of 'coxcombry' which jars on Paul and
puts this quiet rural world in perspective. The Holmans' world is
made to seem small even as we acknowledge that he is going to
betray it. These small events are placed in time by the accompanying seasonal markings, which are inseparable in the presentation
from the events themselves. But the part opens with a skilful
reference to all the time-scales operating in the story:

> Just after this, I went home for a week's holiday. Everything was
> prospering there; my father's new partnership gave evident
> satisfaction to both parties. There was no display of increased
> wealth in our modest household; but my mother had a few extra
> comforts provided for her by her husband. I made acquaintance
> with Mr. and Mrs. Ellison, and first saw pretty Margaret Ellison,
> who is now my wife. When I returned to Eltham, I found that a
> step was decided upon which had been in contemplation for some
> time: that Holdsworth and I should remove our quarters to
> Hornby; our daily presence, and as much of our time as possible,
> being required for the completion of the line at that end.   (III 53)

Paul's time here is the double time-scale of his participation in
events at the farm and his long-term perspective on the whole story.
Historical time and time in the individual lives of the characters are
marked together by the progress of the railway towards completion.
It has brought the work so near to Heathbridge that work and 'hot
town lodgings' can be exchanged every day for a 'balmy hour or
two' in the 'fresh and pleasant country'. There is no easy over-
writing which would convey a sense of threat, only naturalness and

inevitability as the story moves to the climax brought about by the propinquity of the two worlds.

Until this moment at the opening of the climactic part III the passage of real time has been obscured. Parts I and II cover three years. This is a long time in Paul's young professional life, but the time-scheme is not important and a deliberate effort has to be made to add up the months and years as they pass. At the end of this waiting period in the story all Paul's worlds have eventually come into contact with one another and Part III opens with Paul's effort as narrator to get the time-sequence clear, in the passage I have quoted. Before this, one kind of time is marked by the irregular intervals between visits to Hope Farm; otherwise time moves imperceptibly so that Paul assumes he 'took more notice than anyone else' of the 'small event' which marks Phillis's emerging into womanhood. She left off pinafores for 'pretty linen aprons in the morning, and a black silk one in the afternoon', but even Paul, who noticed, claims that he does not know 'why they were banished'. Phillis is 'the centre of the story, not so much as an explored character, which she is not, but as a focus for all the elements of this picture of a changing world. Pictures of her are interspersed throughout the story from the first one in 'the westering sun' (I 8) to the last one before her disappointment, 'standing under the budding branches of the grey trees' (IV 77–8). These pictures have the clear glow and frozen quality of memories, but they also have a structural function. They are the punctuation marks or means of structuring the story, which is centrally about the passage of time and the ways of life which, with passing time, impinge on one another in their own process of change. They represent the points at which the worlds touch briefly, in mutual accord.

Nowhere is this clearer than in the opening sequence of part II. There is no time-gap between this and part I, but at this central moment in the expository section of the book, the waiting period at the end of which all Paul's worlds have begun their interaction, pictures of Phillis flicker in the memory along with other sense impression; the loud ticking of the clock marks a moment when time appears otherwise to be completely still:

> Cousin Holman gave me the weekly county-newspaper to read aloud to her, while she mended stockings out of a high piled-up basket, Phillis helping her mother. I read and read, unregardful of the words I was uttering, thinking of all manner of other things;

of the bright colour of Phillis's hair, as the afternoon sun fell on her bending head; of the silence of the house, which enabled me to hear the double tick of the old clock which stood half-way up the stairs; of the variety of inarticulate noises which cousin Holman made while I read, to show her sympathy, wonder, or horror at the newspaper intelligence. The tranquil monotony of that hour made me feel as if I had lived for ever, and should live for ever, droning out paragraphs in that warm sunny room, with my two quiet hearers, and the curled up pussy-cat sleeping on the hearthrug, and the clock on the house-stairs perpetually clicking out the passage of the moments. By-and-by, Betty, the servant, came to the door into the kitchen, and made a sign to Phillis, who put her half-mended stocking down, and went into the kitchen without a word. Looking at cousin Holman a minute or two afterwards, I saw that she had dropped her chin upon her breast, and had fallen fast asleep. I put the newspaper down, and was nearly following her example, when a waft of air from some unseen source slightly opened the door of communication with the kitchen, that Phillis must have left unfastened; and I saw part of her figure as she sate by the dresser, peeling apples with quick dexterity of finger, but with repeated turnings of her head towards some book lying on the dresser by her.   (II 26)

Phillis, quiet as she is, is mobile almost restless in this somnolent scene. It is Phillis who carries the sense of active possibility in this timeless world. It is also, of course, Phillis who activates the renewal of old patterns at the end. During her illness the family re-forms itself in the light of the Minister's recognition of Phillis's capacity for action springing from mature feeling. Phillis's illness also draws the community close in their respect for Holman and affection for his daughter. The story of Holman's sense of himself in relation to the community parallels the story of Phillis's growth to maturity. Part I shows a remarkable correspondence between the community view of the Minister's way of life and what Paul is told of his life by Phillis. Phillis only adds detail (I 14) to the description of him given by the landlord who answers Paul's inquiry for his relatives (I 7). The two central parts show the Minister 'drinking his dram of forgetfulness'. In Part IV the community gathers round him – ineffectually for the most part, but the farm is kept quiet on the crucial last day of Phillis's illness by Timothy, the half-wit, who 'reckons' Paul 'no better nor a half-wit yoursel'' for not thinking of sending the carts another way to Hornby market. No aspect of the Minister's life can ever be exactly the same after the revelation of his daughter's share in the catastrophe. But in the same way that he will learn to live with his knowledge of her as a woman, he will keep patience with the Elders and adjust to Timothy's slow wit in the knowledge of his good heart. The community is not just the background to this story, it has a part to play. If its stability is set against the volatility of the new technological society, the opposition is no more schematic than the oppositions of other ways of life and modes of perception which make up this story. The underlying contrasts in *Cousin Phillis* are set not so much in opposition as in a temporary interaction. The distance established by the circumstances of the narration – the story told as a personal memory – allows for the sense that the past is carried forward into the present in all the glow of its ideality. Affection and non-commitment in the narrator are perfectly natural. So too is the point of comparative sophistication from which the narrator can survey a world removed from present business but indisputably part of his living consciousness. The perspective from which he can see a multi-faceted but unresolved situation is itself a part of that situation.

Elizabeth Gaskell is alone among the authors I consider in writing an idyllic tale so late in her career. *Cousin Phillis* is marked by the transposition of art into an appearance of naturalness, as *Cranford* is marked by consciousness of style and handling. One reason why the idyllic mode lasted so late in her career is the persistence in her work of the preoccupations which can be handled so well in the mode, a sense of the interdependence but separateness of the individual and his social circumstances, and a vision of the permanence of essential values in a process of change. After *Cousin Phillis* she returned to her memories of Knutsford, reworking the Cranford material once more in 'The Cage at Cranford',[14] and then producing the material for the last time subsumed in the rich comic pattern of *Wives and Daughters*. There the themes, repetitions, contrasts, historical observation of *Cranford* are absorbed in the line of the human story. The narrator has a wider view than Molly Gibson so that, to some extent Molly is seen objectively in relation to her surroundings, but centrally the viewpoint is controlled by the narrator's endorsement of Molly's sensibility. There is some distance, but only between the narrator and some characters. The plan for the ending described by the editor of the *Cornhill Magazine* after Elizabeth Gaskell's death was, of course, for the full resolution of the story in the comic pattern of happy marriages. Central concentration on a single character similarly disposes the elements of *Ruth* in an unidyllic pattern. In *Ruth* the exploration of a social problem through the fate of a single individual does not admit of balance or equilibrium any more than it admits of distance. History and story make a different pattern again in *Sylvia's Lovers*, where the bleakly romantic love-story is told against a carefully reconstructed historical background in the manner of the Romantic historical novel. In the idylls, on the other hand, history is recent and told by a narrator who is as continuously aware of the present as of the past, and who sees the process of change as forcing reconciliation of its opposing pressures in the lives of the characters, whether they are aware or not. This would serve as a partial description of the two remaining large-scale works, the two 'industrial', or condition-of-England novels, *Mary Barton* and *North and South* as well as of *Cranford* and *Cousin Phillis*. Of course, the two longer novels are neither idylls nor idyllic, but it is my argument that isolating the 'poetic' idyllic strain in these realist novels reveals the pastoral mode as one way of turning into art, and thus simultaneously exploring and mediating, oppositions plain to any observer of the mid-century social scene, but difficult to contain in one frame. *Mary Barton* and *North and South* are both illuminated, though in different ways, by distinguishing an idyllic method at work in them, even while the method does not in the end produce the characteristic idyllic effect.

In *Mary Barton* the dramatic conflicts, the violent climax of the story and the suspense surrounding Jem's trial, all belong to another kind of fiction than the idyllic. Nevertheless the germ of the book puts the narrator in a position which has something in common with that of an idyllic narrator. There is a felt need to mediate between a sophisticated readership and characters who, whatever the strength of their feelings, can deliver no message for themselves. Appalled by the conditions of the newly industrialised city, Elizabeth Gaskell saw that 'there [were] many whose lives are tragic poems which cannot take formal language'.[15] Thus, the narrative is designed, as we saw before, to show how a man 'full of rude, illogical thought' might be driven by his sympathy for suffering and lack of power and language, to 'a course of action, violating an eternal law of God'. The narrative must show too what might well not be apparent to potential victims of the 'illogical thought', the 'poetry' of the inner reality which gave these lives truly tragic proportions. In a fiction the continuing capacity for trust, faith and openness can hardly be shown to exist by the violator of God's eternal law. But while, in *Mary Barton*, such capacity is transferred to other characters in the community of the poor and suffering the novel does encounter difficulties. The darkness of the lives is not spiritual but 'real' in a limited and concrete way. The conditions in which Davenport lies dying, and the squalor of the street scenes on his workmates' journey to visit him, leave a stronger impression than the communal feeling and family unity which are also a part of the total effect of the scene. In so far as this is a picture of how people 'really' live, we, as readers, cannot respond to the flickering of the human spirit in such darkness without asking why it should have to struggle against such appalling odds. Which is to make the obvious point, reinforced by contemporary response and recent criticism, that the material itself is too politically explosive to be submitted to satisfactory resolution inside the realistic fiction. The central difficulty of *Mary Barton* as a novel is that the methods by which the outer reality can be made clear are of a different kind from those which signal the inner reality. When, for example, the pace of the narrative slows for the sequence which includes the confrontation of Carson and Barton, Carson's change of heart and the death scene, we are given time to absorb the dramatic link between the murderer and the suffering father.[16] The 'melodrama' of the tableau of forgiveness and death is a move to inner truth, a revelation of what Peter Brooks calls 'the moral occult'.[17] This dimension is rendered, naturally enough, by the least realistic methods. Barton's ghostly presence before his death, for instance, which Raymond Williams sees as a withdrawal of sympathy from him[18] is a reflection of his spiritual state. By his act of violence he has at once killed the spirit in his body and so become a shadow, and put himself beyond the community. His repentance cannot restore him to emotional or communal life, or to physical health. It does, though, release him from complete subjection to the social conditions so vividly described.

The social concerns of modern critics have reduced to mere prettification the dimension by which the characters, by the sheer force of their common humanity, escape the humiliation of their condition. 'A trifling and irrelevant judgment', John Lucas comments when the narrator says of John Barton's reaction to Davenport's death, 'his thoughts were touched by sin'.[19] A Victorian sense of sin is not a failure of imagination, but, apart from the anachronism of such a view, the reading also weakens a significant structural feature of the novel. At a realistic level the story produces crime out of harsh, unjust and undoubtedly realistic circumstances. The crime, however, is not contained by the social dimension of the book, it violates 'the eternal law of God'. But the people whom in this novel society drives so hard are innocent until their capacity for sin is awakened by their own helplessness. The end of the novel, with what Raymond Williams calls 'a glimpse of the uncompromised New World', is a reassertion of fundamental innocence. Williams finds it 'devastating' that it removes the characters outside the situation in which 'a solution might be hoped for . . . the solution with which the heart went was a cancelling of the actual difficulties'.[20] But the 'actual', which here means 'social', forms only half the design of *Mary Barton*. The last two pages of the book contain not only the prophetic leap into the new world but the return and death of Esther, 'as a wounded deer drags its heavy limbs once more to the green coolness of the lair in which it was born, there to die'. At the moment of death, clasping the picture of her child in the locket, she knows both innocence and sin, life and death:

> 'Has it been a dream, then?' asked she, wildly. Then with a habit, which came like instinct even in that awful dying hour, her hand sought for a locket which hung concealed in her bosom, and, finding that, she knew all was true which had befallen her since she last lay an innocent girl on that bed.   (XXXVIII 456)

The Canadian future – the 'long low wooden house with room enough and to spare', its gable-end shadowed by one 'primeval tree', surrounded by a garden and bathed in the light of 'the glory of the Indian Summer' – has a dream-like quality, but its roots are in the reality of the past. The family, Jem, Mary and little Johnnie, are seen living in the letters from home and the last words of the book – ' "Dear Job Legh!" said Mary softly and seriously' – cast the reader's mind back over a long compromising story. In retrospect the dark picture of industrial life is not cancelled, but made more poignant by the indestructible innocence which has been kept alive in the violence and squalor.

As the book ends with a glimpse of the 'uncompromised New World', it begins with a picture of a threatened patch of rural calm, glowing with a beauty given to it precisely because it is compromised by proximity to the city. The city has sprung up in the countryside which still exists in little untouched patches where the buildings belong to another way of life:

There are some fields near Manchester, well known to the inhabitants as 'Green Heys Fields', through which runs a public footpath to a little village about two miles distant. In spite of these fields being flat, and low, nay, in spite of the want of wood (the great and usual recommendation of level tracts of land), there is a charm about them which strikes even the inhabitant of a mountainous district, who sees and feels the effect of contrast in these commonplace but thoroughly rural fields, with the busy, bustling manufacturing town he left but half an hour ago. Here and there an old black and white farm-house, with its rambling out-buildings speaks of other times and other occupations than those which now absorb the population of the neighbour-hood. (1 1)

A still beauty is evoked in the short passage which follows; there is the pond, a farm in its luxuriant garden of flowers in 'most republican and indiscriminate order', an uninterrupted view of the sky, the 'softness' of the spring day which has 'tempted' buds into leaves and turned brown willows 'tender grey-green'. The response here is controlled by the distinct presence of the narrator, a sympathetic but sophisticated outsider. His world is wide enough to afford comparisons, not only of other districts but of accepted ideas of beauty and order. With the manufacturing town only half an hour old in his memory even he falls under the spell of this commonplace spot. The authentic voice of the city worker is heard in the epigraph to the chapter, two verses of a Manchester song, where the singer conjures up the countryside in his mind while he works:

> 'Oh! 'tis hard, 'tis hard to be working
>   The whole of the live-long day,
> When all the neighbourhood about one
>   Are off to their jaunts and play.
>
> There's Richard he carries his baby,
>   And Mary takes little Jane,
> And lovingly they'll be wandering
>   Through field and briery lane. (1 1)

The yearning note is recalled, of course, by Alice, whose babblings during her 'painless approach to death' are a background to the dark events of this late portion of the story. The narrative thread is never interrupted – the visits to the death bed are a realistic necessity and Alice's escape into green fields is perfectly credible at a realistic level; she has, after all, kept more of her country ways in the town than any other of these displaced and struggling souls. Her total innocence is established as a positive force here. Contemplating this peaceful death and faced with Alice's 'unconsciousness of all that was passing around her', Mary, distraught as she is, finds a depth of tenderness and patience in herself to deal with Jem's mother. The narrator speaks partly in his own person and partly in Mary's thought:

. . . she was evidently passing away; but *how* happily!

Mary stood for a time in silence, watching and listening. Then she bent down and reverently kissed Alice's cheek; and drawing Jane Wilson away from the bed, as if the spirit of her who lay there were yet cognisant of present realities, she whispered a few words of hope to the poor mother, and kissing her over and over again in warm, loving manner, she bade her good-bye, went a few steps, and then once more came back to bid her keep up her heart. (XXII 293–4)

The dramatic events of this part of the story can all be seen as variations on the idea of innocence – all the main characters are in some way both innocent and guilty by deed, suspicion, pressures and mistakes. The story moves quickly and the events are played out against the quiet and slow-paced moments like those by Alice's bed. Sometimes the voice of the narrator makes a pause in the progress of events which is otherwise so fast it might seem incredible. When Mary has burned the tell-tale paper the narrator frames events in two contrasting pictures:

Her head ached with dizzying violence; she must get quit of the pain or it would incapacitate her for thinking and planning. . . . Then she sought for some water to bathe her throbbing temples, and quench her feverish thirst. There was none in the house, so she took the jug and went out to the pump at the other end of the court, whose echoes resounded her light footsteps in the quiet stillness of the night. The hard, square outlines of the houses cut sharply against the cold bright sky, from which myriads of stars were shining down in eternal repose. There was little sympathy in the outward scene with the internal trouble. All was so still, so motionless, so hard! Very different to this lovely night in the country in which I am now writing, where the distant horizon is soft and undulating in the moonlight, and the nearer trees sway gently to and fro in the night-wind with something of almost human motion; and the rustling air makes music among their branches, as if speaking soothingly to the weary ones, who lie awake in heaviness of heart. The slights and sounds of such a night lull pain and grief to rest.

But Mary re-entered her home after she had filled her pitcher with a still stronger sense of anxiety, and a still clearer conviction of how much rested upon her unassisted and friendless self, alone with her terrible knowledge, in the hard, cold, populous world. (XXII 285–6)

As we read we accept the pause as one in which Mary has had time to sharpen her sense of her whole situation, without noticing that we have not seen anything of her thoughts. It is we who have taken a fresh look with the narrator from his distance in the midst of quite other scenes. We are given 'a still stronger sense' of the pity of it.

The narrative surface is uninterrupted through the rapid sequence of events to the end of the story. But the separate events reflect on one another thematically. If Alice makes a murmured background, the centre is held by Esther – as 'guilty' as Alice is blameless, as active as the old woman is passive. The piece of paper she brings is a vital link in the story; the way in which she is shown making the decision to bring it is a powerful thematic comment which convinces us without ever showing exactly how she comes to the decision. We do not know what she is going to do, but we know from a few deft strokes that she is in a Hell in which the greatest pain is a knowledge of Heaven. We only see her sitting on the doorstep in her tawdry finery and then looking at herself in the glass in her borrowed respectability; the emotion is narrative comment, though as we read it hardly feels like it:

She looked at herself in the little glass which hung against the wall, and sadly shaking her head, thought how easy were the duties of that Eden of innocence from which she was shut out; how she could work, and toil, and starve, and die, if necessary, for a husband, a home – for children – but that thought she could not bear; a little form rose up, stern in its innocence from the witches caldron of her imagination, and she rushed into action again. (XXI 274–5)

Eden and the cauldron exist together in Esther's imagination, as they exist together in the book within the wider terms of reference of a story against a harshly realistic background. Some clarity of spiritual vision is vouchsafed the 'hero' as he dies with all earthly passion spent. Against the glowing innocence of the final landscape the human figures are shown in relief, healed but scarred. This is not out of keeping in message or method with the way in which inescapable innocence has been kept in the reader's mind as a thread of light in a dark story.

The thoughts to which *Mary Barton* as a 'tragic poem' gives rise are too tragic for an idyll. And yet the book does consistently maintain the distance necessary for a simultaneous description of destructive social conditions and indestructible human spirit, and does not attempt to step outside the bounds of the novel and offer social solution. It says to all who would listen, 'this is what it is like', and it does the characters the sympathetic justice of showing them to be fully human, independent, at least to some extent, of even such conditions as these. Unlike George Eliot and Hardy, who grew more socially explicit in later novels, Elizabeth Gaskell began with her most open and tragic social comment. Hardy grew more involved with his central characters the sharper his social criticism became. For Elizabeth Gaskell identification of the narrative point of view with Molly Gibson in *Wives and Daughters* produced a comedy, rich in psychological and social observation, with change and tragedy absorbed into the developing lives of the characters. Narrative distance produced a balance of inner life and social life, and of content and form in *Cranford* and *Cousin Phillis*. It left its mark on *Mary Barton* in the ambition of the conception, which was defeated by the intractability of the social material.

Elizabeth Gaskell's other large-scale account of social change and its toll on individual lives is, of course, *North and South*. It was begun the year after *Cranford* and precedes *Cousin Phillis* by eight years. The idyllic method here is used to a quite different end. It is part of the history, which has not yet been fully told, of the way in which Elizabeth Gaskell's work reveals a continuous experimentation with kind and mode. In *North and South* the idyllic is not as might be thought thematic,[21] but a part of the fabric of the story. As a

perception of the way things relate and a manner of seeing or
experimenting with the relation of personality and society, it is
rejected at the end of the introductory section of the book by the
narrator and abandoned by the heroine herself. The thematic title
which points up the historical element in the book was given to
it by Dickens for publication in *Household Words*.[22] In letters to
friends during the composition of the novel Elizabeth Gaskell
called it 'Margaret Hale', 'Margaret' or 'M. Hale'.[23]
Restoration of this authorial emphasis removes the opposition
of the North and the South from the pivotal position in the
structure. The book then falls into the shape dictated by
Margaret's role; we see Margaret young, inexperienced and
uncommitted, Margaret active and mistaken, Margaret experien-
ced and chastened, and finally Margaret active and useful. Once
Margaret reaches Milton she takes an active role in making her own
story. At the end the contrasts in the social dimension of the book
reach their resolution in her experience. Her story, once she assumes
an active role is one in which old and new loyalties and perceptions
follow one another in such rapid succession and in so unpredictable
an order that it is quite clear that reconciliation or resolution is the
end towards which the fiction has, of its nature, to move. But the
beginning of the book is not only in another mode, but uses the
mode itself to define what will be so radically altered in the latter
portion of the book, the nature of the relationship between the
heroine and her social background. In the first chapters Margaret
moves between London and Helstone, at home but apart. Lively
but only half aware, in the terms of the story, she is waiting for 'real'
experience. The only means of self-definition available to her are
artistic stereotypes. Margaret as a social being is described in such a
way as to call the stereotypes into question, reassert the kernel of
'truth' in them and to suggest their final inadequacy with an irony
so light as to leave the way open to completion of the story in a
different mode. The idyllic balance of possibilities which marks the
beginning of *North and South* is abandoned for another narrative
method, another perception of the relation of figure and
background.

North and South gave Elizabeth Gaskell more trouble than any
other of her novels, and the beginning most trouble of all. The '76
pages' she first sent to Forster were, she complained, 'dull'.[24] They
were 'all she had written' and they must have taken the story to the
settling in Milton.[25] In a letter three days earlier she is more specific

about *how* she thought it dull: 'flat and grey with no bright clear foreground as yet'.[26] Her sense of these opening chapters as a picture recalls her description of the origin of *Mary Barton*. In *North and South* she attempts to make the picture part of the story.[27] Like the inspirational image of *Mary Barton*, the opening of *North and South* describes only the grounds out of which the story proper grows. But at the length of seven chapters the characters have to be shown in action without advancing the story. In Margaret's biography this proves to have been a waiting period; in the novel it establishes, as action would not have done, a variety of angles or perspectives on Margaret in her setting. An early picture is of Margaret modelling the Indian shawls. Tall and dressed in black, she shows off both the soft folds and glowing colours of the shawls perfectly. But her passivity 'as a sort of block' is an illusion. Her simultaneous enjoyment and amusement is active; it shows in her 'bright, amused face' as Henry Lennox enters, and in the expectation that he will at once share her sense of 'the ludicrousness of being thus surprised'. The activity is touched off by the occasional reflection of herself in the mirror as she turns. It shows Margaret her usual self in an unusual guise. The mirror records but in framing and isolating the facts transforms them into a reflected image at once true and heightened, the 'familiar features in the usual garb of a princess'. The effect of the mirror is to refract the truth, to show it to Margaret in two separable halves – the real and the romantic, or at least the familiar and the romantic. The pattern thus established is the pattern of the opening section of the whole novel. Margaret and the world in which she finds herself are in an uneasy, unresolved partnership; the outside world is a series of idealised images coexisting with the truths they only half accommodate.

The picture of Margaret modelling the shawls is an image not only of the matter of the opening paragraphs but of the method as well. They are full of artistic stereotypes, always, like the reflection in the mirror, slightly at odds with another level of perception. The mockery here is diffuse, because the novel is going to be long and because, equally clearly, the central human interest is going to be emotional. But mediated by a sympathetic and not too obtrusive narrator,[28] the mock-heroic here is of the greatest structural importance, none the less for the fact that the terms are 'artistic' rather than 'heroic'. The book begins with Edith, a 'Titania' in 'a back drawing-room', a 'soft ball of muslin and ribbon, and silken curls' taking a 'peaceful little after dinner nap' on 'a crimson-

damask sofa'. Margaret's life will change with Edith's marriage –
her thoughts are of the future but their tenor is nostalgic; she thinks
of the 'delight of filling the important post of only daughter at
Helstone parsonage' in the picturesque light of her 'bright holidays'
of the past ten years. Edith's mother is delighted by her daughter's
love-match, having married herself for comforts more solid. But
Edith, who has settled for love and a 'picturesque', 'gipsy or
makeshift life', sighs faintly for 'a good house in Belgravia'. Upstairs
in the nursery, in search of the exotic Delhi shawls, Margaret's
childhood memories have simultaneously the naturalistic force of
pre-wedding nostalgia and the heightened form of art. She was
brought, she recalls, 'all untamed from the forest' to the 'dark, dim'
London nursery. These self-conscious adult musings are fed on
remembered childhood fantasies, 'for unless she were in the sky (the
child thought), they [the Shaws] must be deep down in the bowels of
the earth'. When she comes to describe her childhood home to
Henry Lennox, he laughs at her for romanticising but although she
claims to be describing reality the only reference she can find for
vividness is in poetry:

'. . . Is Helstone a village, or a town, in the first place?'
    'Oh, only a hamlet; I don't think I could call it a village at all.
There is the church and a few houses near it on the green –
cottages, rather – with roses growing all over them.'
    'And flowering all the year round, especially at Christmas –
make your picture complete,' said he.
    'No,' replied Margaret, somewhat annoyed, 'I am not making
a picture. I am trying to describe Helstone as it really is. You
should not have said that.'
    'I am penitent,' he answered. 'Only it really sounded like a
village in a tale rather than in real life.'
    'And so it is,' replied Margaret eagerly. 'All the other places in
England that I have seen seem so hard and prosaic-looking after
the New Forest. Helstone is like a village in a poem – in one of
Tennyson's poems. But I won't try and describe it any more. You
would only laugh at me if I told you what I think of it – what it
really is.' (19)

Her turn to laugh comes later at Henry Lennox's idea of country
life, as London society in a rural setting, 'Archery parties – pic-nics –
race balls – hunt balls'. One function of the minor characters in

these opening paragraphs is to set up notions which are clearly unreal, like Aunt Shaw's persisting view of her sister's husband, founded in the days when he had 'that blue-black hair one so seldom sees', as 'one of the most delightful preachers she had ever heard, and a perfect model of a parish priest'. Part of the flatness of effect that was a problem to Mrs Gaskell comes from the fact that Margaret herself is involved in the same process which produces the effect, though this, of course, is what saves the opening from over-simplification.

The second chapter, 'Roses and Thorns', is headed by an epigraph which ignores the thorns:

> By the soft green light in the woody glade,
> On the banks of moss where thy childhood played;
> By the household tree, thro' which thine eye
> First looked in love to the summer sky –   (Mrs Hemans)

It stresses the strength of childhood roots while the restlessness is left for the body of the chapter. The chapter is built up on the pattern of its title: 'her out of doors life was perfect. Her indoors life had its drawbacks'; 'This marring of the peace of home by long hours of discontent was what Margaret was unprepared for.' The style used to describe the 'roses' is heightened, for the 'thorns' it is plain:

> She was so happy out of doors, at her father's side, that she almost danced; and with the soft violence of the west wind behind her, as she crossed some heath, she seemed to be borne onwards, as lightly and easily as the fallen leaf that was wafted along by the autumn breeze. But the evenings were rather difficult to fill up agreeably.   (II 18)

The plot is only advanced in this chapter by hints of Mr Hale's uneasiness, and Margaret's attribution of it to the mysterious cloud over her brother. The chapter ends with Margaret's resolution to encapsulate the fugitive glories of the Autumn in Art and the announcement, straight from the world where such efforts belong, of Mr Henry Lennox:

> But Margaret was at an age when any apprehension, not absolutely based on a knowledge of facts, is easily banished for a time by a bright sunny day, or some happy outward circum-

stance. And when the brilliant fourteen fine days of October came on, her cares were all blown away as lightly as thistledown, and she thought of nothing but the glories of the forest. The fern-harvest was over; and now that the rain was gone, many a deep glade was accessible, into which Margaret had only peeped in July and August weather. She had learned drawing with Edith; and she had sufficiently regretted, during the gloom of the bad weather, her idle revelling in the beauty of the woodlands, while it had yet been fine, to make her determined to sketch what she could before winter fairly set in. Accordingly, she was busy preparing her board one morning, when Sarah, the housemaid, threw wide open the drawing-room door, and announced, 'Mr. Henry Lennox.' (II 21)

The sketching is, of course, central in the next short chapter. Margaret wishes to sketch the cottages; Lennox teases that they will have to do it this year or they will fall down – they must be sketched: 'They are very picturesque.' He hasn't the imagination, however, to choose his own vantage-point, and Margaret has to show him the trunk of a tree, 'just in the right place for the light'. Margaret likes the people of the forest and goes to talk to old Isaac. Lennox's view of Helstone is partly worldly, partly aesthetic, like his assessment of the cottages – unlikely to stand up long, but very picturesque. Helstone vicarage, exquisitely bright outside, is inside 'smaller and shabbier than he had expected, as background and framework for Margaret, herself so queenly'. The conclusion is inescapable: 'The living is evidently as small as she said.' His sketch of the cottages includes the girl and the old man tastefully placed and drawn to the life, but the real girl rejects his proposal with astonishment.

Immediately after the proposal comes the announcement of Mr Hale's intentions, all the bustle of the move, the journey and the arrival in Milton. Margaret is decisive in action and considerate of her parents; this is shown in the direct story-telling and in the dialogue. The progress of the novel is still not fast, however, as to some extent the pace must allow for the lingering regrets which Margaret feels so painfully. On this last evening in Helstone she is shown losing imaginative grasp of it as she leaves:

That morning when she had looked out, her heart had danced at seeing the bright clear lights on the church tower, which foretold a fine and sunny day. This evening – sixteen hours at most had passed by – she sat down, too full of sorrow to cry, but with a dull cold pain, which seemed to have pressed the youth and buoyancy out of her heart, never to return. Mr. Henry Lennox's visit – his offer – was like a dream, a thing beside her actual life. The hard reality was, that her father had so admitted tempting doubts into his mind as to become a schismatic – an outcast; all the changes consequent upon this grouped themselves around that one great blighting fact.

She looked out upon the dark-grey lines of the church towers, square and straight in the centre of the view, cutting against the deep blue transparent depths beyond, into which she gazed, and felt that she might gaze for ever, seeing at that moment some farther distance, and yet no sign of God! It seemed to her at that moment, as if the earth was more utterly desolate than if girt by an iron dome, behind which there might be the ineffaceable peace and glory of the Almighty; those never-ending depths of space, in their serenity, were more mocking to her than any material bounds could be – shutting in the cries of earth's sufferers, which now might ascend into that infinite splendour of vastness and be lost – lost for ever, before they reached His throne. (v 45–6)

The end of the book for Margaret is in a sense her discovery of reality, which she finds in action and a union of heart and mind. This might imply that art, used in the way I have suggested, in the opening of the novel is used to express the unreal and so the 'bad', as against the 'real' to be found in action and so 'good'. The flatness or indistinctness of the beginning comes partly from the fact that this sharp dichotomy is not intended, is carefully avoided in fact, just as the North/South opposition is not at all simple. Art shows a kind of truth, frozen and fleeting like the image in the mirror, but true as far as it goes and of great beauty. Childhood roots and beauty are what Helstone stands for in the novel, which comes full circle with the roses Mr Thornton gathered when he went to see 'the place where Margaret grew to what she is'. Margaret's face is described in the first pages as 'lightened up into an honest, open brightness'; her openness is a version of the pastoral quality of innocence. In the everyday terms of the novel this is a responsiveness to people and to beauty which Margaret is shown to have in the opening of the novel. To people she responds warmly although she has her small snobberies. The world she looks at and shapes into the patterns of beauty she knows. These, naturally, she has acquired in the course of her education. On the journey to Milton, in chapter VII, the seaside stop they make at Heston presents itself to Margaret in a series of 'pictures, which she cared not in her laziness to have fully explained before they passed away'. They are beautiful, and in their familiarity, undemanding:

> the stroll down to the beach to breathe the sea-air, soft and warm on that sandy shore even to the end of November; the great long misty-sea-line touching the tender-coloured sky; the white sail of a distant boat turning silver in some pale sun-beam: – it seemed as if she could dream her life away in such luxury of pensiveness, in which she made her present all in all, from not daring to think of the past, or wishing to contemplate the future.   (VII 66)

The future, however, lies in the middle of totally unfamiliar scenes for which nothing in her education has prepared her:

> For several miles before they reached Milton, they saw a deep lead-coloured cloud hanging over the horizon in the direction in which it lay. It was all the darker from the contrast with the pale grey-blue of the wintry sky; for in Heston there had been the earliest signs of frost. Nearer to the town, the air had a faint taste and smell of smoke; perhaps, after all, more a loss of the fragrance of grass and herbage than any positive taste or smell. Quickly they were whirled over the long, straight, hopeless streets of regularly-built houses, all small and of brick. Here and there a great oblong many-windowed factory stood up, like a hen among her chickens, puffing out black 'unparliamentary' smoke, and sufficiently accounting for the cloud which Margaret had taken to foretell rain. As they drove through the larger and wider streets, from the station to the hotel, they had to stop constantly; great loaded lorries blocked up the not over-wide thoroughfares. Margaret had now and then been into the city in her drives with her aunt. But there the heavy lumbering vehicles seemed various in their purposes and intent; here every van, every wagon and truck, bore cotton, either in the raw shape in bags, or the woven shape in bales of calico. People thronged the footpaths, most of them well-dressed as regarded the material, but with a slovenly looseness which struck Margaret as different from the shabby, threadbare smartness of a similar class in London.   (VII 66–7)

In this often-quoted passage the main action of the story begins in a cutting off from the past. What unifies the passage is not only the point of view of the approaching travellers, but the total un-familiarity of every sign the landscape offers. Margaret supposed the 'lead-coloured' cloud meant rain; Heston, crisp and frosty, 'full of the fragrance of grass and herbage' was familiar, for all its Northernness, compared with the strange absence of Nature in this scene. The 'long, straight streets' are described as 'hopeless' not because Mrs Gaskell did not like Manchester, but because in this sentence she is describing the seeing eye as much as the streets themselves. The eye which has been trained in the picturesque can find no irregularity in the 'regularly-built houses, all small and of brick', nothing to break the picture into manageable parts or cause the mind to pause; its journey down the street in search of the familiar is indeed 'hopeless'. The speed and crush should be familiar to anyone who knew London, but the difference underlying the economic facts of life in the two cities is obvious even to this initial view; the inconceivable uniformity in the loaded wagons betoken a one industry town. Here, to judge by a view of the social scene from the passing carriage window, money does not imply polish or style – these people wear good material made up into indifferent clothes. All the signs by which the newcomers might be able to place themselves in relation to this world uncompromisingly spell 'strangers' to them. The central image is the strange one of the factory 'like a hen among her chickens'. It should be read, I think, as making an effect by its strangeness as though Margaret had to search for an image. The image has a kind of aptness in that the houses, all the same, all small, would not be there but for the factories and 'putting out "unparliamentary" smoke' keeps them protected by insuring that wages go into them. 'Unparliamentary' smoke turns out a short while later to be a perverse gesture of freedom on the part of the manufacturers. The interdependence of house and factory, man and manufacturer, is, of course, the theme of the book from now on. This most unpicturesque of pictures marks the emergence of Margaret from her relation with her past world and signals the growth of her perceptions of her future one.

The idyllic in Elizabeth Gaskell's work is the primary way in which she saw social change and individual characters coping with their lives in the inevitable historical flow. It is a mode which allows for the focus of opposing realities and perceptions in one frame, and demands the conscious making of equivalences between what is seen and the means by which we understand what we see. An uneasy balance of inner and outer realities in *Mary Barton* was followed by an achieved balance in *Cranford* which absorbed personal memory into a comic consciousness of the artistic means by which the historic past of ordinary lives could be shown to live on into the present. The characteristic idyllic distance from which a complex view can be maintained, and the balance of active and unresolved possibilities which can be seen from it, are absorbed into character in *North and South* and *Cousin Phillis*. The absorption in *North and South* is incomplete, because Margaret Hale is presented initially from her own indecisive view of herself and subsequently from the narrator's view of her in action. Narrator and character are perfectly merged in Paul in *Cousin Phillis*. That short, totally idyllic story is part picture, part history, both a natural memory and an elaborate reconstruction of a real historical moment in which two worlds touch in the lives of four invented characters.

4 George Eliot: *Adam Bede* – the Bounds of the Idyll

Adam Bede is George Eliot's only idyllic novel. It approaches the bounds of the idyll at a number of points, but ultimately, in not taking the development of either the characters or of some aspects of the story as far as they might have tempted their author to go, *Adam Bede* retains the distanced view of a balanced prospect and remains inside an idyllic frame. George Eliot conceived the characters in a pattern of relationships. Events change the constitution of the pattern which remains the central interest, not the individuals. The world is unfamiliar and is described for readers who do not know it at first hand, but who do know it from literature and painting. The novel is a picture of a world in which none of the characters is fully self-conscious. Each one has to live with what he comes to see he has helped to bring about. The reader, however, is not allowed the complacency which might result from this relation with the characters. He is persuaded in this novel to examine the stereotypes of his own thinking, and to make the effort required to see freshly what is being described. The narrator's function in the expository section of *Adam Bede* is to establish the relation with the reader in which he simultaneously shows him the picture and persuades him to adjust his conventional focus. This is as distinct a use of the narrator as the naturalistic recall which harmonises disparate elements in *Cousin Phillis*. More than in any other of the idyllic novels I consider, the narrator in *Adam Bede* directs his attention to the reader. When 'the story pauses a little' in chapter XVII, narrator and reader may be said to have come to terms. As a dialogue between narrator and reader the chapter provides in itself, as I shall show below, a model of the relationship between them in which the reader's thinking has been brought into harmony with the narrator's. It is retrospective in that it summarises both the ideal or representative character of the refocused world and the process of refocusing. The narrator reflects on his narration, and persuades the reader to reflect on his response. The fictional world is established as a 'real' one at the same time as the reader is induced to look at it freshly. The strategy was evidently successful with contemporary readers who greeted the book as both real and fresh.

The immediacy of contemporary response to this most interesting of Victorian idyllic novels has given way to critical unease. Ian Gregor names the difficulty as uncertainty of mode, and sees the uncertainty lodged in the novel not in the reader.[1] He is not alone, particularly among critics who see *Adam Bede* primarily as a step on the way to *Middlemarch*.[2] He identifies a conflict between the 'country story' and the novel of 'serious moral purpose', which gives this novel a particular historical interest as one of those which mark 'a notable change in the art of fiction':[3]

> Though an interpretation of 'the seen' must be the task of every novelist, George Eliot ensures that it is the form of her novels that will make this quite explicit. She acts both as guide and creator. With James and subsequent fiction the guide has become superannuated, and the reader is left to personal exploration. We no longer look at things so much as find them out. With this shift from contemplation to participation, the subject matter itself has altered; the social community in moral action gives way to the individual consciousness in moral reflection. 'Innocence' is translated into 'integrity'.

Clearly the novel in which the narrator promises 'to give a faithful account of things as they have mirrored themselves in my mind' is one which, in an historically interesting way, is declaring its place in the history of realistic fiction. But *Adam Bede* may be seen not so much as facing both ways at this moment of literary time as making a remarkable fusion of two after all compatible narrative roles. While there is obviously no need to stress that the narrator's moment of superannuation has not yet arrived in *Adam Bede*, he does, however, do more than *show*. The narrator's role here is to arrange for the reader's active participation in contemplation, balancing the two reading processes. He asks – indeed since he is as much goad as guide he demands – that we continually adjust our focus so that we can first make out, then contemplate, what is actually there, the 'reality' to which convention blinds us.

Highly structured, elaborately patterned, with a cast of ideality over scene and character alike and with every evidence of a strong

mind reflecting on the process of narration – all indications of
narrative self-consciousness which disturbs a modern critic – *Adam
Bede* nevertheless impressed first of all with its sense of immediate
reality. Blackwood's comments as he received the parts of the
manuscript only precede a chorus of praise for the reality of the
book. His comment, sent with the first cheque, remarks on the
clarity of the figures and the scenes and may stand for much of the
initial response. 'The whole story', he wrote, 'remains in my mind
like a succession of incidents in the lives of people whom I know.'[4]
Not 'popular' or 'agreeable' it would appeal to those who looked for
'power, real humour and true natural description [who] will stand
by the sturdy Carpenter and the living groups you have painted in
and about Hayslope'.[5] Theodore Martin recognised in the book the
art which conceals art. Thanking Blackwood for the gift of the new
publication, he wrote:[6]

> The views of life and character are so large, so Shakespearian in
> their breadth of sympathy, the pathos so natural and searching,
> the humour so genuine, the style so pure, that one almost forgets it
> is a book and loses himself in the reality of the incidents.

Dickens, who hoped to persuade her to write for *All the Year Round*,
had recognised in 'George Elliott' both woman and writer. In a
letter of 10 July 1859, in which he tells her of the 'absolute and
never-doubting confidence with which I have waved all men away
from Adam Bede and nailed my colours to the mast with "Eve"
upon them', he sees clearly that it is high art which creates the
reality of the new book:[7]

> Adam Bede has taken its place among the actual experiences
> and endurances of my life. Every high quality that was in the
> former book, is in that, with a World of Power added thereunto.
> The conception of Hetty's character is so extraordinarily subtle
> and true, that I laid the book down fifty times, to shut my eyes
> and think about it. I know nothing so skilful, determined, and
> uncompromising. The whole country life that the story is set in, is
> so real, and so droll and genuine, and yet so selected and polished
> by art, that I cannot praise it enough to you. And that part of the
> book which follows Hetty's trial (and which I have observed to be
> not as widely understood as the rest), affected me far more than
> any other, and exalted my sympathy with the writer to its utmost
> height.

Dickens's response is to the book as a whole, his expression of it analytic. Jane Carlyle responded to her first reading of *Adam Bede* with a personal and wholly unanalytic expression of the traditional response to pastoral – a willing surrender to the restorative power of its associations and reconciliations:[8]

> Oh yes! It was as good as *going into the country for one's health*, the reading of that Book was! – Like a visit to Scotland *minus* the fatigues of the long journey, and the grief of seeing friends grown old, and Places that knew me knowing me no more! I could fancy in reading it, to be seeing and hearing once again a crystal-clear, musical, Scotch stream, such as I long to lie down beside and – *cry* at (!) for gladness and sadness; after a long stifling sojourn in the South; where there [is] no *water* but what is stagnant and muddy!

To this George Eliot asked Blackwood to respond by telling her 'the sort of effect she declares herself to have felt from "Adam Bede" is just what I desire to produce – gentle thoughts and happy remembrances'.[9] Jane Carlyle's response is first to the overall impression but she too comments on the singularity and realism of the detail:[10]

> In truth, it is a beautiful most human Book! Every *Dog* in it, not to say every man woman and child in it, is brought home to one's 'business and bosom', an individual fellow-creature! I found myself in charity with the whole human race when I laid it down – the *canine* race I had always appreciated – 'not wisely but too well!' – the *human*, however, – Ach! – *that* has troubled me – as badly at times as 'twenty gallons of milk on one's mind'!

As a professional reader Eneas Sweetland Dallas gave critical expression to what is essentially the same view in his review in *The Times*, 12 April 1859.[11] Like so many other critics, he comments on the individuality of the characters who are all 'so true, and so natural, and so easy that we love to hear them talk for the sake of talking'. But he comments too on the levelling intention of the sympathetic drawing of simple characters. Thackeray and George Eliot he thought were original in demonstrating 'with broad sympathy and large tolerance combined with ripe reflection and finished style' the essential oneness of the human heart. But where Thackeray is continually asserting that we have all got an evil corner in our hearts, and little deceitful ways of working, Mr Eliot is good enough to tell us that we have all a remnant of Eden in us, that people are not so bad as is commonly supposed.

An idealising tendency does not rob the characters of individuality, but it does make for a particular kind of art with particular kinds of effect. Its strength does not derive from movement; 'there is not much of a story it will be seen', he says, but in the description of the 'wonderful monotony in the great world of life which never comes into the light', the novelist 'crowds the canvass' with portraits and sketches. 'We have not here one great and real character in the midst of a mob of lay figures. The subordinate personages are in their way quite as well pictured as the leading one.' Henry James,[12] while less convinced of the reality of the book, also felt the analogy with the more static art of painting. A second reading left him totally convinced only by Hetty. Mrs Poyser no longer seemed 'a representative figure', her 'wisdom' smelled 'of the lamp'. The drama the book so signally lacks James would have supplied not only by a summary end to Hetty by execution, but by bending the 'stiff-backed' Adam under temptation and leaving Dinah wedded only to her calling. His is not a sympathetic view of the book but, grudging as he is with his praise, he does describe some of its essential nature, notably its reflective quality. Over 'the objects furnished by her observation' there is 'a constant play of lively and vigorous thought', which is the source of 'that lingering, affectionate, comprehensive quality which is . . . the chief distinction of her style'.[13] Lacking in movement (even the wholly successful Hetty is drawn, he points out, without development), the book is most valuable for James 'as a picture or rather a series of pictures', in which 'attitudes of feeling' are more successfully drawn than 'movements of feeling'.

Drama of the kind that James felt could have been provided in *Adam Bede* by 'allowing passions and foibles to play themselves out' would, of course, have had to be in terms of individual character. As the book stands, its centre is in relationships not in character. In this way individual characters do not stand out so far from the background as they are sometimes thought to, and so should not arouse expectation of the psychological depth in which George Eliot herself was later to excel. As is well known, George Eliot started from a remembered story of a visit paid by her Methodist aunt to a girl about to be executed for child murder. The account in her journal of the rest of the book as it existed at the moment of starting to write is a description of a pattern of relationships:[14]

> When I began to write it, the only elements I had determined on besides the character of Dinah were the character of Adam, his relation to Arthur Donnithorne and their mutual relation to Hetty, i.e. to the girl who commits child-murder: the scene in the prison being of course the climax towards which I worked. Everything else grew out of the characters and their mutual relations.

The distance sustained by the author who is not centrally engaged with one main character does not mean that scenes of passion are not both present and structurally important. The confrontation of Adam and Arthur in the grove and Hetty's hopeless journey (written 'without the slightest alteration of the first draught')[15] carry the weight of the past, and the passion is in the inevitable eruption of the past within the necessary constraints of the present moment. The scene in the prison carries the forward movement of the book and is the moment when the redemptive pattern emerges. 'Peaceful sunshine and happiness will come –' Lewes wrote, 'like the fifth act of *The Merchant of Venice* when R. H. Horne [who played Shylock disastrously] has left the stage'.[16] Dinah's marriage does not break the pattern of the book since the end for all four entails, in varying degrees of consciousness and acceptance, renunciation of vital hopes this particular world will not hold. The book is a picture of a world which determines, strains and reabsorbs the characters in an inevitable pattern to the limit of their worthiness. It is a world of which the reader has a more heightened consciousness than any of the characters, since Adam and Dinah, hardly less than Arthur and Hetty, come late to a realisation of the self which acts. The reader not only sees the patterns clearly, but, in being in part recalled to his own Eden, comes to an understanding of their necessity. 'If she is not a great dramatist', James said, 'she is at least a great describer.'

The author as describer has a peculiar relation with the reader. He does not, as Wordsworth says in defining the idyllium, teach or persuade. He simply shows, but in narrative this will present problems, notably in ending. James thought 'the art of story-telling cannot be said to have approached perfection until the 'secret' of making the reader do his share of the task' is found out, and that the end of *Adam Bede* should have been deducible not stated. But the 'sympathetic reader' who is, as James puts it, as much 'made' by the writer as the characters are, is engaged in a different kind of activity when he is engaged with a 'descriptive' work; progress outside the book along the continuum of time set up by the story, which is necessary if he is to frame an end for himself from the author's directions, is pointless. The end of the idyllium for the reader is acceptance – the poem has no continuance outside itself except in a circular pattern of repetition. To achieve this end in a story the lines must be closed off, the end cannot be open. Acceptance, however, is not necessarily a passive process; the reader is as actively engaged in accepting the qualifications of the happiness at the end of *Adam Bede* as he would be in constructing an ending. James's own *Bostonians* engages the reader in the same way. In both books there is an elaborate playing off and balancing of heroic and pastoral modes of perception, and in the eventual mitigated triumph of the pastoral an acceptance of life in a minor key. In both books history and individual lives, public and private histories, are seen bound up of necessity in the two modes and not, in either case, in any simple or schematic way. The reader must linger over the parts in order to focus them in relation to one another. More movement in *Adam Bede*, whether of action or passion, would have entailed a stronger story line or development of individual motivation and reaction. Either would have brought the characters outside the pattern of relationships in which they were conceived and, particularly, have disrupted the harmony between figures and background in the picture of Hayslope and its people. If in response to such a book the reader must suspend his curiosities and disappointments, the author must suspend any temptation to engage too heavily with any single aspect of the work.

George Eliot thought *Adam Bede* a more perfect whole, and better balanced than '*The Mill on the Floss*, because of the way in which her love of the childhood scenes' had distorted the pattern of *The Mill*.[17] While writing *Adam Bede* she saw the story as 'so closely knit together that it must lose by being read in fragments'.[18] The following examination of *Adam Bede* as a pastoral attempts to see the 'closely knit' parts inside the 'perfect' and 'balanced' whole. It assumes that while the book undoubtedly contains auguries of the author's future it is primarily interesting because it is moving, and moving in a distinct way. *Adam Bede* presents to an urban audience a picture of rural life, remote in time and nature; its story is slight; description and dialogue are lengthy and do not advance the action. Nevertheless its impact on publication was of immediacy and reality. For that reason I shall begin with what is often remarked on but rarely considered closely in the context to which, like the other closely knit parts of *Adam Bede*, it inextricably belongs – the deceptive artistic credo in chapter 17. In this chapter, 'In Which the Story Pauses a Little', it becomes clear, I think, how the reader is being involved in the active construction of a reality he can accept; it is, in fact, a model of the interaction of narrator and reader on which the structure of the novel is based.

Chapter 17 begins with a hypothetical reader exclaiming on the handling of the breakfast-time interview between Mr Irwine and Arthur:

> How much more edifying it would have been if you had made him give Arthur some truly spiritual advice! You might have put into his mouth the most beautiful things – quite as good as reading a sermon. (221)

With the interview fresh in his mind the real reader reacts with a sense of how improbable this would have been. In response to a number of cues the reader has seen the inevitability of Arthur's failure to confess virtually all the way through the last chapter of book 1. The meeting between Arthur and Adam has stressed the contrast between them and, for Arthur, reinforced his sense of his own benevolence and importance. The cultivated ease of the rectory breakfast scene, the rector in the 'radiant freshness' of 'his morning toilet', the open Aeschylus by the silver coffee pot, is not conducive, we know from the start, to the rigour of confession or to the recall of 'those little scenes in the wood' which Arthur can hardly bear to recall to himself. The rector's dismissal of his own faint glimmer of understanding is entirely credible. Ironically he likes breakfast-time, he says, because 'no dust has settled on one's mind then, and it presents a clear mirror to the rays of things'. The narrator speaks of his own mind as a mirror too. He rejects the 'arbitrary picture' his exaggeration of the hypothetical reader's case has suggested and claims that in contrast his 'strongest effort' is 'to give a faithful account of men and things as they have mirrored themselves in my mind'. The mirror may be defective but only because of the limits of the narrator's understanding and he feels 'as much bound to tell you as precisely as I can what that reflection is, as if I were in the witness-box, narrating my opinion on oath'. This is appealing in its apparent conventional honesty, but it cannot be received as the simple statement of intention it appears to be. It is an over-simplified answer to an exaggerated case the narrator has constructed himself. The mirror in *Adam Bede* is not a simple reflecting instrument. 'With a single drop of ink for a mirror,' the narrator will, he tells us at the opening of the novel, like 'an Egyptian sorcerer' undertake 'to reveal to any chance comer far-reaching visions of the past.' Further, inside the story, real mirrors have already been shown, as witnesses on oath will later be shown, not always to be the most reliable tellers of relevant truth. The 'small red-framed shilling looking-glass' at which Hetty worships, aided by the secretly purchased candles, gives back a clearer image than the blotched . . . glass on her old chest of drawers. The antique glass, with only the light through the blindless window would have been quite adequate, 'considering that she had only to brush her hair and put on her night cap'. But the unblotched image tells only the betraying truth that there is plenty to attract Arthur. The two stories told in the witness-box by Sarah Stone and John Olding are the two halves of the 'truth' which convict Hetty. She did have a child and she did bury it in the chips. These truths are enough for the court, but though they add up to guilt the reader has hardly had to wait for these stories to know of it and they take no account of what the reader alone knows – the desperation of Hetty's pitiful journey. Another kind of truth is left for Dinah to elicit in the prison – Hetty's own acknowledgement and acceptance. Chapter 16, which is the subject of the discussion in this chapter 'in which the story pauses a little', makes its impression on the reader with ripples of passing thought and social nuance no mirror can reflect and of a kind which is not considered relevant in the court-room. Chapter 17 is built in its entirety on this model. No single statement can be extracted as George Eliot's. Each is part of a self-contained rhetorical structure in which a case is stated, argued and answered; the reader is being challenged to find and explore his own relation to the story, midway between the deprecatory and elusive narrator and a hypothetical reader of idealising tendency. The illustrations and analogies used are relevant to the whole book and relate directly to it.

This elaborate *pas de deux* of narrator and reader is nowhere more interesting than in the most famous passage of all about the narrator's preference for Dutch paintings of 'monotonous homely existence' over those of 'cloud-borne angels, prophets, sybils, and heroic warriors'. Often taken to be about subject-matter, its real concern is treatment, which gives it a relevance to the novel as a whole which is more far-reaching than a simple correspondence of subject. Even the 'idealistic friend', brought in again to overstate a case, is concerned, certainly, with the vulgarity of the 'phase of life' depicted in such paintings, but equally with the 'pains' taken over it. 'It is for this rare, precious quality of truthfulness' that the narrator delights in the Dutch pictures. Such truthfulness is difficult to achieve. The paintings are an illustration of the kind of 'sympathy' which can be generated for simple subjects if the 'delightful facility' with which the pencil can draw an imaginary griffin is abandoned for the sobering effort to 'draw a real unexaggerated lion'. The two paragraphs, not usually quoted together, are mutually dependent and parallel. 'So I am content to tell my simple story' corresponds to 'I delight in many Dutch paintings'. The difficulty of depicting the 'truth' is shown in the example of the Dutch paintings to be resolvable by focus. By skilful handling of the 'noonday light, softened perhaps by a screen of leaves, [which] falls on her mob-cap, and just touches the rim of her spinning-wheel, and her stone jug' the painter makes a statement about the status of 'these cheap common objects' as 'necessaries of life' to the old woman. In the second example of a generic Dutch painting, 'that village wedding', the imaginary artist has penetrated beyond the appearance of the rustic couple and their clownish guests to the 'truth' of the feelings involved in this communal display of goodwill. The reader, it is implied, who sees the narrator's story as a 'simple' one without giving himself up to the care, or art, which is needed for truth-telling, will make a judgement as irrelevant as that of the superficial viewer of the pictures of common life. He must be prepared to dwell with the author's pen wherever the light falls, be it only on the edge of a mob-cap.

In this chapter life and the work of art, the engagement of the reader, and the relation he thus makes between art and life, are shown to be mutually dependent. By the end of the chapter the reader is convinced of the simple truth of the story, which has here paused a little, because he has been manœuvred into a position where the only clearly defined common ground between himself and the narrator is a common-sense and humane attitude to real life. Everywhere 'ease' is the enemy. In the story it is Arthur's 'ease' and Hetty's 'carelessness' which is their undoing. In wishing to simplify the relation of Arthur and Mr Irwine and hypothetical reader is craving for ease of reading, in the way in which it is easier to accept picturesque 'lazzaroni' than the suffering poor. Chapter 17 deceives if it is thought to be a statement of authorial intention directly made – if it were that it would be as ponderous and roundabout as it is sometimes accused of being. Instead it teases the reader in one way and another with successive possible points of view and in suggesting that the narrator is taking him into his confidence in fact simply forces him to explore the stereotypes of his own thinking. Chapter 17 halts the story to bring author and reader to an understanding. It demonstrates, in another kind of language than that of the story, the relation between narrator and reader in which the true reader's characteristic creative activity so far in the book is shown to grow out of being made aware of the limitations he is accepting in settling for familiar and so easy modes of perception. The reader's stereotyped, because inattentive, thinking is seen to approximate to the false pastoral in which Hetty and Arthur wreak havoc on one another and on the community. When at the beginning of the chapter the 'idealistic' reader complains of lack of edification in the interview between Arthur and Mr Irwine, and the narrator replies that truth and not edification was his aim, both positions, in relation to the story, are discredited. Edification of the reader by means of the edification of Arthur would have gone further than making the story pause a little to preventing outcome altogether – no human error, no story. On the other hand, a mirror reflects only the surface and a court of law admits only the provable. In the gap arranged by the author between the imaginary reader and the assumed narrator, the real reader must find his position *vis-à-vis* the story.

'Sixty years ago', the narrator continues, and apparently assumes the role of historian as he picks up the story. But the reader is not destined to find a resting-point in any easy relationship with the past. This, it turns out, is mock-history:

> Sixty years ago – it is a long time, so no wonder things have changed – all clergymen were not zealous; indeed, there is reason to believe that the number of zealous clergymen was small, and it is probable that if one among the small minority had owned the livings of Broxton and Hayslope in the year 1799, you would have liked him no better than you like Mr. Irwine. Ten to one, you

would have thought him a tasteless, indiscreet, methodistical
man. (221)

The measured language appropriate to the objective historian,
'there is reason to believe', 'it is probable that', 'one among the small
minority', is mocked by the simplicity of the finding that, 'all
clergymen were not zealous' and by the colloquial jocularity – 'no
wonder things have changed', 'you would have liked him no better'
and 'Ten to one'. Mock-history is succeeded by mock-philosophy;
'It is so very rarely that facts hit the nice medium required by our
own enlightened opinions and refined taste.' And the mockery
continues through the following speech of the hypothetical reader
('Perhaps you will say') into whose mouth are put words which do
not represent a single point of view, but simultaneously a point of
view and the narrator's judgement of it. Whatever vestiges of a
longing for simplicity the real reader may be harbouring, he will not
accept them in this unspeakable form: 'Do improve the facts a little
then, make them more accordant with those correct views it is our
privilege to possess.' It is, of course, tempting to be able to 'see at a
glance whom we are to condemn and whom we are to approve', but
the moral logic of 'that true ruminant relish which always belongs to
undoubting confidence' makes the position demonstrably
unacceptable.

 . If the real reader is unable to accept the sketched reader as his
surrogate self, is he any more likely to respond to the *captatio
benevolentiae* of 'But, my good friend' as the narrator takes up his
address? And yet, of course, you accept entirely the real-life position
in which you cannot straighten other people's noses, 'nor brighten
their wit' and that 'it is needful you should tolerate, pity, and love'
them as they are. This is analogy, not exhortation, and the irony of
'So I am content to tell my simple story' is twofold. The 'simple
story' requires an effort from the real reader as hard and as
constructive as loving the irritating people who surround us in
everyday life, and an effort from the narrator as concentrated and
selective as it takes to draw a living lion rather than an hieratic
griffin. The narrator continues to draw on the parallel with life; the
significance which artistic treatment may give to commonplace
things and people is like the beauty bestowed on perfectly ordinary
people by love. 'Yes! Thank God; human feeling is like the mighty
rivers that bless the earth: it does not wait for beauty – it flows with

resistless force and brings beauty with it.' This unqualified acclam-
ation is in a different tone and concludes a paragraph which begins
with the narrator assuming a commonsensical persona, daring a
touch of iconoclasm:

> But bless us, things may be lovable that are not altogether
> handsome, I hope? I am not at all sure that the majority of the
> human race have not been ugly, and even among those 'lords of
> their kind', the British, squat figures, ill-shapen nostrils and dingy
> complexions are not startling exceptions.   (223)

The mockery which follows is again directed against a simplified
view, which assumes that outward form gives rise to love. But the
mockery is not simple:

> And I believe that there have been plenty of young heroes, of
> middle stature and feeble beards, who have felt quite sure they
> could never love anything more insignificant than a Diana, and
> yet who found themselves in middle life happily settled with a
> wife who waddles.   (224)

It is directed towards modes of self-perception equally with modes of
perceiving others.

It might be thought that the parallel between art and life is
incomplete, life lacking the necessity of artistic mediation. But the
careful avoidance here of the simple assumption that beauty lies in
the eye of the beholder seems to suggest a more complicated process
nearer to the art the narrator is talking about. Love may transcend
them, but squat figures, sallow cheeks and middle stature are facts of
life. Beauty is conferred by relationship in life, and in Art, as the next
paragraph shows, by 'human sympathy'. To allow into the realm of
Art 'those old women scraping carrots with their work-worn hands'
is to have, as viewers, constantly to remember that to see truly is
difficult. To accept only 'picturesque sentimental wretchedness' in
Art is to forget that real life is not a 'world of extremes'. Art must
continue to remind us that our philosophies must not be too lofty for
the facts. That is, Art and life interact as well as lying parallel to one
another. Artists are needed who will 'give the loving pains of a life to
the faithful representing of commonplace things, and delight in
showing how kindly the light of heaven falls on them'. Assuming
now the role of someone who looks at Art, and so aligning himself

with the real reader, the narrator takes up a position from which it is
impossible to dissociate oneself because of its impeccably humane
attitude to real people in real life. Life and Art are one in fact and
language; while in the first half of the sentence the terms of artistic
perception are shown not to be totally applicable to life, in the
second life is seen as if in a picture:

> There are few prophets in the world; few sublimely beautiful
> women; few heroes. I can't afford to give all my love and
> reverence to such rarities; I want a great deal of those feelings for
> my everyday fellow-men, especially for the few in the foreground
> of the great multitude, whose faces I know, whose hands I touch,
> for whom I have to make way with kindly courtesy. (224)

Artistic stereotypes are no use in real life. A mental set of a
'handsome rascal in red scarf and green feathers' will not go any
way in providing a 'fibre of sympathy' for 'that vulgar citizen who
weighs out my sugar in a vilely assorted cravat and waistcoat'. Still
in the role of any one of us who may live in a parish and read novels,
the narrator says, persuasively enough, that he needs sympathy with
'the clergyman of my own parish' who is not likely to be an Oberlin
or a Tillotson, and he rejects 'the sublimest abstract of all clerical
graces that was ever conceived by an able novelist'.

At this point, with the words 'And so I come back to Mr Irwine',
the narrator returns to the avowed role of narrator of the story. His
strategy has been to set up roles for the reader in such a way as to
provide a point of agreement; this he has done in relation to life and
through examples from painting. Stories are not mentioned in those
parts of the argument intended to persuade. By substituting life the
narrator leaves the assumption unspoken that the story is 'real'. The
reader has been manipulated to the point where he makes that
assumption himself. In this chapter, which seems so full of the voice
and personality of the narrator, any brief appearance he makes
apparently in his own persona, as in the sentence about human
feeling flowing with the 'resistless force of a mighty river' or in the
statement of the difficulty he shares with the reader in summoning
sympathy for those around him, he is a man looking at life not a
teller of a tale, this or any other. He is no sooner back as story-teller
than he hands over to the elderly Adam, becoming himself the
faceless interviewer successful in getting the historical survivor to

talk authentically of the past. The language is itself comment, recessed one stage further by Adam's quotation from Mrs Poyser:

> she said, Mr Irwine was like a good meal o' victual, you were the better for him without thinking on it, and Mr Ryde was like a dose o' physic, he gripped you and worreted you, and after all he left you much the same.   (227)

Here as elsewhere in the book Mrs Poyser's heartfelt wisdom is of a piece with its homely expression; it sums up and closes off any avenue to further discussion. Her voice, though always endorsed by the narrator, is qualified by being only one voice so corroborated. For the reader this picture of a rural world remains open to interpretation because he is required to see it from so many angles. This is evident when the narrator appears again at the end of the chapter as narrator. 'You will perceive', he says, 'that Adam was a warm admirer, perhaps a partial judge, of Mr Irwine as, happily, some of us still are of the people we have known familiarly.' Adam, having stepped outside the confines of the story into old age, is established as 'real' and we hardly need the 'happily' in this sentence to notice not only the narrator's approval, at least of the attitude, but his assumption that Art and life are one.

It is as the observer of life that the narrator ends the chapter, aligning us this time with his views by the sour little anecdote of Mr Gedge, the landlord of the Royal Oak, who thought if he moved far enough away he would find neighbours worthy of his attention. Mr Gedge is presented as a 'real-life' example of 'those lofty minds who pant after the ideal', who, in relation to the narrator's story, will no doubt despise 'as a weakness' Adam's partiality as a judge of Mr Irwine. But these 'select natures' are easily deceived and have frequently been so, he says, by the narrator's hypocritical assent to their views, reinforced by 'an epigram on the fleeting nature of our illusions, which anyone moderately acquainted with French literature can command at a moment's notice'. The easy and falsifying nature of literary assumptions is the basis of George Eliot's attack on 'our picture exhibitions' in 'The Natural History of German Life'.[19] The painter, she says, has been 'under the influence of idyllic literature, which has always expressed the imagination of the cultivated and town-bred'. The rendering of peasant life in English art is inferior to that of Teniers or Murillo because the subjects are treated 'under the influence of traditions and prepossessions rather than of direct observation'. It is interesting that, in this review of Richl, the true peasant George Eliot compares with the idyllic rustic – who shows 'a row of sound teeth' as he is caught in a 'typical moment' cracking a joke – is unpromising literary material outside the broadest comedy:

> The slow gaze, in which no sense of beauty beams, no humour twinkles, – the slow utterance, and the heavy slouching walk, remind one rather of that melancholy animal the camel, than of the sturdy countryman, with striped stockings, red waistcoat, and hat aside, who represents the traditional English peasant.

Adam Bede turns the situation round; the novel takes painting as a model and in claiming realism recasts idyllicism. The cultivated and town-bred preoccupy the narrator and determine the fabric of the telling. In the way in which chapter 17 manœuvres the reader into a reassessed position among the stereotypes of his thinking it is a scale model of the whole book. The Dutch paintings with their selective focus, which induces contemplation of meaning and relationship behind the commonplace surface of the picture, are a model for that part of *Adam Bede* on which, his stereotypes undermined, the reader is asked to focus with 'sympathy'. The chapter clearly shows the narrator persuading the reader to fill the gap made by the undermining of preconceptions with a more active, and thus more difficult, appreciation of the real.

Chapter 17, at the beginning of book II, is a crucial point in the exposition. In the expository section of the novel, which may be said to be the whole of books I and II, the reader creates what seems to him real and true in a continuous dialogue with the narrator. As the novel proceeds, the narrator speaks increasingly in an unequivocal voice. The struggles of Adam, Hetty's journey, Mr Irwine's decisions, Dinah's role in the prison and afterwards are all presented in a plainer, more completely lucid though often 'high' style, than the earlier portions of the story. The later Dinah, indeed, is presented in so plain a way as to be unconvincing to many readers, who find the heavily metaphoric descriptions of Hetty more vivid, as, immediately, they are. This Wordsworthian plainness is used as Tennyson used plainness in 'Dora' in an effort to construct an inner world by means of a contrasted style. Dinah has a particular place in George Eliot's pastoral vision which is revealed by her particular place in the stylistic pattern of the novel. In chapter 17 the narrator speaks only rarely in an unequivocal way and then only, as I hope I have shown, when the reader has been brought to a point when agreement is virtually certain. The dynamism and open nature of the story is derived from the way in which the reader creates his viewing-point by being constantly required to adjust the lenses with which he has hitherto been used to focusing the rural scene in life and literature. The plot, considering the potential drama of the story of seduction, is surprisingly static, as James first noted. The characters are shown in book 1, as George Eliot first conceived them, in a pattern of relationships, representative figures in a country background. Not surprisingly in this case, the unequivocal narrative voice is used in the exposition to pictorial ends. The ambiguities of the relation of narrator and reader in the whole of the exposition are designed on the mock-heroic pattern of the opening to establish a relationship with the past which acknowledges at once its glamour *qua* past and its continuing life in the present as communal and individual memory.[20] By the end of *Adam Bede* the reader is in creative possession of a reconciling capacity which endows the conclusion with an idyllic, qualified happiness. At the beginning he is alternately involved closely, on the model of chapter 17, in examining the expectations he brings to the judgement of fictional characters and situations, and placed at a distance in front of a series of pictures of the peopled rural scene familiar to him only in stereotype.

In book 1 all the major locales of the story are introduced in pictures. Other senses than sight are called on, but the scenes are pictures in the sense that they are presented in a way that relates strictly to what may be perceived from a distance. The first seven chapters all begin in this way. By chapter 8, which begins with the meeting of Dinah and Mr Irwine, we have a general sense of Hayslope, its relation to neighbouring countryside, the location, at least roughly in terms of distance from one another, of the homes of the main characters, and some pictured interiors. We have glimpsed the people who make up this rustic world and, in the dramatic sketches which follow the pictorial introductions, have heard their language. We have entered into some appreciation of the main characters who stand in the 'foreground' of the total picture. The 'pictures' range from the briefest sketch at the beginning of chapter 4, 'Home and its Sorrows', to the lengthy placing of Hayslope in its geographical position in the second chapter, 'The Preaching'. The framing of most of these essential views in book 1 is done at least in

part through the device of the 'elderly horseman', who is struck by
Adam's stalwart appearance at the end of chapter I. This is, of
course, in some ways a very obvious device and, if we respond to his
introduction with the reading habits more proper to plot and
mystery, he is bound to be a disappointment, if he does not also
irritate as a piece of creaking machinery. But the pace of the
opening 'goes on with a pleasant andante movement' as George
Eliot described the pace of composition,[21] and it seems to me that
curiosity about the stranger becomes absorbed by what the stranger
sees, especially as his point of view is only a starting-point in any
single case. It alternates at need with that of the narrator and by
chapter v when with his 'Let me take you into the dining-room' the
narrator speaks with the total assurance of story-teller as guide,
the traveller is forgotten and the reader has imperceptibly become
the stranger moving around the neighbourhood.

The description of Hayslope in Loamshire in chapter 2 begins
with the traveller putting his horse 'into a quick walk up the village',
but being deflected from his unnamed purpose by mingled interest
and curiosity. The order in which his response to the situation is
recorded is, in miniature, the pattern of the book; the village is
shown in its setting, then from a large group of more or less
anonymous characters the main characters emerge. In the metaphor from Art sanctioned by chapter 17, a particular meaning is
attached to the relation of grouped and individualised figures, just
as in the setting, the foreground is only interesting in its relation to
the background. The traveller's immediate view of the village is
limited to what he can see from the green; he serves only as a focus
for the narrative present in what is really a generalised description.
The traveller can see only certain things, but the alternation
between his point of view and the narrator's, smooth and not
particularly noticeable (partly because we are by now not interested
in the traveller as a character) generalises the scene to the typical.
Hayslope is both Hayslope and a generic village. Variety in the
landscape is measured by riding time and the single traveller has
become any traveller:

> and in two or three hours' ride the traveller might exchange a
> bleak treeless region, intersected by lines of cold grey stone, for
> one where his road wound under the shelter of woods, or up
> swelling hills, muffled with hedgerows and long meadow grass
> and thick corn; and where at every turn he came upon some fine

old country seat nestled in the valley or crowning the slope, some homestead with its long length of barn and its cluster of golden ricks, some grey steeple looking out from a pretty confusion of trees and thatch and dark-red tiles.   (101-2)

This traveller first saw Hayslope Church as any traveller might have done and 'now from his station near the Green he had before him in one view nearly all the other typical features of this pleasant land'. It is the narrator who knows that though the sheep appear as stationary white specks they are in fact moving, that the mountains themselves are unaffected by seasonal changes of light, and that the 'tender green of the ash and lime on which 'the eye rested' below the mountains will shortly deepen to become 'the uniform leafy curtains of high summer'. It is possible for the eye to make out 'faint blue summer smoke' from a 'tall mansion' but 'our traveller' cannot see what 'doubtless' was there, 'a large sweep of park and a broad glassy pool' in front of that mansion. The narrator claims no special knowledge in this last instance, just a sense of the typical. While the dual point of view, the single traveller's and the narrator's, makes this scene visually both particular and general, the vision is also effectively extended in time beyond the present early summer into regularly changing seasons by the embodiment of the now and the always in two alternating points of view. The traveller is ostensibly the perceiver, but there is nothing personal about the observation. The description ends with the inclusion of the reader:

> It was that moment in summer when the sound of the scythe being whetted makes us cast more lingering looks at the flower-sprinkled tresses of the meadows.   (62)

This is the foreground of the picture picked out in 'transparent gold' by the 'level sunlight'. The light has the isolating and focusing effect described by the narrator in the 'Dutch picture' of an old woman bending over her flower-pot or eating a solitary dinner. The traveller himself is sometimes a figure in the picture, watched in turn by the narrator, who only infers his response from what can be seen. He turns from the beauties of the landscape 'apparently' more interested by 'the living groups close at hand', but through the rest of the chapter his remains the main focal viewpoint. He is the excuse for the external view of the villagers and once again, as in the description of the landscape, his view and the narrator's generalising comment alternate without very noticeable transition.[22]

In the immediate foreground the villagers and the Methodists make two groups, each conscious of the other. Every generation is there from 'old "Feyther Taft" in his brown worsted night-cap' to the babies 'with their little round heads lolling forward in quilted linen caps'. The men cluster round the blacksmith's door, the women, silent and curious, draw nearer the meditative and melancholy Methodists. The men are distinguished as they would be to the eye by their different callings, Chad's Bess by her earrings, which single her out for 'peculiar compassion' from the Methodists. The traveller's eye holds the scene, the narrator sketches in the relationship of the two groups and characterises the peculiarly rustic quality of their curiosity about the preacher. The narrator in this scene assumes the role of teacher about the real characteristics of real rustics. 'Villagers never swarm,' he says, and 'a whisper is unknown among them.' The assured didactic note and the touch of patronage in the thumb-nail sketches might seem alien alike to story telling and to pastoral. John Goode remarks that the novel at times has 'the air of an anthropologist's notebook'.[23] But the relation of the anthropologist to his material, certainly in his notebook, is a direct one, an effort to come to terms with it himself. In *Adam Bede* the author's view of rustic life is a given, the artistic effort is one of mediation. The mediation is complicated by the narrator's knowledge of the conclusions he wishes drawn and his need to make the uninformed see freshly for the first time. This particular scene is held inside the frame of the novel by the contrast and interdependence inside the whole picture of the two groups, and by the harmony of the visual and the linguistic. In both these aspects the central and reconciling force is Dinah. The loosely grouped villagers marked by family and interdependent calling, and the quiet, alien but homogeneous Methodists focus their attention, as the traveller does his, on the figure of the preacher. From her eyes the light of compassion shines on all, but the focusing and characterising light of the picture falls on her:

> She stood with her left hand towards the descending sun, and leafy boughs screened her from its rays; but in this sober light the delicate colouring of her face seemed to gather a calm vividness, like flowers at evening. (61)

The traveller's response is to suppose 'nature never meant her as a preacher'. The narrator's comment on this disposes of another stereotype:

Perhaps he was one of those who think that nature has
theatrical properties and, with the considerate view of facilitating
art and psychology, 'makes up', her characters, so that there may
be no mistake about them.   (67)

Like the shepherds of classical pastoral, George Eliot's characters
live in the country and their callings are country callings, but the
drama of their lives is a human one and Nature is a background
only. Wiry Ben's response, not uttered but recorded by the narrator
in words appropriate to him, is an earth-bound recognition of
difference, not wholly reductive of him and with a reminder of the
previous anticipatory comments on the young woman preacher and
her connections in the village. The villagers' argument turns on the
interpretation of the codes which govern social relations:

A strappin' young carpenter as is a ready-made Methody, like
Seth, wouldna be a bad match for her. Why, Poysers make as big
a fuss wi' Adam Bede as if he was a nevvy o' their own.   (66)

This is language which is continuous in the book; it is spoken with
more thoughtfulness by Adam and more force by Mrs Poyser but
both expression and underlying values are the same through major
and minor characters. The emergence of the main characters from
the 'living group' is the emergence of people we end by knowing
better than others, but they are not different in kind and live in the
same relation with their background as the one painted here
between landscape and figures. Adam himself is, of course, an
heroic figure with his broad chest, and 'a back so flat and a head so
well poised that when he drew himself up to take a more distant
survey of his work, he had the air of a soldier standing at ease'. But
this is a description of an ordinary countryman, cast in an heroic
mould and destined to hold the centre of the stage in this fiction.
The strength is such as is seen at country fairs and the delicacy,
proper to a hero, signifies skill rather than elegance. Adam has an
historic ancestry which shows in his features as would any 'hero's'
but his is of the common people not the invading aristocrat; it could
be discovered in the face of any man if you looked hard enough and
chose to describe what you saw in those terms. His beauty is not a
distinguished singularity, but proceeds from an openness and an
honest acceptance of himself in relation to others:

The sleeve rolled up above the elbow showed an arm that was likely to win the prize for feats of strength; yet the long supple hand, with its broad finger tips, looked ready for works of skill. In his tall stalwartness Adam Bede was a Saxon, and justified his name; but the jet-black hair, made the more noticeable by its contrast with the light paper cap, and the keen glance of the dark eyes that shone from under strongly marked, prominent and mobile eyebrows, indicated a mixture of Celtic blood. The face was large and roughly hewn, and when in repose had no other beauty than such as belongs to an expression of good-humoured honest intelligence. (50)

The traveller is interested in this 'fine strapping fellow' and says, 'We want such fellows as he to lick the French.' He errs in his admiration of Adam and of Dinah, in not seeing either totally inside the situation in which he finds them. As readers we do not see Adam settling the disputes in the workshop as a likely soldier anymore than we can see the fervent preacher in the conventional role of 'sweet woman'. We do not know these characters, but already we have disassociated ourselves from one cultivated response.

The traveller leaves at the end of the preaching to reappear again only as the magistrate who lets Dinah into the jail. His departure from the scene functions for the reader at more than one level. It is naturalistic – at that late hour he clearly had to go, and in the still evening air he will hear the hymn as he rides for some distance. His riding thoughtfully away and so setting the scene at a physical and mental distance apparently distances it for the reader:

Dinah had been speaking at least an hour, and the reddening light of the parting day seemed to give a solemn emphasis to her closing words. The stranger, who had been interested in the course of her sermon, as if it had been the development of a drama – for there is this sort of fascination in all sincere un-premeditated eloquence, which opens to one the inward drama of the speaker's emotions – now turned his horse aside and pursued his way, while Dinah said, 'Let us sing a little, dear friends'; and as he was still winding down the slope, the voices of the Methodists reached him, rising and falling in that strange blending of exultation and sadness which belongs to the cadence of a hymn. (76)

Distancing devices are not always, as they are sometimes thought to be, faintly immoral invitations to lull sensibilities which would otherwise be strenuously awake to rigorous and painful possibilities; they function effectively in Victorian pastoral as focusing devices. As the picture is withdrawn the reader is intended to contemplate it whole with its parts in relation to one another, not simply to let it go in complacent acceptance. The traveller's perception of what he has seen and so, briefly, ours, is shaped like 'the development of a drama', of which, of course, Dinah's audience is an integral part; her eloquence is not self-generating and the exchange with Bessy is quite as revealing of her audience as her sermon is of Dinah's 'inward drama'. Dinah brings the fictional proceedings to an end with, 'Let us sing a little, dear friends' but the lingering cadence of the evening hymn affects the reader independently of the effect of the preceding 'drama'. The reader has seen, through the drama of the scene, Dinah's responsiveness to others and her power to touch the hearts of her audience, but it is also a part of the power of the book to touch the reader too. The open purity of the language of the hymn gives lyrical expression to what has been perceived dramatically. This is, of course, at one remove from the reality of the scene but near the heart of the reality the reader can construct for himself. The necessity of personal recall in the process of reader participation is actually described by the narrator in chapter 7, 'The Dairy':

> I might mention all the divine charms of a bright spring day, but if you had never in your life utterly forgotten yourself in straining your eyes after the mounting lark, or in wandering through the still lanes when the fresh-opened blossoms fill them with a sacred silent beauty like that of fretted aisles, where would be the use of my descriptive catalogue?   (128)

In its context, however, this is paralipsis; it is part of the 'catalogue' of detail which 'it is of little use for me to tell you . . . unless you have seen a woman who affected you as Hetty affected her beholders'. It has the double effect of making Hetty crystal clear and of conveying that there is little more to know than you can see. In these instances neither the distancing nor the direct invitation to the reader to do his own imagining functions in the way indicated by the surface technique. What is clear is that here, as elsewhere in the expository section of the novel the narrator is, in James's phrase, 'making' his reader.

The clearest indication to the reader of where the emotional focus of the book is most truly located is a painterly use of light. The description of light is never incidental or self-indulgent; it functions exactly as the narrator describes in chapter 17 to make the eye linger and convey meaning. The meaning, as in the Dutch pictures, lies in the relationships. The sun shines, in Jonathan Burge's workshop, on the small working community and, making them exquisite, on the fine particles of the material they work with. The 'level sunlight' falls on the foreground meadows under the traveller's eye, not on the mountains; in the sober light of the setting sun through leaves Dinah strikes her simple rhetorical attitude and 'the reddening light of the parting day' emphasises her closing words. The working part of the Hall Farm is also bathed in sunshine in contrast to its neglected front. In the description of this central location a change of style signals the transition to the value-bearing description. The introduction to the farm is made up of two pictures in contrasting styles. The approach is a picture of a ruin in the picturesque style:

> It is a very fine old place, of red-brick, softened by a pale powdery lichen, which has dispersed itself with happy irregularity, so as to bring the red brick into terms of friendly companionship with the limestone ornaments surrounding the three gables, the windows, and the door-place. (115)

The picturesque is comic – 'two stone lionesses . . . grin with a doubtful carnivorous affability above a coat of arms surmounting each of the pillars' – and nostalgic:

> For it is a solid, heavy, handsome door, and must once have been in the habit of shutting with a sonorous bang behind a liveried lackey, who had just seen his master and mistress off the grounds in a carriage and pair.

Narrator and reader approach the house together and, imagination being 'a licensed trespasser', climb the walls of the garden 'with impunity'. With their view of the neglected interior 'the history of the house is plain now'. This exercise in fictional social-history in a popular, mock-heroic style gives way to a picture as conventional in its way and as far from the urban life of the reader. The difference is that the reader is clearly meant to approve and to respond with a 'fibre of sympathy' for a life unlike his own. The 'picture' is, of course, bathed in light:

Plenty of life is there, though this is the drowsiest time of the year, just before the hay-harvest; and it is the drowsiest time of the day too, for it is close upon three by the sun, and it is half-past three by Mrs Poyser's handsome eight-day clock. But there is always a stronger sense of life when the sun is brilliant after rain; and now he is pouring down his beams, and making sparkles among the wet straw, and lighting up every patch of vivid green moss on the red tiles of the cow-shed, and turning even the muddy water that is hurrying along the channel to the drain into a mirror for the yellow-billed ducks, who are seizing the opportunity of getting a drink with as much body in it as possible. There is quite a concert of noises; the great bull-dog, chained against the stables, is thrown into furious exasperation by the unwary approach of a cock too near the mouth of his kennel, and sends forth a thundering bark, which is answered by two fox-hounds shut up in the opposite cow-house; the old top-knotted hens, scratching with their chicks among the straw, set up a sympathetic croaking as the discomfited cock joins them; a sow with her brood, all very muddy as to the legs, and curled as to the tail, throws in some deep staccato notes; our friends the calves are bleating from the home croft; and, under all, a fine ear discerns the continuous hum of human voices.   (116–17)

The human voices belong to the men working in the great barn who are viewed by Mrs Poyser as, much like the animals, the natural enemies of cleanliness. The weight of the narrator's approval is conveyed only by the description of the light. The frame for both pictures of the farm, neglect at the front, work and warmth at the back is the simple historical fact: 'It was once the Hall, it is now the Hall Farm.' The suggestion of a *probable* reason, the 'dwindling' of the family 'down to mere spinsterhood', makes typical rather than particular history of the process:

Like the life in some coast town that was once a watering-place, and is now a port, where the genteel streets are silent and grass-grown, and the docks and warehouses busy and resonant, the life at the Hall has changed its focus, and no longer radiates from the parlour, but from the kitchen and the farmyard.   (116)

This piece of neutral historical writing separates the two pictures. While they are slightly humorous, the emotion we are intended to attach to the representation of the living present is indicated in the second by the transforming light.

The quality of the light, of course, is a part of most of the evocative scenes of *Adam Bede*. In the Bedes' cottage,

> the small window, which had hitherto freely let in the frosty moonlight or the warm summer sunrise on the working-man's slumber, must now be darkened with a fair white sheet, for this was the sleep which is sacred under the rafters as in ceiled houses. (148)

And when Lisbeth comes downstairs the bright afternoon's sun shone 'dismally' on the dirty kitchen. From her window in the same cottage Dinah watches the 'growing light' of morning and from her window at the Hall Farm 'the unresponding stillness of the moonlit fields'. These are atmospheric descriptions mirroring mood and situation which were to become so usual a feature of romantic fiction that we hardly notice them. A very clear example is the sparkling sunshine after rain as Arthur makes his heedless way into the fateful wood. The painterly use of light I have described in the 'set piece' descriptions has a different function. It is a direction of the reader's attention, an indication of the openness of the scenes to his interpretation provided he will linger long enough over them. It is an indication of the dynamism in a static method. The reader has by sympathetic interaction with the text to activate the movement between one picture and another. The characters will step out of their frames and speak and act as well as gesture, but the wholeness of the book for any reader will depend on how far he can keep both action and frame in mind. The world of Loamshire is itself only relative – there is another world outside to which the characters, dramatically, penetrate, but in all its frailty the world of Hayslope is real in the sense of being a part of everyone.

The narrator of *Adam Bede* takes, characteristically, in the first part of the book the mildly embattled position sketched in chapter 17 where the enemy is the rigidity and conservatism any reader is likely to bring to the new. Like any good fighter though, this narrator uses the known characteristics of the enemy on his own behalf. Chapter 17 brings attention most clearly to the analogy of story-telling and painting. The way in which painting can be used to place characters through the familiar is illustrated by the introduction of Mr Irwine in chapter 5. His old-fashioned virtues of mind and manner are reflected in the elegant conversation piece revealed as the narrator stands with the reader at the door of the rectory dining-room. Adam and Dinah are introduced in verbal genre paintings and only then revealed in the little 'dramas' of dialogue, and Dinah, of course, in the sermon. These are the characters in whom the values of the book are embodied. We may again recall here the method of Tennyson's 'Dora', where the undermining of patriarchal authority is signalled by pictorial interruptions in the Biblical style. Where criticism is intended, in the descriptions of Hetty and Arthur, the allusions are literary. Here the distance is ironic and the reader closely involved in judging. Hetty is described in an alternating series of detail and metaphor and authorial statement; played off one against the other, the detail brings her vividly before the eyes, and the statement makes clear that she is limited to this impression; she has no hidden resources, only subterfuges; no religion beyond Hetty. She is drawn as a temptation, and she both links and separates the two young men in the story. But the weight of the story is carried by the drawing of Adam and Arthur. It is in these two meticulously differentiated portraits that the idyllic manner of stylistic allusion brings most clearly into simultaneous focus new and old perceptions.

Arthur was conceived, as is clear from George Eliot's journal, in relation to Adam. That the socially humbler character is morally the more upright goes without saying. But aesthetically these are complementary portraits. Other novels have unheroic heroes but while Pendennis, for example, is provided with a foil in George Warrington, that amiable and suffering young man never approaches the centre of the novel. In *Adam Bede* the tradesman, a 'surprising' hero, not only displaces the young squire, the 'natural' hero, but remains his friend in the life described and shares the novel's space with him. The portrait of Adam is initially strongly pictorial; thereafter his inner struggles are presented directly, with the sympathies of the narrator actively engaged. Arthur's portrait, on the other hand, though it gives the appearance of psychological truth, is in fact a continuous narrative comment on the expected, and the handling of Adam cannot be seen apart from it. While Adam initiates nothing, Arthur's sole 'heroic' function is to instigate the single action of the story. This he does by a kind of inattention against all his own conception of conduct which would be more appropriate to his sense of himself. As the misplaced hero of the novel he is shown in terms of the reader's association of the upper classes with certain kinds of artistic modes which have to be called on, and, if not entirely discredited, modified to fit the unheroic facts.

On his return to Hayslope, and his introduction to the book (in chapter 5, 'The Rector') the community may open its arms to him, but the central figure himself makes but an indeterminate impression. The noise of friendly greeting indicates his footing at the rectory; he has a name, but he is 'known in Hayslope variously as "the young squire", "the captain" and "the heir"'. The tenants have an exaggerated view of his military position, his captaincy in the Loamshire militia outshining any such rank in the regulars 'as the planet Jupiter outshines the Milky Way'. As for his appearance, the reader is invited to imagine it for himself in a way which says that he is an ordinary young man who could as easily be dressed in present-day clothes but for the accident of the time of the story – his actions, that is, are not to be judged by any special standards we might be inclined to employ for a character in an historical novel:

> If you want to know more particularly how he looked, call to your remembrance some tawny-whiskered, brown-locked, clear-complexioned young Englishman whom you have met with in a foreign town, and been proud of as a fellow-countryman – well-washed, high-bred, white-handed, yet looking as if he could deliver well from the shoulder and floor his man: I will not be so much of a tailor as to trouble your imagination with the difference of costume, and insist on the striped waistcoat, long-tailed coat, and low top-boots. (105)

When he first speaks at length it is in the mixture of young man's slang and scraps of learning which characterises his mind. Adam is 'a regular trump', who 'shall manage my woods for me', and Dinah struck him as 'like St. Catherine in a Quaker dress'. 'It's a type of face', he says grandly, 'one rarely sees among our common people'. He later offers to Mr Irwine a similarly distanced view of Hetty as 'a perfect Hebe', to which Mr Irwine replies, with worldly good sense, that he hopes Arthur will continue to see Hetty in this purely 'artistic light'. The sophisticated view of Dinah is placed for the reader by its position in an inconclusive exchange with Mrs Irwine, who says she can 'tell what men are by their outsides. . . . An ugly, piggish or fishy eye, now, makes me feel quite ill; it's like a bad smell.' Arthur replies:

'Talking of eyes', ... 'that reminds me that I've got a book I
meant to bring you, Godmamma. It came down in a parcel from
London the other day, I know you are fond of queer, wizard-like
stories. It's a volume of poems, "Lyrical Ballads". Most of them
seem to be twaddling stuff, but the first is in a different style –
"The Ancient Mariner" is the title. I can hardly make head or
tail of it as a story, but it's a strange, a striking thing. . . .'   (109)

He has made a Gothic mystery of 'The Ancient Mariner', caught by
the glittering eye, and has been completely deceived by the surface
simplicities of Wordsworth's poems. He also has some pamphlets the
rector may like, but the 'fellow' has been instructed to send no more
literature on any subject ending in 'ism'. Arthur, the reader must
infer, is neither a very sensitive nor a very thoughtful young man,
but in so far as the reader needs teasing into a proper perspective on
reality, he may have much in common with Arthur.

The whole of chapter 5 is about impressions and the narrator's
object is to keep the reader's impressions shifting. The two final
paragraphs are again in the form of a picture, but one shown to be
oddly inappropriate. In it the conventional harmony between
figure and landscape has been deliberately unsettled by the
immediately preceding passage of some length on the various ways
in which it would be possible to consider Mr Irwine as a clergyman.
The bright sunlight shines over the whole of this picture, but the
context of its presentation suggests a scepticism about the relation of
its parts:

But whatever you may think of Mr Irwine now, if you had met
him that June afternoon riding on his grey cob, with his dogs
running beside him – portly, upright, manly, with a good-
natured smile on his finely turned lips as he talked to his dashing
young companion on the bay mare, you must have felt that,
however ill he harmonised with sound theories of the clerical
office, he somehow harmonized extremely well with that peaceful
landscape.

See them in the bright sunlight, interrupted every now and
then by rolling masses of cloud, ascending the slope from the
Broxton side, where the tall gables and elms of the rectory
predominate over the tiny whitewashed church. They will soon
be in the parish of Hayslope; the grey church-tower and village

roofs lie before them to the left, and farther on, to the right, they can just see the chimneys of the Hall Farm. (113)

Landowner and cleric are going to fail in this story precisely in the social responsibility assumed by the mode of this picture. Handsome men on spirited horses in pictures are assumed, in social life, to have a responsibility to the land they ride about in. The incompatibility of mode and story under the flat surface of light makes for an ominous effect here, and suggests the frailty of the harmony specifically referred to between figures and landscape.

The action of the story begins in the crucial chapter 'In the World' when the social gap is disastrously bridged. The writing again draws attention to a parallel mismatching of modes. 'It may seem a contradiction,' the narrator says, 'but Arthur gathered a certain carelessness and confidence from his timidity.' Contradictions such as this form the fabric of the chapter. The kind of carelessness which goes properly with confidence arises from courage not timidity and makes possible heroic deeds performed by men lifted temporarily out of common humanity in history or idealised beyond it in art. Contemplating his 'well-looking British person', Arthur is stared at in the fixity of old-fashioned rhetorical gesture from the 'dingy' tapestry by 'Pharoh's daughter and her maidens who ought to have been minding the infant Moses'. Feeling that he has made an heroic renunciation by planning the fishing expedition, he strides along the corridor singing Macheath's best-known song. The narrator's account of the self-image of this 'good fellow' is in language sharply contrasted with the colloquial reality:

> he had an agreeable confidence that his faults were all of a generous kind – impetuous, warm-blooded, leonine; never crawling, crafty, reptilian. It was not possible for Arthur Donnithorne to do anything mean, dastardly or cruel. 'No! I'm the devil of a fellow for getting myself into a hobble, but I always take care the load shall fall on my own shoulders.' (169)

His picture of the future is similarly simplified in a hint of his own generalising and inadequate language:

> [he] would be the model of an English gentleman – mansion in first-rate order, all elegance and high taste – jolly house-

keeping, finest stud in Loamshire – purse open to all public
objects . . . (170)

Society and, the narrator implies, novel-readers would endorse
the promising appearance of this young 'hero'. He seemed to be 'a
sea-worthy vessel that no-one would refuse to insure'. But the
hidden flaws of his nature are to come to light at his first real trial. In
this chapter Arthur moves out of Hall and drawing-room into the
seclusion and treachery of the woods. The words 'nature' and
'natural' run through the chapter raising questions about their
meaning:

> One thing is clear: Nature has taken care that he shall never go far
> astray with perfect comfort and satisfaction to himself; he will
> never get beyond that border-land of sin, where he will be
> perpetually harassed by assaults from the other side of the
> boundary. He will never be a courtier of Vice, and wear her
> orders in his button-hole.
>
>   It was about ten o'clock, and the sun was shining brilliantly;
> everything was looking lovelier for the yesterday's rain. It is a
> pleasant thing on such a morning to walk along the well-rolled
> gravel on one's way to the stables, meditating an excursion. But
> the scent of the stables, which, in a natural state of things, ought
> to be among the soothing influences of a man's life, always
> brought with it some irritation to Arthur. (171)

Natural laws, Arthur's nature, what we regard as natural, what
Arthur regards as natural are all distinguishable in the introductory
paragraphs of this chapter. It is clear that by 'natural' Arthur
always means 'easy' and sometimes 'convenient'; the context
presents a scale of comparison and judgement. In action Arthur's
nature is revealed as unheroically pettish when he is thwarted of an
anticipated ride on Meg: 'It seemed culpable of Providence to allow
such a combination of circumstances.' And when the narrator says,
'So nothing could seem simpler and more natural: meeting Hetty
was a mere circumstance of his walk, not its object', Arthur is
interpreting 'natural' in one way, narrator and reader, while seeing
his meaning, attach their own from an ironic distance. As Arthur
strolls along 'carelessly' through the wood, the reader is implicated
in the seductive charm of the Grove and made to feel the danger to
which Arthur is indifferent. On this 'afternoon in which destiny

disguises her cold awful face behind a hazy radiant veil, encloses us in warm downy wings, and poisons us with violet-scented breath', the natural world evoked is shifting and amoral. Generally pagan, it recalls particularly the *Metamorphoses*. The nymphs it is so easy to imagine behind 'the light silver-stemmed birch trees . . . make you believe that their voice was only a running brooklet', or 'metamorphose themselves into a tawny squirrel that scampers away and mocks you from the topmost bough'. The restlessness of this world of fleeting shapes and flickering light is anti-pastoral. True ease of spirit might have come in 'a grove with measured grass or rolled gravel', but not in this dangerous world made as if 'by the free will of the trees and underwood, moving reverently aside to look at the tall Green of the white-footed nymphs'. Arthur's 'ease' is mere 'carelessness', and narrator and reader share a view of it summoned by literary associations. That part of the reader's response which has survived the impulse to criticism of this particular kind of charm is disposed of in the recognition of the absurd conventionality of the only kind of story where such an encounter in such circumstances could have had a happy ending at all, one in which consciousness of time does not exist:

> Poor things! It was a pity they were not in that golden age of childhood when they would have stood face to face, eyeing each other with timid liking, then given each other a butterfly kiss, and toddled off to play together. Arthur would have gone home to his silk-curtained cot, and Hetty to her home-spun pillow, and both would have slept without dreams, and tomorrow would have been a life hardly conscious of a yesterday.   (195)

Nowhere in *Adam Bede* is it clearer that modes of perception are being set against one another. The reader's involvement with the effort to see what is actually there saves him from complacency even while he knows that for these unknowing characters the outcome of the story cannot be good.

When Hetty makes her parallel approach to the Fir-tree Grove in the evening she is as indifferent as Arthur was to the present beauty around her:

> She thought nothing of the evening light that lay gently in the grassy alleys between the fern, and made the beauty of their living

green more visible than it had been in the overpowering flood of
noon: she thought of nothing that was present.   (181)

Hetty's dream is described in terms inaccessible to Hetty herself, but
which the narrator and reader can share, as the narrator
acknowledges:

> Mr Arthur Donnithorne coming to meet her again along the Fir-
> tree Grove. That was the foreground of Hetty's picture; behind it
> lay a bright hazy something – days that were not to be as the other
> days of her life had been. It was as if she had been wooed by a
> river-god, who might at any time take her to his wondrous halls
> below a watery heaven. There was no knowing what would
> come. If a chest full of lace and satin and jewels had been sent her
> from some unknown source, how could she but have thought that
> her whole lot was going to change, and that to-morrow some still
> more bewildering joy would befall her? Hetty had never read a
> novel; if she had ever seen one, I think the words would have been
> too hard for her; how then could she find a shape for her
> expectations? They were as formless as the sweet languid odours
> of the garden at the Chase, which had floated past her as she
> walked by the gate.

The narrator's 'I think' here establishes the relation between
narrator, reader and character, and indicates some sympathy in
what might otherwise have grated as rather patronising. The
description of their meeting and its immediate effect is neither
distanced nor ironic. The unspoilt feelings of the two young people
are shown to be as uncorrupted and 'natural' as the pair are
momentarily without consciousness of social situation. But Arthur
and Hetty, one educated, the other ignorant, are shown to be alike
in the ease with which they give way to languor. Art is not
corrupting in itself, but it can provide a form for dreams. In the face
of what is urgent and natural, classic stories of innocent love are
beside the point; but the reader does not, with Arthur, entirely lose
the power to discriminate:

> Ah, he doesn't know in the least what he is saying. This is not
> what he meant to say. His arm is stealing round the waist again; it
> is tightening its clasp; he is bending his face nearer and nearer to
> the round cheek; his lips are meeting those pouting child-lips, and

for a long moment time has vanished. He may be a shepherd in Arcadia for aught he knows, he may be the first youth kissing the first maiden, he may be Eros himself, sipping the lips of Psyche – it is all one. (182)

The springs of this unfortunate idyll are unpolluted, but effort is a necessity in the pastoral world if natural feeling is to survive.[24] The elaborate techniques of *Adam Bede*, employed to produce the apparently simple effect of 'gentle thoughts and happy remembrances', are an appeal for a more distinct consciousness, such as was given for a brief and unavailing moment to Arthur in the story, to replace the inflexible modes of seeing which become established in sophisticated conventions. The sophisticated reader is being urged to look freshly.

Although at the beginning of book II, in the middle of the exposition, the story is said to 'pause a little' for the direct address to the reader of chapter 17, in fact, the fiction and the process by which the reader plays his part in creating it are not interrupted at this point more than at any other. The remaining five books have many 'pauses' of one kind and another and are probably as remarkable for their variety of pace as for any other single feature. By the end of book III the whole of which is taken up by Arthur's birthday celebrations, Arthur has still only reached the point of intending to give up Hetty and, like her, wishing their dance at the party would 'last for hours', for, the narrator says, 'a man never lies with more delicious languor under the influence of a passion than when he has persuaded himself that he shall subdue it tomorrow'. It has been often commented, inside a variety of critical arguments that the gatherings, in the Church for the funeral, at the birthday celebrations and at the harvest supper, carry the values of the community in the novel. My concern is with their placing and with their relation to the techniques in the exposition of the novel. Immediately after 'the story pauses a little' is the long chapter called 'Church'. In this chapter Hetty misses Arthur from Church and learns that he has gone to Eagledale fishing, and Adam faces the loss of his father. For the rest, Hayslope gathers in the Church, the Poyser family is watched out of sight by Martin Poyser and occupied by thoughts of shorthorns and butter and damp hay that ought to be turned, and Thias Bede is lowered to his grave 'off-stage'. The chapter ends with desultory talk of the weather and the war, amongst which is the information about Arthur's whereabouts. The chapter advances the main plot by a very short step. At greater length it shows something of Adam's inner life which makes credible the resources he calls on in the adversity of later in the story. Its main function, though, as has often been remarked is to show the community, but, more particularly, to do so in a way which further clarifies the reader's conscious acknowledgement of the realities of this remote scene. The chapter repeats the pattern of picture and voice found in the initial scene on the Green. Colloquial talk, personal reverie and the words and music of the church service mingle. But at the centre is a picture of the congregation and its pastor, a still moment between animated scenes.

Once again the apparent detachment of the presentation of the picture is in fact a rhetorical appeal to the reader. The narrator is first concerned to establish that he and the reader share old-fashioned aesthetic standards, after which he 'paints' the picture they are both to contemplate; 'this will not be greatly to your taste', he pretends to say, 'but if you see it truly you will see its charm', which, of course, we do:

> I cannot say that the interior of Hayslope Church was remarkable for anything except for the grey age of its oaken pews – great square pews mostly, ranged on each side of a narrow aisle. It was free, indeed, from the modern blemish of galleries. The choir had two narrow pews to themselves in the middle of the right-hand row, so that it was a short process for Joshua Rann to take his place among them as principal bass, and return to his desk after the singing was over. The pulpit and desk, grey and old as the pews, stood on one side of the arch leading into the chancel, which also had its grey square pews for Mr Donnithorne's family and servants. Yet I assure you these grey pews, with the buff-washed walls, gave a very pleasing tone to this shabby interior, and agreed extremely well with the ruddy faces and bright waistcoats. And there were liberal touches of crimson toward the chancel, for the pulpit and Mr Donnithorne's own pew had handsome crimson cloth cushions; and, to close the vista, there was a crimson altar-cloth, embroidered with golden rays by Miss Lydia's own hand. (241–2)

The congregation is described in the next paragraph, in generalities – 'half a dozen well-to-do farmers with their apple-cheeked families' – or with well-chosen evocative detail – 'the clean old women . . . their bits of snow-white-cap-border under their black bonnets, and with their withered arms, bare from the elbow, folded passively over their chests –.' The narrator guesses – the effect of Mr Irwine 'must have been' cheering –, tells – 'not one of them could read' – and takes the reader's attention for granted – 'one of those lively psalm-tunes which died out with the last generation of rectors and choral parish clerks'; he ends the paragraph as story-teller placing his hero in his social setting. Before the story recommences the scene in the Church is held for one more still pictorial paragraph. The narrator 'beseeches' the reader to imagine the fine figure of Mr Irwine and seems to be putting the finishing touch to the group. The effect is to hold the whole scene with its irregularities and particularities smoothed out. This high moment is, of course, bathed in light:

> I beseech you to imagine Mr Irwine looking round on this scene, in his ample white surplice that became him so well, with his powdered hair thrown back, his rich brown complexion, and his finely cut nostril and upper lip; for there was a certain virtue in that benignant yet keen countenance, as there is in all human faces from which a generous soul beams out. And over all streamed the delicious June sunshine through the old windows, with their desultory patches of yellow, red, and blue, that threw pleasant touches of colour on the opposite wall. (242)

Hetty's disappointment is the only advancement of the plot in this long chapter and it is introduced here after this vignette of the gathered community as a restlessness under the smooth idealised surface, the lightest disturbance in Mr Irwine's general benignancy:

> I think, as Mr Irwine looked round today, his eyes rested an instant longer than usual on the square pew occupied by Martin Poyser and his family. And there was another pair of dark eyes that found it impossible not to wander thither, and rest on that round pink-and-white figure. But Hetty was at that moment quite careless of any glances – she was absorbed in the thought that Arthur Donnithorne would soon be coming into church, for the carriage must surely be at the church-gate by this time. (243)

The narrator's 'I think' draws attention to the disjunction in a way which does not entirely dispel the impression of the whole in the change of focus. The light comedy of Moll's well-meaning effort to restore Hetty with a bottle of stale smelling-salts gives way to the description of Hetty's 'selfish tumult' against the solemn words of the 'Absolution' and of the unruffled surface of her beauty. Adam's sensitivity to this 'did not deafen him to the service'.

If Hetty is shown here as out of key with the community, Adam, for all his heightened 'heroic' consciousness is shown as a natural part of its harmony. The terms in which he is shown responding to the service are not such as would have been available to Adam himself. The narrator sees him in an historical succession of simple worshippers and identifies himself and the reader with the psychology of association:

> And to Adam the church service was the best channel he could have found for his mingled regret, yearning and resignation; its interchange of beseeching cries for help with outbursts of faith and praise, its recurrent responses and the familiar rhythm of its collects, seemed to speak for him as no other form of worship could have done; as, to those early Christians who had worshipped from their childhood upwards in catacombs, the torch-light and shadows must have seemed nearer the Divine presence than the heathenish daylight of the streets. The secret of our emotions never lies in the bare object, but in its subtle relations to our own past: no wonder the secret escapes the unsympathizing observer, who might as well put on his spectacles to discern odours. (245)

Though this presentation of Adam has been often enough remarked on, its context has not. Adam is not the only humble person so ennobled in this religious and communal vignette. Considerably more space is given, in fact, to a description of Joshua Rann's reading. Only the beginning of Adam's spiritual progress is sketched at this point. Book II is largely concerned with a very precise placing of Adam in his background, the community. Though 'not an ordinary man', he is not a very extraordinary one either. Bartle Massey had many other pupils besides Adam, and in Church the peculiar gift Nature has bestowed on the 'narrow soul' of Joshua Rann is the narrator's opportunity to bow out of the special relationship he has with Adam for the brief while that Joshua holds the stage: 'any chance comer' to this service would have found it more impressive than 'in most other village nooks in the kingdom – [for] a reason of which I am sure you have not the slightest suspicion'. The unaccountable occurrence of a great gift of Nature in 'our friend Joshua Rann' serves to establish the heroic village carpenter of inarticulate but tender sensibility as no more and yet no less surprising to one who might contemplate this world than the parish clerk with an untaught capacity to render the scriptures. The relation between what the reader might expect of Adam from what he could see, and what he can know by the mediation of the narrator, is spelled out at length in the next chapter, 'Adam on a Working Day'. In this chapter, 'Church', the two modes of speaking about Joshua Rann – the poetic and the mock-heroic – are demonstrated together and joined by an explicit comment on handling:

> The way he rolled from a rich deep forte into a melancholy cadence, subsiding, at the end of the last word, into a sort of faint resonance, like the lingering vibrations of a fine violoncello, I can compare to nothing for its strong calm melancholy but the rush and cadence of the wind among the autumn boughs. This may seem a strange mode of speaking about the reading of a parish clerk – a man in rusty spectacles, with stubbly hair, a large occiput, and a prominent crown. But that is Nature's way: she will allow a gentleman of splendid physiognomy and poetic aspirations to sing woefully out of tune, and not give him the slightest hint of it; and takes care that some narrow-browed fellow, trolling a ballad in the corner of a pot-house, shall be as true to his intervals as a bird.   (245)

Rann's passing with 'a sense of heightened importance' from 'the desk to the choir' holds the haunting words of the psalm-based hymn:

> 'Thou sweepst us off as with a flood;
> We vanish hence like dreams'

in the same precarious balance with the commonplace. With 'the closer application than usual in the death of poor Thias' the words of the hymn focus on the story again. Against the solemnities of the Church service, the melancholy thoughts it gives rise to in Adam are touching in their sincerity. The reductiveness of his expression of them aligns Adam effectively with the other rustic characters. 'There's no real making amends in this world, any more nor you can mend a wrong subtraction by doing your addition right' is different from Mrs Poyser's wisdom only in being drawn from the kind of experience appropriate to Adam's work. The rigidity of which this mode of thought is capable is criticised later by the narrator; it can transform any 'proposition' into a 'principle'. The criticism is both moral and social comment: 'Perhaps here lay the hardness he had accused himself of: he had too little fellow feeling with that weakness that errs in spite of foreseen consequences.' The mode of expression, the reader is free to notice, be it Adam's or Mrs Poyser's matches the hardness exactly. It touches the source of feeling, but freezes the flow into immobility. But Adam is portrayed as genuinely moved by the Church service and he is later said to have 'learnt the alphabet' of sympathy for weakness by his father's death. Sympathy with Adam, short of identification on the one hand and of patronage on the other, is possible in this chapter because, in its 'andante' movement, the reader is himself touched by the timeless grandeur and relevance of the words of the service. He has at the same time acknowledged that the reminders have come via a man insignificant to plain in appearance and comically vain. The stillness of this long chapter does in fact contain significant movement in the growing definition of the reader's awareness of the way in which sophisticated assumptions must be renewed to attach themselves to a new conception of worth.

The weaving together of pictorial and linguistic modes of perception and expression in 'Church', with the slightest possible movement of the story to its inevitable end, can tell us much about the way in which that end is intended to make its impact. The courtship and marriage of Dinah and Adam has made many including some contemporary readers uneasy. George Eliot reported Sir Edward Lytton as saying that 'the two defects' of *Adam Bede* were 'the dialect and Adam's marriage to Dinah'. Modern critics do not complain of the dialogue, though some, like John Goode,[25] do complain of the inadequacy of Adam's language, and many more would still see the end as a disappointment. George Eliot, however, was equally attached to both: 'of course I would have my teeth drawn rather than give up either'.[26] More integral to the inspiration and method of *Adam Bede* than has often been allowed, the presentation of the marriage is interrelated with the representation of speech. The bare simplicity and speed of the ending are moving in the way they offset Adam's ponderous and rather reductive musings before the betrothal. If in the earlier chapter, 'Church', at the beginning of Adam's moral education, he is only learning the 'alphabet of sympathy', he has the syntax of judgement which he retains to the end. But the moment at which he faces the joint guilt of Hetty and Arthur robs him of that:

> 'but then, that's the deepest curse of all . . . that's what makes the blackness of it . . . *it can never be undone.* My poor Hetty . . . she can never be my sweet Hetty again . . . the prettiest thing God had made – smiling up at me . . . and was good . . .'   (468)

Although the inveterate novel-reader in most of us tends to simplify this part of the story into Adam's loss of Hetty, another look at the chapters surrounding the trial will show Adam as at least as preoccupied with Arthur as he is with Hetty and, in his dealings with Mr Irwine, more explicitly so. Mr Irwine's instinctive sympathy with Arthur, and his failure to see what he should have seen, is a kind of betrayal too. The pattern of Adam's world has been shattered with the rupture of the relationships which constitute it, and he stands, briefly, entirely alone. The literary language of emotion without relationship is melodrama,[27] and Adam's theatrical outburst is a measure of the social rubble around him.

The end of the novel, book VI, presents a new relation of voice and picture, which is effective because of its implied commentary on what has gone before. After the eighteen-month gap which follows the muted 'Goodbyes' of Adam and Arthur, book VI opens with a conversation between Mrs Poyser and Dinah. This is a colloquy of the two most distinct voices of the book – the one noisy and racy, the other quiet and limpid. Dinah has been used in contrast all through the book – with Hetty of course and with Mr Irwine. The moment in which she and Arthur are joined in Hetty's 'rescue' is the most dramatic. Her stillness in the cart has implicit in it all the words in the prison, just as the clatter of Arthur's last-minute dash has implicit in it the goodwill and tragic mistakes of the past. There is less room for criticism of the melodrama of the reprieve, I think, when it is seen in the total moment of which it is a part. In the scene at the Hall Farm Mrs Poyser and Dinah both speak from the depth of feeling, however differently. The months have not left Dinah as she was. The growth of Adam's friendship is convincingly portrayed; she has been converted 'into a convenient household slave' by the Poyser children, who feel free to tease and play with her as they will. Under Aunt Poyser's direction she 'has advanced in household cleverness', but with Dinah this means letting in 'the fresh air and the smell of the sweet-briar, and the bright low-slanting rays of the early sun, which made a glory about her pale face and pale auburn hair as she held the long brush'. She sings 'in a very low tone', while she works, one of Wesley's hymns, of which three verses are quoted. They extend and comment on the cheerful performance of homely duties by what they say and by the shapely lyric form given to the pictured scene:

> Eternal beam of Light Divine,
>   Fountain of unexhausted love,
> In whom the Father's glories shine,
>   Through earth beneath and heaven above.
>
> Jesus! the weary wanderer's rest,
>   Give me thy easy yoke to bear;
> With steadfast patience arm my breast,
>   With spotless love and holy fear.
>
> Speak to my warring passions, 'Peace!'
>   Say to my trembling heart, 'Be still!'
> Thy power my strength and fortress is
>   For all things serve thy sovereign will.   (535)

The 'pictures' of book VI are of a different kind from the previous ones. There is a matching pair of domestic interiors with figures, for instance, one on either side of the fireplace in Lisbeth's cottage. Each is animated with a little characteristic dialogue but the analogy with pictures is explicitly made:

> There were two pretty pictures on the two sides of the wall in the cottage. On one side there was the broad-shouldered, large-featured, hardy old woman, in her blue jacket and buff kerchief, with her dim-eyed anxious looks turned continually on the lily face and the slight form in the black dress that were either moving lightly about in helpful activity, or seated close by the old woman's arm-chair, holding her withered hand, with eyes lifted up towards her to speak a language which Lisbeth understood far better than the Bible or the Hymn-book.

The matching picture on the other side is of two brothers 'so like each other in the midst of their unlikeness', independently occupied but mutually aware and caring. Relationship binds the two pictures; it is the subject of each one and the two are of course complementary. Domesticity closes in convincingly on Dinah, provided the reader is prepared to accept the sweetness as it is conceived. It is domesticity rather than the community which does absorb her; she is, for instance, absent from the Harvest Home with its good cheer and peasant politics, where she could hardly have found a voice. There is loss for her though. Personal feeling comes first to Dinah in agitation and an uncontrollable tendency to tears. 'I have felt as it were a division in my heart.' But most significantly from the reader's point of view, what in one aspect can be seen as Dinah's sacrifice of vocation in domesticity, can also be seen as the taking up of the *difficulties* of silence in place of the 'ease' of speech. Dinah's preaching on the Green, for all its accomplished and authentic[28] rhetoric, is in the story, ineffective; it is her power to make almost wordless human contact that gives her her distinctive part in the story. It is not her arguments in 'The Two Bed-Chambers' which touch Hetty for a brief moment of chill fear, but the 'solemn pathetic distinctness' with which they were uttered. And in the prison Hetty stumbles into her sad tale in the gap left between them by Dinah's passionate prayer. The dimension which the union of Adam and Dinah adds to the picture of the created world is fittingly shown in the scene of their final promise to one another:

> He chose this spot, almost at the top of the hill, because it was away from all eyes – no house, no cattle, not even a nibbling sheep near – no presence but the still lights and shadows and the great embracing sky. (575)

The absence of feature in a story so full of detailed description leaves us free to follow them where words will not direct us. The narrator has 'made' us as readers up to this point: we are no freer of our preconceptions than Adam of his past, but like him we too are in possession of a firmer sense of what is real.

In approaching the hamlet where Dinah is working, Adam is treading again the path he trod in search of Hetty. The two loves are placed in relation to one another by means of landscape and in this the narrator has the last word – we have heard the last of Adam's reflections:

> It was more than two o'clock in the afternoon when Adam came in sight of the grey town on the hill-side and looked searchingly towards the green valley below, for the first glimpse of the old thatched roof near the ugly red mill. The scene looked less harsh in the soft October sunshine than it had in the eager time of early spring, and the one grand charm it possessed in common with all wide-stretching woodless regions – that it filled you with a new consciousness of the overarching sky – had a milder, more soothing influence than usual, on this almost cloudless day. Adam's doubts and fears melted under this influence as the delicate weblike clouds had gradually melted away into the clear blue above him.   (574)

Adam's active choice of the lonely spot at the top of the hill completes a process by which the significant landscapes of the story have been internalised by Adam. At first, after the church service, Adam's thoughts are of Hetty in the sunshine of 'the summer morning in his heart'. It is only the reader for whom the 'slanting rays that tremble between the delicate shadows of the leaves' are a reminder of the Grove and sadly illumine Adam's mistake. Everyman, the narrator says, can recall the scene of the 'mere feather touch' of first love returned and so Adam will remember Hetty in the garden. But the memory of the discovery of Hetty and Arthur in the Grove is the beginning of Adam's suffering and as such is particularised as are other significant scenes by the artist's eye and the beam of light. 'What grand Beeches!', Adam thinks as he enters the Grove. He has a practised eye for trees but though that is the eye of a skilled workman, the shaping of a fine beech as a memory is aesthetic. And it is at that heightened moment of perception that the revelation comes:

> He kept them in his memory, as a painter does, with all the flecks and knots in their bark, all the curves and angles of their boughs, and had often calculated the height and contents of a trunk to a nicety, as he stood looking at it. No wonder that, notwithstanding his desire to get on, he could not help pausing to look at a curious large beech which he had seen standing before him at a turning in the road, and convince himself that it was not

two trees wedded together, but only one. For the rest of his life he remembered that moment when he was calmly examining the beech, as a man remembers his last glimpse of the home where his youth was passed, before the road turned and he saw it no more. The beech stood at the last turning before the Grove ended in an archway of boughs that let in the eastern light; and as Adam stepped away from the tree to continue his walk, his eyes fell on two figures about twenty yards before him.   (341)

The memory always recurs in the same visual form and when he resolves after the trial to look once more at the spot to mourn the past he believes dead at 'the boundary mark of his youth', the first stirrings of old affection, have occurred before the chastened Arthur actually appears. With Hetty, of course, there is no such internalisation – only Dinah penetrates briefly to that part of Hetty where regeneration could begin if it were destined to do so at all. She exists entirely separated from the background of the story in community and landscape. Her plight at the beginning of her journey with her 'hidden dread' is brought home to the reader in the image of the suffering God in the beautiful landscapes of foreign countries, in other respects, the narrator says, so reminiscent of Loamshire. The reality of Hetty's suffering goes on against the most 'joyous' natural beauty.

Critics have used this and other statements of the narrator as evidence of George Eliot's philosophical and aesthetic views at the time. But generally, I believe, they are not extractable from their context. They are woven in to the fabric of the book in the same way that the marriage of Dinah and Adam is continuous with the whole in spirit and method. The whole book can be seen as a complex rhetorical gesture in which the narrator is engaged with the reader at every point. He *describes* a world which he assumes is strange to the reader and 'beseeches' him to look at it freshly. Distanced as any pastoral or idyll is, it demands an active sympathy of the reader which makes it seem not remote. Perhaps because we know the later George Eliot, perhaps because the mode, like genre-painting, is strange to us, modern critics do not respond with the freshness of her contemporaries. At the time it moved even the impassive Herbert Spencer to uncritical pleasure: 'What am I to say? That I have read it with laughter and tears and without criticism. Knowing as you do how constitutionally I am given to fault-finding you will know what this means. . . . I feel greatly the better for having read it.'[29] It describes a social world which will not return, but it asks the question which is relevant at any time – 'What is "real"?' It forces the contemporary reader to adjust his assumptions, notice where they come from, and focus on the simple, but for that reason extremely difficult truth. It appears to be showing people not like 'us' – unsophisticated and rooted in the ways of the past. But it is, of course, saying that their inner life, the human 'reality', is exactly like ours.

The idyllic mode is not repeated in George Eliot's work. The book exists in a balance of interest between four main characters and a background of landscape and grouped figures. The balance, though precarious, is sustained and extends like that of other idylls into the modes of presentation both used and recalled. If *Adam Bede* is seen not as a failure in psychological realism, but as a remarkable work in its own right, it can be judged more rightly as a success in a mode which George Eliot, in company with other pastoral artists, soon abandons. One main distinguishing feature separates this early work from the later novels. It shares its origin in early memory with *The Mill on the Floss*, its humble subject-matter with *Silas Marner*, the intimate weaving of picture and story with *Romola*, a sense of the relationship of individual and community with *Middlemarch*, a vision of tangential worlds touching with *Felix Holt* and *Daniel Deronda*. Its narrator, however, the stance he assumes and the function he performs, are unique in George Eliot's work. In *Silas Marner*, where the subject-matter is the most pastoral, the narrator's vision is, in contrast to that in *Adam Bede*, single-minded. He directs the attention of the reader to a single figure, who is shown from a single point of valuation. The simple line of his story – of an outcast and resentful solitary who, in the moment of losing all he values, finds what he should have been valuing all along – is, for all the realism of the presentation, part legend, part parable. The resolved story confirms a single system of values which we are never asked to question, and which, of course, remove the possibility of the idyllic balance found at the end of *Adam Bede*. In *The Mill on the Floss* the narrator's sympathy is given so unequivocally to the heroine that there can be no question of distance. George Eliot's own fondness for the childhood scenes, she thought, upset the balance of the book. They are recalled with an affection and clarity which might in themselves have suggested an idyllic method, but in the book as a whole they serve to direct our sympathies to the place where they remain undisturbed, with the ardent and frustrated Maggie. The story is framed in two verbal genre pictures, the first of the little girl with the jumping dog by the mill, the last one of the grave with two names on its stone in the partially restored landscape. But this idyllic and generalising frame does not remove the concentration of the story of a passionate life at odds with circumstances. The end of the book is a total resolution in which Maggie's and Tom's death proceeds from an inexorable aesthetic logic rather than realistic necessity. In *Middlemarch* the narrator attempts to discover by telling. His position has perhaps been best described by J. Hillis Miller, who shows him entangled in his own metaphors for the historical processes he describes.[30] A balanced idyllic view only results when the narrator withdraws to show a multi-faceted picture of mutually relating parts. In *Adam Bede* the comparative distance of the narrator from the scene is dependent on the closeness and directness of his relation with the reader, who is being persuaded to engage with the narrator rather than directly with his story. The active possibilities balanced inside the idyllic calm at the end of *Adam Bede* are circumscribed by the marriage of Adam and Dinah. But the marriage, in closing the circle, allows the possibilities to be more clearly apparent. Smallness of scale is an essential idyllic quality.

Oddly, *Adam Bede* is most closely related in method with *Daniel Deronda*. *Daniel Deronda*, ambitious and engaged beyond any conception of pastoral, nevertheless returns in its lack of resolution and complicated mirroring of part and part to essential elements in idyllic strategy. The end shows the protagonist of each of the interwoven stories not only at the beginning of a new phase of life, but in a separate and altered relation to moral and historical issues. The breadth of the conception dictates a structure which allows parallels and reversals, connections and contrasts to take a shape in the reader's mind the more haunting for its lack of completeness. The comparative mode operates between and within the parts. The minuscule scale of individual life seen in relation to the concerns of the larger world, the living present in historical flux – these conceptual foundations underly the idyllic vision of *Adam Bede* and the historical vision of *Daniel Deronda*. In pastoral the narrator takes a stand on the values of the simple world. He is aware that breadth and sophistication, complexities of all kinds, at once threaten and provide a scale of measurement for the described world. Such consciousness is a part of the description, whether overtly or by reference to other modes of telling. Further the luminosity of the idealised moment must glow against a continuing sense of passing time. If the narrator ceases for a moment to be aware of flux the narrative can fall into sentimentality – all too 'easy, vulgar and therefore disgusting'. If he becomes exclusively aware of it the pastoral calm disappears into the process of narrative or history. To take a stand on the values of the larger world is to move into the heroic.[31] The heroic narrator keeps the grand scale of his enterprise in his own and his reader's mind by recalling the simple, commonplace or static, as the coexistent world of Homer's similes is one means of measuring the momentous chances of an historical struggle in which the Gods are involved along with men. Of their nature neither the pastoral nor the heroic can offer resolution. Comparison, on which they are based, implies repetition or continuity. The two parts of *Daniel Deronda* function in relation to one another, I suggest, on the basis of this pattern. They balance the public and the private, and each contains within itself the means of measuring its own scale. The potential tragedy of the two stories puts pressure on the fictions to resolve themselves in a united end, but in fact they draw further apart and continue beyond the end of the fiction only in mutual reflection.

Adam Bede and *Daniel Deronda*, the beginning and end of George Eliot's major fiction, remind us how close, in Clough's words, are 'the Muse of great Epos, and Idyll the playful and tender'. If the story of *Adam Bede* is not 'playful' it is 'tender', and the narrator brings the reader to a proper focus on it by means which are fundamentally 'playful'. If *Daniel Deronda* contains stories of human weakness, its conception of the individual as a part of inevitable historical process is, nevertheless, epic. Henry James thought George Eliot gave 'exaggerated attention' to 'general considerations', and blamed the 'age' which forced the artist to confront so many issues.[32] But she might rather be thought in her final handling of this recalcitrant material to have learnt much from having written her first full-length novel in the reflective, comparative, balanced mode of the idyll.

5 Thomas Hardy: Character and Environment

All through his career as a novelist Hardy wrote not only about, but from within, the world which gave rise to his pastoral vision. His excursions into wider spheres produced what are generally considered his 'minor' novels. The works which steadily chart the growth of Wessex as an imagined scene are not, of course, all pastorals. As 'Novels of Character and Environment', to use Hardy's 1912 classification, they increasingly focus on character. In *The Mayor of Casterbridge, Tess of the d'Urbervilles* and *Jude the Obscure* the focus on the fortunes of a strong central character dictates the generic nature of the novels. But Wessex is vividly portrayed in all of them, and *Jude* depicts the end, in Hardy's vision, of an historical process in the 'Environment' which he has been recording since *Under the Greenwood Tree.* The replacement of Mellstock 'quire' and Fancy's self-conscious choice of customary ceremonies for her wedding – the events in that first book which represent the movement towards the new and the emotional ties to the past – are not the stuff of which tragedy are made, but they indicate a tension in the observed world which is a part of the structure of Hardy's imagined world wherever, in any single novel, the emphasis may fall. In *Under the Greenwood Tree, The Woodlanders* and *Far from the Madding Crowd*, the 'idylls' in my terms among Hardy's major works, the emphasis falls not on individual character but on the novel's world of grouped figures in a distinctive landscape. In *Under the Greenwood Tree* the narrator is at pains to make the reader *see* the life with which he himself is so familiar.[1] Subtitled 'A Rural Painting of the Dutch School', the novel in fact does not present a clear picture in strong Dutch colours so much as invite, in George Sand's words, 'ceux qui ont les yeux à regarder aussi'. *The Woodlanders*, fifteen years and eight novels later, returns to the wooded scene of *Under the Greenwood Tree* and Hardy's own earliest recollections. If the underlying melancholy in the early narrative voice has become more marked over the years, the emphasis remains on showing the described world as it is. The painting is no longer a realist one; Hardy's techniques like his interests have moved with the times. Later I shall try to show the literary techniques which make a Dutch or realist 'picture' of *Under the Greenwood Tree* and an 'impressionist' one of *The Woodlanders*. Here I want simply to stress the descriptive emphasis of these two books which takes precedence over a separate concentration on either character or story. The lack of final resolution in *The Woodlanders* thus becomes a characterising generic feature not a failure to reach a satisfactory end.

These two novels represent two versions of the landscape in which Hardy's imaginative life is rooted. They are both in their different ways meditative and poetic. Their sharp realisation of the fictional worlds is a triumph of aesthetic distance over involvement. *Far from the Madding Crowd*, on the other hand, is the least personal of all Hardy's novels. The life of the farms is one he knew thoroughly but not intimately, and the novel is the one most shot through with references to the pastoral tradition. In Hardy's development *Far from the Madding Crowd* indicates a sudden sense of mastery of his craft. As in other idylls I have described, consciousness of the fiction-making is incorporated into the telling. The result is a happy picture in spite of the tragedies of death and madness, and the most vivacious novel Hardy ever wrote. Everything – the landscape, the work of the farms, the community, the figures who act out their story in front of this rural backdrop – all in their turn interest this narrator. Not least he is fascinated by his own creative power to make a fiction out of what is real to him and strange to others. He peoples his world of stubborn realities and magical beauty with strong characters isolated in their passion. As narrator he is not involved with one of these elements more than another, and so remains free to see them in constantly surprising relationships. *The Woodlanders* depicts a world of separate elements, but in that novel they are shown to be to some extent incompatible, held in a melancholy unity by the voice of the contemplating narrator. *Under the Greenwood Tree* is realistic and immediate. But the present moment observed with such clarity is seen to carry with it the historical and traditional past, just as the tree in the Days' garden gives a physical reality to the Shakespearean reference of the title.

Its shade unites in one picture the nameless wedding guests and the known principals gathered in the dance underneath it, and the narrator presents a view which encompasses both the continuity of life and the perpetually dissolving modes of apprehension to which the dancing generations subscribe. More like one another than they are like those of Elizabeth Gaskell or George Eliot, Hardy's 'idylls' still employ the idyllic method to very different ends.[2]

Under the Greenwood Tree is a 'painting' of a world at a single moment of precarious balance in a continuous process of evolution. It is not, as is sometimes assumed of pastoral, under threat from outside. Growth or historical movement is as 'natural' as stasis. Of the two linked stories, the displacement of the choir tells of the relinquishing of the past, Fancy's love-story of its uneasy continuance into an altered future. The two stories are fairly separate in the structure of the book. Though Dick is smitten during our first acquaintance with the choir on the Christmas Eve round, the first half of the book tells the story of the choir and its roots in the past and present of the community. From chapter vi of 'Spring' the story is wholly Dick's and Fancy's. Nevertheless the effect of fusion and wholeness is strong on putting the book down; besides being a story in its own right, the story of the choir establishes the communal setting of the love-story. The dialogues between the villagers have a double function of story and background. After the return from the vicar's in chapter v of 'Spring' there is no rustic dialogue till the wedding day. In 'The Knot there's no Untying' the dialogue between the women upstairs helping Fancy to dress and the men below waiting for the tardy bridegroom, the extent to which Fancy is a part of the community is demonstrated. J. Hillis Miller has written on the 'thick texture of speech in the rustic chorus which constitutes a kind of background or context for the experiences of the central characters, a context as circumscribing and limiting as the natural scene'.[3] In fact, innovation and the way it impinges on tradition is also embodied in language. Reuben's awkward tact in the interview with the vicar is a struggle to cope with things close to his heart in language which is to some extent foreign to him. Fancy enjoins 'propriety' for the brief duration of her wedding and 'as an additional precaution in this direction had strictly charged her father and the tranter to carefully avoid saying "thee" and "thou" in their conversation, on the plea that those ancient words sounded so very humiliating to persons of newer taste'. The sentence as a whole, though, adroitly separates the narrator not only from

Fancy's little snobbery but from the sentimentality of the reader who might warm to the idea of preserving 'thee' and 'thou' but would be less happy, presumably, with other remnants of antiquity; it continues, 'also that they were never to be seen drawing the back of the hand across the mouth after drinking – a local English custom of extraordinary antiquity, but stated by Fancy to be decidedly dying out among the better classes of society'. There is no final voice in the matter. In the last rustic chorus of the book as the wedding party draws to a close, the tranter encourages Thomas Leaf to tell his pointless story in marked departure from new-fangled ways of speech; 'Let's hear thy story, Leaf', he says, and 'Silence all of ye! Mr. Leaf will tell a story.' 'Better than the history of England, my sonnies!' is his extravagantly kindly comment. In the crucial visit to the vicar Leaf was allowed along 'for a trate' and because 'we don't know what we should do without 'en for an upper G'. Like the Cumberland beggar he might be seen as a drag on progress but a community which proceeds at the old pace can accommodate such poor creatures, and, while closed to the rest of the world, remains open to its own members to the mutual benefit of weak and strong. As the happy pair drive away in Dick's 'excellent new spring-cart', openness is just what there is not between them. Mrs Dewey sees the couple as ideally matched, or, as she puts it, 'exactly in tune with one another'; but their voices are last heard by the reader in a 'song' where we are more aware of the separated notes which make up the harmony than the perfect chime of unison. The picture of the end with the two figures together on the cart in a landscape suffused with moonlight, the lonely road between the two dark copses, is made ambiguous by the talk between the two. Fancy and Dick never, in talk, approach the instinctive harmony they establish in their first wordless dance together at the Deweys' Christmas party.[4] Throughout the story their talk has revealed the gaps in their conscious understanding of one another. In dance, music, tears and kisses Dick and Fancy are one, but every conversation reported between them reveals the gap in their mutual understanding and the partial nature of their communion. But the beauty and tenderness of the first evening of their married life remains and is not marred by the gap between them. The narrator, at least, is completely open to impression and dispassionate in his recording.

Throughout *Under the Greenwood Tree* the narrator remains continuously aware of the reader's unfamiliarity with the described world. He is, necessarily, sophisticated, but consistently unpartial;

the reminders of the sophisticated world are not, for instance, used to shape the fictional world in mock-heroic proportions. The remarkable number of elements which go to make up this dispassionate involvement can be seen in a detailed examination of the description of Mr Penny's shop (part II, chapter II). Here the two kinds of sympathetic knowledge available to the narrator are clearly separated. The visual description is sharp and clear as the scene might appear to a passing stranger. The 'stranger' does not, like George Eliot's traveller in *Adam Bede* or her stage-coach passenger in *Felix Holt*, make an appearance which has to be justified by story or structure. Hardy's narrator assumes the point of view of either the strange or the knowledgeable observer at will, sometimes even in the same sentence. The first paragraph of the chapter is brief:

> It was the evening of a fine spring day. The descending sun appeared as a nebulous blaze of amber light, its outline lost in cloudy masses hanging round it like wild locks of hair. (83)

The first sentence seems to be a straightforward piece of narrative timing. It certainly serves as that, but would have done equally well for the purpose as, 'It was the evening of a fine day in spring'. 'A fine spring day' is a seasonal not simply a narrative placing and means, of course, 'a fine day of a particular kind peculiar to spring'. In the loosely constructed second sentence, where all three parts are given an equal presentness which deliberately avoids the underlying hypotaxis, the narrator as stranger responds to the immediate impression and seems less to be describing than searching for an accurate way of doing so. The sentence mimics the responsive mind's effort to name. The narrative persona is not itself unstable or various so much as able like a good conversationalist to sympathise with the response of his hearer as he speaks. The fact in the next paragraph that the 'lowness of the source of light render[ed] the brims of their hats of no use at all as a protection to the eyes' is of no narrative significance. It simply persuades the reader to come closer to the scene than he would only by visualising the figures with their shadows. The purely visual is not the intended effect of the opening description of this chapter. You are to be made to feel the texture of life in the village and the three paragraphs progress from the visual to a sense of the personal relations in the community with a speed and smoothness which makes the introduction of a surrogate figure for some part of the narrator's function quite unnecessary. The narrator's sympathetic knowledge of characters and reader is manipulated in several ways in the third paragraph. The sunken position of Mr Penny's house is described from the 'passer's' point of view but not at a particular time – cartwheels and horses legs were always 'about level' with the shop window-sill. 'About level' rather than 'level' repeats the impression of an effort at accuracy – the reader's process of visualising is to be a felt activity, not an instantaneous apprehension. In this context the description of Mr Penny as 'invariably seen working inside like a framed portrait of a shoemaker by some modern Moroni' is an acknowledgement of the fact that we see, name and so comprehend in terms of Art, that impression is mediated by familiar representation.[5] Mr Penny's movements are described and the hypothetical 'passer' actually summoned in the sentence which takes the shoemaker out of the 'frame' into the village street:

> He sat facing the road, with a boot on his knees and the awl in his hand, only looking up for a moment as he stretched out his arms and bent forward at the pull, when his spectacles flashed in the passer's face with a shine of flat whiteness, and then returned again to the boot as usual.   (83)

The white flash of the spectacles in the sun gives the impression of a single instant in the story, but is not incompatible with 'invariably' and 'as usual'. This is a bold handling of a double time-scale, the always and the now. *Under the Greenwood Tree* portrays a fragile moment at the end of a way of life by craftmanship of great delicacy, characteristically in moments of balance such as this. In the shadowed interior of the shop,

> Rows of lasts, small and large, stout and slender, covered the wall which formed the background, in the extreme shadow of which a kind of dummy was sitting, in the shape of an apprentice with a string tied round his hair (probably to keep it out of his eyes).

This is a visual not a comic description; it follows the process of peering into the interior, separates out the human figure and explains his strange appearance by the string which has a practical reason. But from then the description becomes a description of things as they 'always' were – the apprentice was 'never known' to answer remarks in Mr Penny's presence, a Wellington boot 'usually' hung outside. The comparison of Mr Penny's shop with 'old banks and mercantile houses' in the matter of a common distaste for advertising when the 'trade came solely by connection based on personal respect' seems to me to be without the comic or mock-heroic effect which might be expected and to suggest instead an effort a 'passer' might well need to make to focus with understanding on the scene in front of him.

The small adjustments of focus close reading requires of the reader is the source of the realism of this 'rural painting'. They mime the effort of the painter to delineate precisely. Sometimes at the level of sleight of hand a 'picture' which appears still can be seen to be made up of small 'strokes' many of which denote movement. The still moment in the picture of Fancy at the window (part I, chapter v) which imprints itself so indelibly on Dick's heart is one of some theatricality; she appears,

> a young girl framed as a picture by the window architrave, and unconsciously illuminating her countenance to a vivid brightness by a candle she held in her left hand, close to her face, her right hand being extended to the side of the window. She was wrapped in a white robe of some kind, whilst down her shoulders fell a twining profusion of marvellously rich hair, in a wild disorder. (53)

All the charm and delicacy which gives the image of the girl permanence for Dick and a touching transience for the reader arises from the description of how 'thirty concentrated eyes' focus on the window as the candle approaches the blind remaining, like the girl, still for a passing second, long enough for the watchers to register its 'exact position'; their intrusion has roused the girl with her hair not at all as it might be seen during the day; the paragraph ends with the delicately described process by which 'courage defeats shyness' in Fancy and the expression in her grey eyes 'transforms itself to resolution'. The effect is pictorial, but, in fact, the completely still and pictorial is only a part of the whole.

By means such as these Hardy keeps the relation of fictional and historical time and the underlying concepts of stasis and flux at the centre of his first portrayal of a woodland scene. The first description of the tranter's 'long low cottage', for instance (part I, chapter II) is strongly visual, though what the narrator adds in explanation from knowledge which the reader cannot have, relates to how what can be seen has evolved and how the appearance alters at other times. The distorted shapes of the codlin trees comes from their having been trained as espaliers in the first place and then climbed – by pickers and children – without any regard for the consequent weakening of the branches. The description is of a winter evening but the narrator knows also that 'by day' the doorway in the middle of the beaten back creepers looks like 'an old keyhole'. The marks of time in this description are the marks of human activity. Another dimension is given to it by the spelling out by the narrator of the reader's probable response to the scene in terms of pictorial cliché:

> Light streamed through the cracks and joints of outbuildings a little way from the cottage, a sight which nourished a fancy that the purpose of the erection must be rather to veil bright attractions than to shelter unsightly necessaries. (35)

Workaday daily life is suggested by the noise of activity – the splitting of the wood and the munching and shifting of the feeding horses. But this is not a simple opposition of picturesque beauty and the hard reality of toil. The sounds denote toil certainly, and equally the satisfaction of the viewer's curiosity by the identification of them in the dark. An earlier sentence has linked the effect of light shining into surrounding darkness and a sense of generations of human activity, and has coloured the connection with emotion and obvious approval in the choice of the verb 'radiated forth': 'The window-shutters were not yet closed and the fire- and candle-light within radiated forth upon the thick bushes of box and laurestinus. . . . '

A whole incident may follow the pattern of this description from clearly focused time-levels into poetic evocation. The fictional time of 'Honey-taking and afterwards' is plainly plotted: 'Saturday evening saw Dick Dewey journeying on foot to Yalbury Wood, according to the arrangement with Fancy.' The paragraph which follows, a mixture of evocative details, scientific explanation, and Dick's own impressions, holds four time-levels in suspension – the present moment on Dick's walk, his whole walk, the day and the scientific and seasonal generalities the one day implies:

> The landscape being concave, at the going down of the sun everything suddenly assumed a uniform robe of shade. The

evening advanced from sunset to dusk long before Dick's arrival, and his progress during the latter portion of his walk through the trees was indicated by the flutter of terrified birds that had been roosting over the path. And in crossing the glades, masses of hot dry air that had been formed on the hills during the day greeted his cheeks alternately with clouds of damp night air from the valleys. He reached the keeper-steward's house, where the grass-plot and the garden in front appeared light and pale against the unbroken darkness of the grove from which he had emerged, and paused at the garden gate.   (147)

The first sentence does not become visual until the reader has applied his own experience, actual or theoretical, to make it so. The second is centred on Dick, but keeps the time focus vague. 'Had advanced' would have held it to a particular moment but the whole 'progress' of his walk is suggested by the indefinite past tense and the unspecific moment of the disturbing of the birds on 'the latter portion' of it. The scientific explanation of the changing physical sensations describes conditions of the environment as timeless and inevitable, but felt immediately and intimately 'on the cheeks' by an individual. Dick's particular perceptions are transitory, belonging only to the moment when he 'emerged' and 'paused' – 'the garden in front *appeared* light and pale against the unbroken darkness of the grove'. In the light of this particular moment the slow-moving scene of the honey-taking is almost hallucinatory and shares briefly, at least in its initial stages, the unpredictable but instinctive movement of the startled birds.

If still or brief moments of fictional time also simultaneously yield a sense of flux or of the passing of historical time, the rustic 'choruses' work quite differently. The rustic speech is of a startling naturalism, but the dialogues are separated from the flow of the narrative. This is a function partly of the shapeliness of their construction. Their repetitive, circular motion works at once like poetry to evoke the timeless stasis of the rural world and like drama to enact the warmth and inclusiveness of its social life. While at the level of representation the authentic texture of the dialogue gives the illusion of complete truth to reality, the reader acquiesces in the process of shaping as with expectation set up in poetry by the repetition of form and the circularity suggested by refrain. The distance maintained by the narrator allows, of course, for generalisation and an application beyond the circumstances of the dialogue to the themes of the book. The distance is shaped characteristically in a grotesque not a mock-heroic mode.

There is an element of the grotesque, of course, in the introduction of the heroine into the story by means of her boot; the spare visual description in the accompanying dialogue is in a correspondingly grotesque style. Before going on the Christmas round with the choir, Mr Penny interrupts the talk on the difficulty of 'number 78' to empty his pockets of what, 'thirtingill as a chiel', he has brought with him. The assembled choir gather round the last originally made for Fancy's grandfather, and, as a climax to this little family pageant stage-managed by Mr Penny, they gaze at the boot, 'small, light, and prettily shaped', of Fancy herself. The first of the extended rustic conversations, in the previous chapter, circled round the untapped cider barrel and ends simultaneously with the tapping of the barrel and the appearance of grandfather William. The passing of the generations and the timeless ways of the country are picked up again in the conversation so comically focused on the metonymic boot. Gesture and movement are pared down to a remarkable simplicity and, robbed of individuality and even, at times, humanity, so acquire a comparable weight of apparent meaning:

During the latter part of this speech Mr Penny's left hand wandered towards the cider-cup as if the hand had no connection with the person speaking; and bringing his sentence to an abrupt close all but the extreme margin of the bootmaker's face was eclipsed by the circular brim of the vessel.

'However, I was going to say,' continued Penny, putting down the cup, 'I ought to have called at the school' – here he went groping again in the depths of his pocket – 'to leave this without fail, though I suppose the first thing tomorrow will do.'

He now drew forth and placed on the table a boot – small, light, and prettily shaped – upon the heel of which he had been operating.

'The new schoolmistress's!'

'Ay, no less, Miss Fancy Day; as neat a little figure of fun as ever I see, and just husband-high.'

'Never Geoffrey's daughter Fancy?' said Bowman, as all glances present converged like wheel-spokes upon the boot in the centre of them. (43)

In its circularity much of the language serves as gesture too. Take Mr Spinks's comment, for instance, when Mr Penny wonders at his own absentmindedness:

> 'The brain has its weakness', murmured Mr Spinks, waving his head ominously. Mr Spinks was considered to be a scholar, having once kept a night-school, and always spoke up to that level. (43)

However dehumanising or placing the narrative voice may be, as here, the actual words of the rustics are uninterruptedly naturalistic even while they voice the themes of the novel. The unresolvable tensions and melancholy of the end are enacted in this conversation in the response to Mr Penny's dramatic story of how he identified a dead man by the 'family voot':

> I was a-bearing across towards Bloom's End, and lo and behold, there was a man just brought out o' the Pool, dead; he had un' rayed for a dip, but not being able to pitch it just there had gone in flop over his head. Men looked at en; women looked at en; children looked at en; nobody knowed en. He was covered wi' a sheet; but I catched sight of his voot, just showing as they carried en along. 'I don't care what name that man went by,' I said, in my way, 'but he's John Woodward's brother; I can swear to the family voot.' At that moment up comes John Woodward, weeping and teaving, 'I've lost my brother! I've lost my brother!' (44–5)

This passage functions, like the interlude of the porter in *Macbeth*, to enact underlying themes in the whole work. It may be seen by the end of the novel to pose the basic question of how far a man is knowable from the stamp with which nature ties him to his family and so to the past. What status, in the final instance, has what a man learns in relation to what he inescapably *is*? Is he fixed in the patterns of immemorial time or subject to process, and some of that willed? The passage dramatises the tensions inherent in pastoral in the particular terms of this book. It is no less serious as comment in offering, instead of a contrast of mode like the comic porter in the tragic play, one variation on the consistently comic mode of the novel. When grandfather William 'absently' dissents from the tranter's view that it is hard enough to tell 'what a man is from all his members put together, oftentimes', with 'But still, look is a good deal', he thinks of Fancy:

'By the way,' he continued in a fresher voice, and looking up, 'that young creature, the schoolmis'ess, must be sung tonight wi' the rest? If her ear is as fine as her face, we shall have enough to do to be upsides with her.' (45)

So with this light foreshadowing, plot and themes are joined in the 'chorus'.

These remarks of grandfather William are separated by another of the narrator's curiously dehumanising pictorial descriptions. As he remarks on the importance of 'look', he balances his head 'till the tip of grandfather James's nose was exactly in a right line with William's eye and the mouth of a miniature cavern he was discerning in the fire'. The described world is made to appear remote in time and space by the very constriction of the art forms which evoke it. The narrator, with his disengaged sympathy, is an acceptable character in the fiction. His restricted visual impression of this scene, Mr Penny's hand wandering towards the cider-cup, which 'eclipsed' his face, or the exact relation of the eye of one grandfather with the nose of the other verge on the grotesque and so enhance the comic effect. But they also give the air of a man struggling for scientific accuracy, which implies the intrinsic worth of the object described, while the dialogue retains the capacity to reflect the deeper concerns of the book. The focus of the book is particularly restricted. The world outside these related hamlets in the deeply wooded landscape has only the vaguest outlines in *Under the Greenwood Tree*. Apart from Fancy's education and the new church organ it has no realised form in the book. As the old ways give way to the new the disturbance to rural peace is non-existent measured in economic or social terms. But in the pattern of the novel as a pastoral the narrator shares with Fancy the role of defining the inherent frailty of the described world. The story is one of growing gaps of understanding. The narrator's sense of the passing of time, secure throughout the multiple perspectives of his vision, maps the lacunae between modes of perceiving the rural world. Fancy's simultaneous acquiescence in the life she has always known and her consciousness of other ways enacts the same inevitable duality inside the fiction.

By such unnaturalistic means does the narrator of *Under the Greenwood Tree* paint what he presents as a 'real' picture of the Dutch school. It is perhaps his most perfect pastoral. Distance, affection and delicacy are its hallmarks. With the growth of confidence in his own powers and the development of his idiosyncratic style so perfectly to mirror his 'idiosyncratic mode of regard' Hardy pushes any genre he chooses to the edge of its capabilities. *The Woodlanders* is frequently felt to be a tragedy[6] but is, I believe, more revealingly discussed with *Under the Greenwood Tree* and *Far from the Madding Crowd* as a pastoral. Generic labelling has its comic side, but Polonius never got round to discussing individual works. If I file *The Woodlanders* under 'tragical-pastoral' I separate it both from *Tess of the d'Urbervilles* and *Jude the Obscure*, with which as a tragic story it can only be compared to its great disadvantage, and from *Under the Greenwood Tree*, with its lighter claims to the 'comical-pastoral'. *The Woodlanders* does share an idyllic perspective with *Under the Greenwood Tree*, though, in the similar distance from which the narrator establishes his vantage-point. The evolutionary view which informs *The Woodlanders* may be tinged with gloom, but it is too accepting to be called 'pessimism'. Of course, in coming so near to pessimism Hardy may be thought to have overstepped the bounds of pastoral, especially in the matter of Giles's death. I shall argue that the death of one of the main characters would have to be structurally more central than it is for it not to be absorbed into the other incompletely resolved aspects of the ending. I shall consider *The Woodlanders* next, out of its chronological sequence, because what has been felt to be its problematic nature is illuminated by its relation to *Under the Greenwood Tree*. It was probably conceived as early as 1874 or 1875, close to both the other idyllic works.[7]

If it was indeed the story 'laid aside', in response to criticism which typecast Hardy as a rural writer ignorant of the sophisticated world, for *The Hand of Ethelberta*, a novel in a very different mode, it has a close connection with *Under the Greenwood Tree* in origin. What form it took in Hardy's mind at that early time, except as a 'woodland story', it is of course impossible to say. In its final execution *The Woodlanders* is another look in a later style at related material.[8] The reference in the *Life* to his father's cider-making, at the time when he was writing *Far from the Madding Crowd*, supports the impression of the books themselves that there is much nostalgia attached for Hardy to the wooded world of *Under the Greenwood Tree* and *The Woodlanders*:[9]

> This autumn Hardy assisted at his father's cider-making – a proceeding he had always enjoyed from childhood – the apples being from huge old trees that have now long perished. It was the last time he ever took part in a work whose sweet smells and oozings in the crisp autumn air can never be forgotten by those who have had a hand in it.

The recall in both books extends to detailed listing and describing of appurtenances and processes – furniture in the Dewey and Day households, the tranter's barrel-tapping in *Under the Greenwood Tree*, tree-planting, spar-making and apple-pressing in *The Woodlanders*. In the richer harmony of the later book, the processes which tie Giles and Marty to the world of their origins is contrasted with the pointless studies of Fitzpiers, in their way as self-centred and unproductive as the romantic musings of Felice Charmond. Interpretation of *The Woodlanders* must take into account an elaborate pattern of oppositions[10] of which this is one thread. But the pattern is such that no single opposition is ever a simple one.[11] Even this one, which would seem to offer a pre-determined judgement in favour of Giles as a pillar of the rural world, is undermined by the ultimate carelessness Giles shares with Fitzpiers. He loses his cottages and has to make do with a diminished way of life from something not altogether unlike the inattentiveness which disperses Fitzpiers's Hintock practice. What Robert Drake has called 'the essential dualism of pastoral'[12] is undoubtedly present in *The Woodlanders*, but Mr Drake sees the serpent in this particular garden as 'the existence of subversive forces within the natural world itself', foreshadowing 'the human conflicts which will imperil this Arcadia'. The natural and human worlds so interact across this patterning, though, that in separating them so neatly he fails to see that Fitzpiers and Grace going forth 'like a chastened Adam and Eve' would be more accurately put as Grace leaving Eden with the serpent, and he, temporarily anyway, ennobled rather than chastened. Professor Millgate answers Robert Drake's argument by pointing out that the details of traditional pastoral are not as relevant as the 'general strategy of pastoral'.[13] He sees this strategy as accounting for the central features of *The Woodlanders* which he lists as multiple oppositions and contrasts, a mixture of tragedy and comedy, moral ambiguity and narrative irresolution.[14]

Robbed of the highly appreciative tone in which Mr Millgate's criticism is always offered this summary might lead one to ask how the book is even readable. Indeed to some contemporaries it was not. R. H. Hutton thought the descriptions of Nature 'all perfectly wholesome as well as rich in beauty'; this was more than could be said for the pictures of men and women, in which if there could have been less 'abstract humanism' and more 'human piety' 'we should find his stories not only more agreeable, but more lifelike also'.[15] To readers coming to a novel with the assumption that its first concern was to give a true picture of life, *The Woodlanders* offered so much affront to their primary moral concerns as to be disgusting. Less indignant but equally disappointed, the reviewer in *The Dial* thought it ought to be a tragedy but that it failed 'from lack of seriousness'.[16] He gives priority to faithfulness, to a general sense of 'real life', but also assumes that form is an essential affective component of the final novel. 'The story' he says 'is tragic enough but the accessories are not in keeping', and 'to say that people act thus in real life does not justify their so acting in the novel, at least upon the principles of a higher school of fiction than the photographic one'. Some more recent formalistic criticism gives a priority to the expectations aroused by form over the requirement that a novel conform to our conception of real behaviour, though that remains – only the order of priorities is reversed. But these can stand between the reader and his willingness to submit to the demands the novel makes on him as successfully as any preconceived notions about natural behaviour. Dale Kramer acknowledges that *The Woodlanders* is not a tragedy 'measured against conventional tragic theories' and he cites Beach and Carpenter in support.[17] He still, however, thinks that *The Return of the Native*, *The Mayor of Casterbridge*, *The Woodlanders*, *Tess of the d'Urbervilles* and *Jude the Obscure* all 'take tragedy for their major mode'.[18] The distinguishing feature of *The Woodlanders* in this list is, of course, its most notable formal feature. Whatever emphasis is placed on it, the dispersal of interest over a number of characters and the consequent ambivalence of Giles (part Nature God, part less lucky Gabriel Oak), is important in most modern critical contexts. While Giles's role in the pattern of the book makes him an impossible tragic hero, the oblique focus on him actually creates the pastoral distance. The narrator of a tragedy is closely involved with the protagonist. In *Tess of the d'Urbervilles* he is, perhaps, half in love with her; in *Jude the Obscure*, J. Hillis Miller has suggested, narrator and protagonist have moved so close together as to render 'the disjunction between them necessary to [Hardy's] kind of fiction . . . no longer possible'.[19] The multiple focus of *The Woodlanders* makes such disjunction not only possible but inevitable, and there is a sense, supported by Hardy's later expression of preference for *The Woodlanders* over his other novels,[20] in which the essential qualities of Hardy as a novelist reach their most perfect (though very different) expression in the two great pastorals *Far from the Madding Crowd* and *The Woodlanders*.

Though Professor Kramer invokes modern tragic theory,[21] his own case for *The Woodlanders* as a tragedy is most convincingly put in thematic terms rather than formal ones. He does describe some formal features in an interesting way;[22] on the lack of central focus, for instance, he says:

> The formal principles of the novels before *Tess of the d'Urbervilles* can be thought of as at once proportional and spatial; that is, they help to determine emphases within the material as the plot progresses, and they imply that significance is at least partially external to the individual.

The 'formal principles of the later novels' he sees as 'concepts of consciousness' – a Hardyean version of concentration on character. The spatial principle, of course, leaves room for the importance of setting equal to that of character. In *The Woodlanders* Kramer says

> the superficial impression is one of calm reflection existing in a woodlands retreat disturbed only by relatively mild fluctuations of romantic love. But along with the external beauty of landscape and the delicacy and toleration of individual personality, the novel presents an interpretation of such pervasive frustration that the inevitable miscalculations with human relationships and the constrictions of rigid social decrees can be approximated only by images of bleeding tree trunks and predatory animals.

In this view the setting is subordinated to the human story in that it is assumed to provide an appropriate mode of expression – the miscalculations of the love-story determining the emphasis in the natural description. But setting and story have, in my view, a nearer equality in *The Woodlanders* than this. As much as Egdon Heath in *The Return of the Native* the woodland has a strange, independent, coterminous life. The famous passage about the Unfulfilled Intention (chapter VII) reverses the common order where Nature is used as metaphor or analogue to describe civilised life or human affairs:

> They went noiselessly over mats of starry moss, rustled through interspersed tracts of leaves, skirted trunks with spreading roots whose mossed rinds made them like hands wearing green gloves; elbowed old elms and ashes with great forks, in which stood pools of water that overflowed on rainy days and ran down their stems in green cascades. On older trees still than these huge lobes of fungi grew like lungs. Here, as everywhere, the Unfulfilled Intention, which makes life what it is, was as obvious as it could be among the depraved crowds of a city slum. The leaf was deformed, the curve was crippled, the taper was interrupted; the lichen ate the vigour of the stalk, and the ivy strangled to death the promising sapling. (82)

Human and, most forcefully, urban life, is here assumed to be the better known and is used to explicate the natural scene. A melancholy attachment to scene and character informs the observations of this narrator and it is sustained with an almost dispassionate impartiality throughout the book. Ian Gregor writes of the 'atmosphere, pervasive and persistent, of deep melancholy' established by the woods, but finds the impression of the book nevertheless 'mellow' rather than 'pessimistic' or 'tragic'. He is describing story and setting in *The Woodlanders* as interconnected, equally a part of the 'network or tissue which quivers in every part when one point is shaken, like a spider's web if touched',[23] but he does incidentally point to what, in my view, is the centrally defining characteristic of modern pastoral, the capacity of the narrator to hold a complete, and consistent, even when multiply focused, picture up to the reader for his appreciative contemplation:[24]

> Remembrance of things past, the pastoral mood, allusions to poetry and music, all these help to create what we might think of as the 'gauze of story enclosing the novel softening its outlines, giving it unity' and turning tragedy into mellowness because that story brings with it an implicit assurance that this experience has been encompassed and assimilated by this narrator or nearly so.

The nature of the picture – not so much its content as its style or method of communication – is illuminated by the comments in *The*

Life written in Hardy's diary during the composition of *The Woodlanders*. Those written as the novel neared completion are particularly interesting when considered together.[25] The layers of time represented by the selection of diary entries for inclusion are interesting everywhere in *The Life* – nowhere more so than here. He 'finished *The Woodlanders*' on 'February 4, 8.20 P.M.' He kept in the record of his relief and he, or Mrs Hardy, adds, 'In later years he often said that in some respects *The Woodlanders* was his best novel.' Though it is impossible to say how much of the diary was discarded, the entries from December 1886 to February 1887 have, after the reflection which selected them, an interesting double focus. *The Woodlanders* is what he is working on; it is the centre of *our* interest and his practical concern ('Talked to Lady Carnarvon about the trees at Highclere in relation to my work in hand.' Lady Winifred, 'serious and thoughtful' about her coming marriage, wanted 'me to call my heroine "Winifred" but it is too late to alter it'). On the other hand he represents himself as continuously interested through these months in the relation of what is seen to some kind of inner reality. 'The beginning of December', *The Life* ambiguously records, 'covers this entry':

'I often view society gatherings, people in the street, in a room, or elsewhere, as if they were beings in a somnambulistic state, making their motions automatically – not realizing what they mean.'

the second entry for 13 February reads:

'I was thinking a night or two ago that people are somnambulists – that the material is not real – only visible, the real being invisible optically. That it is because we are in a somnambulistic hallucination that we think the real to be what we see as real.'

Most of the retained entries of these three months are about looking and seeing; people and landscape lend themselves alike to the piercing eye of the observer and his shaping mind transforms the perception of their inner life to the corporeal reality:

You may regard a throng of people as containing a certain small minority who have sensitive souls; these, and the aspects of

these, being what is worth observing. So you divide them into the
mentally unquickened, mechanical, soulless; and the living,
throbbing, suffering, vital. In other words, into souls and
machines, ether and clay.

A man on a train tells him he 'wore out seven sets of horseshoes in
riding from Sturminster Newton to Weymouth when courting a
young woman at the latter place'. Hardy 'fancies' he married her
and with his natural economy as a story-teller has indicated 'a tone
of bitter regret' in the man's voice, as preparation for his own
conclusion. He is much preoccupied with pictures. The landscape
viewed from the train has with the coming of winter 'turned from a
painting to an engraving'. Mrs Jeune, 'in a rich pinky-red gown',
conflates in his mind 'curiously enough' with 'Whistler's study in
red that I had seen in the morning at the gallery'.

Two aspects of these pages seem to me most interesting in relation
to the novel he is writing at this time; one is the demonstrated
closeness of picture and story, the other the fact that he was
consciously reflecting on this parallel at the time. The little vignette
of the December view from the window of the train includes like
many such economical sentences in his novels a great range of point
of view. The general visual impression is in technical artistic terms,
the naturalist's observation – 'the birds that love worms fall back
upon the berries' – could pass for scientific except for its context;
followed as it is by the comment on the backs of the houses no longer
screened by leaves and the wry little story about the wasted
horseshoes, the words 'love' and 'fall back on' come near to
anthropomorphic. The 'squalidness' of the backs of the houses
suggests Hardy's disgust, but the rest of the sentence his une-
motional acceptance of the fact that people do not think about what
the backs of their houses reveal of the ordinary rubbish-producing
process of daily life. Still under December he comments on an
exhibition of the Society of British Artists where the 'impressionist
school is strong'. He makes the analogy of painting and literature
himself and explains exactly what he means:

> The impressionist school is strong. It is even more suggestive in
> the direction of literature than of art. As usual it is pushed to
> absurdity by some. But their principle is, as I understand it, that
> what you carry away with you from a scene is the true feature to
> grasp; or in other words, *what appeals to your own individual eye and*

heart in particular amid much that does not so appeal, and which you therefore omit to record. (Hardy's italics.)

It will be evident that to consider these passages from *The Life* as closely connected to the novel he was writing is to grant them the status of informal preface. As a late selection from his interests at the time they do in fact bear a relation to the novel comparable with that of the prefaces to the 1895 and 1912 editions. Immediacy has been edited out of both, and, since they are all we have, they can usefully be made to supplement one another. A year before, some months after *The Woodlanders* was taken up again (with a return to the 'original plot' followed by a sick headache!) his mind had swept on to methods of rendering underlying realities, realised only long after 'the end of prose' in *The Dynasts* where 'the abstract thoughts of the analytic school' are rendered 'as visible essences'. Meanwhile, feeling that 'Novel-writing as an art cannot go backward', that it had to 'transcend' analysis by 'going still further in the same direction', he still had to wrestle with the inescapable corporeality of character and setting. The attraction for him of the tenets of the Impressionist school, applied to literature, is easy to understand. Both halves of the preserved diary entries for January 1887 are interesting in relation to *The Woodlanders*. The landscape in the drawing-room prompts reflections that have a direct bearing on the description of the Hintock woods, and, whether a 'much decried, mad, late-Turner rendering' is an antithesis to the drawing-room landscape or the logical extension of a tendency perceptible there, it is clear that Hardy is searching for a means of giving expression to an awakened sense of 'tragical mystery' behind the observable surface of things:

'After looking at the landscape ascribed to Bonington[26] in our drawing-room I feel that Nature is played out as a Beauty, but not as a Mystery. I don't want to see landscapes, i.e., scenic paintings of them, because I don't want to see the original realities – as optical effects, that is. I want to see the deeper reality underlying the scenic, the expression of what are sometimes called abstract imaginings.

'The "simply natural" is interesting no longer. The much decried, mad, late-Turner rendering is now necessary to create my interest. The exact truth as to material fact ceases to be important in art – it is a student's style – the style of a period when the mind is serene and unawakened to the tragical mysteries of life; when it does not bring anything to the object that coalesces with and translates the qualities that are already there, – half-hidden, it may be – and the two united are depicted as the All.'

The comparison of Realism and Impressionism in painting, in the terms which Hardy uses here, may furnish a means of comparing *The Woodlanders* and *Under the Greenwood Tree*. The 'rural painting of the Dutch school' is a Realist picture; *The Woodlanders* was written at a time when Hardy was not only exploring the implications of Impressionism, but extending them to literature as well. Alastair Smart comments that any doubt of the completeness of Hardy's understanding of Impressionist technique can be dispelled by an examination of his handling of detail in *The Woodlanders*. He cites the passage in which Mr Percomb watches Marty, where 'such telling use is made of one of the principal canons of Impressionist theory– that all forms lying outside the immediate focus of the gaze are inevitably blurred and indistinct and that it is therefore legitimate for the particular painter having selected his focal point, to treat them as such'.[27] And as an instance of the use of reflected light he quotes the picture of Grace as 'a sylph-like and greenish white creature, as toned by sunlight and leafage'. Hardy's grasp of the technique is, I believe, observable on a wider scale than this – the detail in such instances supports a conception of the whole structure as Impressionist in outlook, as *Under the Greenwood Tree* is Realist. To stop in Hardy's diary entries is to be reminded how privately functional they were intended to be; there are no concessions here to a reader presuming to read concurrent thoughts as a surrogate preface. But what Hardy seems to imply of the different relation between inner and outer reality in Realism and Impressionism illustrates the difference in technique and simultaneous closeness of conception of the two novels. Presumably Hardy would not have characterised the Dutch school as a 'student style', but in his own chosen medium *Under the Greenwood Tree* is a young man's book in the terms of Hardy's definitions in this passage from *The Life*. The external world as the subject of artistic representation is, he implies, separate from the interpretive mind, but in Realism object and significance are, nevertheless, *presented* as one. The picture of the world in *Under the Greenwood Tree* is, as it were, a static picture of movement. The picturesque Dewey cottage is picturesque precisely because it bears the marks of time; it can only, however, stay as it is for the briefest of moments. The gnarled and pocked tree in the Days' garden shelters the wedding party, observed with humour and humanity; here, not the manner of description but the pressure of the antecedent story suggests that Fancy is one of the last brides who will make the choice to marry in the old way. The interlocking of picture and process, stasis and movement, is characteristic of *Under the Greenwood Tree*. It can show in the delicate suggestion of movement by which first the candle and then Fancy herself appears at the window on Christmas Eve, or it can show under the total pressure of the story, as an old way of life pictured at the very moment of its passing. In Impressionistic art, the more mature art as Hardy presents it, the artist has grown so aware of his consciousness of inherent mystery that it takes precedence for him over the surface of things and his art becomes, though not necessarily in T. S. Eliot's pejorative sense, self-expressive.[28] The story of *The Woodlanders* shows the woodland life invaded to a more dramatic or startling effect. The old ways of life are under severe strain, but there must, in spite of the descriptions of forest work, be as little sociological emphasis in this as in any of Hardy's novels. The preface suggests that the divorce laws are of central importance, but they do not seem so in the reading. *The Woodlanders* records an awareness of a 'tragical mystery' underlying appearances, whether fictional, historical or natural. The human and the natural world are shown as alike subject to decay even while life itself goes on. The undramatic continuity of life removes the possibility of a formally tragic ending and it remains for the narrator to present his morbid perception without resolution.

The technique by which the prevailing gloom of the abstracted point of view is transformed into the mellowness of the total effect of *The Woodlanders* ought to be capable of formal description. David Lodge, in his preface to the New Wessex Edition considers it as a 'novelistic adaptation of the pastoral elegy'. His argument is sharp and interesting. Cyclic nature, the close association of Giles with the vegetation, the 'religious and ritual overtones' attached to Marty's and Grace's mourning, the verbal play on the idea of resurrection in the course of the reconciliation of Grace and Fitzpiers – all these elements in the novel, together with the external evidence of the appearance in *Macmillan's Magazine* during the serialisation of *The Woodlanders* of a new translation of Moschus's 'Lament for Bion', are related in Professor Lodge's preface to the pastoral elegy. But they remain, to my mind and, ultimately, in the preface's final view of the novel, elements rather than generic signals which can inform our response to the whole book. In the splitting of the convention-ally upbeat ending to a classical pastoral elegy into two, so that 'Grace and Fitzpiers go off to "fresh woods and pastures new" . . . with their love at least temporarily revived and renewed, while Marty is left behind in Hintock woods to nourish the memory of Giles', it seems to me that the conventions of realism have 'displaced' (Lodge uses Northrop Frye's word) the elegiac mode so successfully that the two halves do not unite to make a common effect. They are so separate as almost to seem to comment on one another, but the comment does not bridge the gap. The two endings are divergent and each separately is unresolved. Grace's future happiness is problematic and it is not as Nature God or vegetation spirit that Giles is remembered (that is an image that belongs to Grace's convalescence), but as a skilled rural workman. It was always their unthinking skill that Marty and Giles shared. When they plant the trees (chapter VIII) the narrator describes the 'sympathy between [Giles] and the fir, oak or beech that he was operating on', but Giles 'seems' careless of what he is doing and at this time is thinking of Grace and Mrs Charmond and his evening party. Marty heroically holds one tree upright after another, but is absorbed in her miseries, a bad cold, a dying father and unrequited love. Giles's epitaph is spoken with a moving but none the less restricted understanding entirely in character. Of the five main characters, two are now dead and the three remaining ones hardly closer together than any of the combinations of the five have been in the rest of the book. No element of the ending corresponds to the formal demands of the elegy. The consolation at the end of Moschus's 'Lament for Bion' is in terms of the myth of the descent of heroes into Tartarus – Orpheus, Odysseus and Hercules. The continuation of Bion's 'music' is assured by the power of the stories to draw the imagination of the reader to a sense of continuation beyond death. As a Christian adaptation of the form, 'Lycidas' is a complex blending of separate elements. Lycidas has 'mounted high / Through the dear might of him that walked the waves', a literally everlasting life had been vouchsafed the poet's friend. The poet himself is left not only to sing the passing of the shepherd, but to continue his pastoral care of the sheep in a way both like and unlike that of the dead shepherd. Neither the imaginative transfiguration of grief accorded by myth nor the combined resignation and self-involvement possible to the Christian poet with his acute sense of what is God's and what is Caesar's is available to Hardy. The realistic parts of the ending remain resolutely separate. Michael Millgate says the novel ends in 'narrative irresolution'; David Lodge describes the power of the book as residing in the

> delicate, precarious balance which Hardy manages to hold between these conflicting and logically incompatible value systems and knowledge systems that makes *The Woodlanders* the powerful, absorbing and haunting work of fiction it is.   (32)

The living Giles is the centre of a part of the action, which is a part of the 'web' of the whole, but he is not the centre of the book. Pastoral elegy as much as tragedy requires for formal resolution a concentration of interest at the centre.

The diffusion of interest over five characters in *The Woodlanders*, Ian Gregor says, 'makes way for the author', who sets his characters in a 'setting' of 'pervasive melancholy' suggested by the woods.[29] The line between this argument and mine is a fine one, but I see the interest as diffused not simply over five characters but equally over their story and its setting, which makes the woods, although a setting for the story, an equal component in the view presented by the narrator. The 'purely descriptive' mode of the idyllium allows for diffusion of interest, 'irresolution' or ambiguity in the ending and the precarious balance of the whole. The balance, of 'incompatible value-systems and knowledge systems', is a balance of inner or interpreted realities. The narrator, with the resigned, mature melancholy of a man 'awakened to the tragical mysteries of life', presents an Impressionist picture of the world to which his sensibilities are open. Behind the natural world of the setting and the human world of the story lies the same pattern of decay, adaptation and endurance. The techniques of *Under the Greenwood Tree* maintain a constant tension between the still surface of the Realist painting of the Dutch school and the movement of historical as well as fictional time. In the Impressionist technique of *The Woodlanders* the separate parts of the total vision – the natural and the human – are brought together in a multiplicity of facets which produces an amazing uniformity of tone and mood. A truly 'mad, late-Turner effect' is hardly possible within the confines of realistic fiction; the human situations emerge with a form and definition which inevitably tones down the hectic vision. The shimmer is maintained in *The Woodlanders* by the constant but surprising interplay of story and setting over the time, which, of its nature, the fiction requires to unfold itself.

The pattern of the narrator's mediation of this vision is set very early in chapter 1; in the opening paragraphs, in fact, the narrator has revealed himself. The chapter begins with a generalised evocation of a past time and as little temporal precision as there is sign of a single person with whom the reader may identify. There is, in fact or fiction, no rambler, 'who, for old association's sake, should trace the forsaken coach-road', no dreaming and responsive loiterer. The narrator invents him to say some things he wishes to say himself without engaging himself in generalities of that kind. The scene itself is described partly in scientific/geographic language – the road running almost in a meridional line', 'the trees, timber or fruit-bearing as the case may be'. This cool approach throws into sharper relief the poetic description which works through all the senses. 'The trees . . . make the wayside ragged by their drip and shade' is both visual and tactile. The next sentence works by sight and sound:

> At one place, on the skirts of Blackmoor Vale, where the bold brow of High-Stoy Hill is seen two or three miles ahead, the leaves lie so thick in autumn as to completely bury the track.

The sound of the words, 'bold brow', alerts the reader to a sense of muffled footsteps on the thick leaves which are not described, but are picked up implicitly in 'the loiterer's, sense of all the perished wayfarers. There is a suggestion here of the pattern of clear distance and enclosed autumnal foreground which is, of course, an important element in the whole book. Here too, as in well-developed ways later, the personified external world has an active, independent life. The distant hill has a 'bold brow', the trees '*make* the wayside ragged, *stretch* their lower limbs across the way' as though '*reclining* on the insubstantial air'. The deserted highway has a 'physiognomy' which addresses the observer, bespeaking 'a tomblike stillness more emphatic than glades and pools'. This stance is typical of the narrator of *The Woodlanders*. The passive recipient of active impression he, most characteristically, takes on a reflective role. Without seeming to shape the actual impression he allows his thoughts to run on in response to it. About the 'tomblike' stillness of the highway he says, in the tone of a man required to explain facts, 'The contrast of what is with what might be, probably accounts for this.' And he continues, putting himself in the place of someone who might, in stepping out of the woods on to the road, if he paused 'amid its emptiness for a moment . . . exchange by the act of a single stride the simple absence of human companionship for an incubus of the forlorn'. The move into story at this point is effected by the introduction of a man in just this situation. But if he was affected in any way as the narrator was by the scene, it lasts only a moment. His 'finical' dress labels him out of place and he is 'mainly puzzled about the way'. It seems that this is not an introduction to anyone who is going to be important in the story. He is picked up in a lumbering van with an old horse and quaintly dressed carrier, all described so minutely that it seems completely natural in its time and place and grotesque at the same time. As the van lurches towards 'the Little Hintock of the master-barber's search' it becomes increasingly clear that the object of his search rather than the barber himself is going to interest us as readers, that and the place where he expects to find it.

It is the narrator's description of that place which has led many to the assumption that Hardy conceived *The Woodlanders* as a tragedy:

> Thus they rode on, and High-Stoy Hill grew larger ahead. At length could be discerned in the dusk, about a mile to one side, gardens and orchards sunk in a concave, and, as it were, snipped out of the woodland. From this self-contained place rose in stealthy silence tall stems of smoke, which the eye of imagination could trace downward to their root on quiet hearthstones, festooned overhead with hams and flitches. It was one of those sequestered spots outside the gates of the world where may usually be found more meditation than action, and more listlessness than meditation; where reasoning proceeds on narrow premises, and results in inferences wildly imaginative; yet where, from time to time, dramas of grandeur and unity truly Sophoclean are enacted in the real, by virtue of the concentrated passions and closely-knit interdependence of the lives therein.   (39)

With another writer the inference that this is a hint, even a statement, that the ensuing story will be such a Sophoclean drama, might well be justified. Here such an inference misreads this narrator and Hardy's habitual opening methods. Detached and meditative, the narrator first describes the signs of Little Hintock as they appear to the traveller, 'gardens and orchards sunk in a concave' and 'tall stems of smoke'. 'The eye of imagination' follows the smoke down to the hearths, but the live eye retains the impression of enclosure. The cultivated spaces seem only 'clipped out of the woodland'. Just as the lonely highway struck him as like the tomb of countless buried travellers over time so the almost hidden village suggests by the scant signs of its existence which penetrate the encompassing woodland the nature of the lives half-buried there. The possibility of Sophoclean intensity of passion is not more emphasised in this sentence than the suffocated mental life with which it coexists. Light does not penetrate to the mind in this dark place – the imagination may soar without any sense of its baselessness; the passions may well reach Sophoclean intensity 'by virtue of the closely knit interdependence of the lives'. The point is a Wordsworthian one, that remoteness and enclosure dull the mind and intensify the passions. The story we are to read will surely be about life in this place, probably a dark story of people with unenlightened minds and a potential intensity of feeling. The misleading 'Sophoclean' describes the feelings not the form of the story which is to follow.

The way in which this narrator will tell the story is more clearly indicated by the ending of the chapter from this point. The barber descends from the van and plunges into the 'umbrageous nook'. The things he is not interested in are described by the narrator as the barber passes them by. The end of the search is bathed in light, but it is hardly the eye of the purposeful barber that is caught by the picture, nor by the stray moth or two in the single shaft of light from the door:

> Half a dozen dwellings were passed without result. The next, which stood opposite a tall tree, was in an exceptional state of radiance, the flickering brightness from inside shining up the chimney and making a luminous mist of emerging smoke. The interior, as seen through the window, caused him to draw up with a terminative air and watch. The house was rather large for a cottage, and the door, which opened immediately into the living-room, stood ajar, so that a riband of light fell through the opening into the dark atmosphere without. Every now and then a moth, decrepit from the late season, would flit for a moment across the outcoming rays and disappear into the night. (40–1)

The only personality to emerge from the first chapter is that of the narrator. He is a perceptive, brooding and humane man and one, we might think, 'who used to notice such things'. Only at the beginning of *The Woodlanders* and *Under the Greenwood Tree* does the narrative persona emerge as central in this way. In the dramatic presentation of a strong situation in a well-realised social setting in *The Mayor of Casterbridge*, in the 'sublimely'[30] atmospheric and animating description of Egdon Heath, or in the sardonic little sketch of the drunken John Durbeyfield, the parson and the little boy, the narrator is subordinated to what he chooses to present. In chapter 1 of *Jude the Obscure* the narrator is a felt presence, but it is the strength of his sympathy with the sharply focused child at the well which sets the mournful tone of the opening. If maturity is, as Hardy described it, being awake to the 'tragical mysteries of life' then *Jude* is obviously from the opening going to be a very-grown up book indeed, but it presents the reality and the interpretation as one coherent whole and is thus a picture in a 'student' or realistic style. At the time of writing *The Woodlanders*, to judge from the diary entries, he would have regarded the style and content of *Jude* as incompatible, and the whole novel an attempt to present a mature sense of ineluctable tragedy fused in a stylistically youthful way with the 'real' surface of things. The coherent Impressionistic picture of a struggling world governed by the Unfulfilled Intention painted in *The Woodlanders* is built up, paradoxically, by a pervasive instability in the detail of the vision.

One of the few incontrovertible promises of the opening of the book is that this will be a story of people in a particular setting – a story of woodlanders. I have spoken of the independent and equal life of the natural and human worlds in this book. It is an ambiguous way of speaking since even for the most attentive and sophisticated reader the human world is at the centre of a nineteenth-century novel. But it is an impression which can be supported from the book. The common 'brutal and ruthless evolutionary struggle' which, as David Lodge points out in his Preface, replaces 'the conventional pastoral antithesis between town and country' is itself a part of it and extends to a general sense of Nature as independently active and struggling. Some arms of ivy on the roof of the Melbury out-house, for example, 'had crept through the points of the tiles and were groping in vain for some support', and others were 'pushing in with such force at the eaves as to lift from their supports the shelves that were fixed there'. Not only is some ivy stronger than other ivy, but the strong ivy threatens man's small contrivances. Activity is not necessarily related, though, to the evolutionary struggle. Grace's final reconciliation with her husband, for instance, takes place 'just at that transient period in the May month when beech trees have suddenly unfolded large limp young leaves of the softness of butterflies' wings'. Except as a reflection of what in this novel is a pervasive view of nature as constantly active, there is no reason in the context why the description should have been phrased in this way. A view of the relation of the natural and the human world in this place where, in the distance, it looks as though cultivated patches have been merely 'snipped out of the woodland', is nowhere more clearly suggested than in the sentence describing morning in chapter IV:

> Owls that had been catching mice in the outhouses, rabbits that had been eating the winter-greens in the gardens, and stoats that had been sucking the blood of the rabbits, discerning that their human neighbours were on the move discreetly withdrew from publicity, and were seen and heard no more till night fall. (55)

Space is shared, activities are self-determined and exist in precarious balance. An hour or so earlier, under the weird pattern made in the grey morning mist by the air-holes in the top of the lantern, Giles and Marty have walked in their mutual loneliness, 'part of the pattern in the great web of human doings', to look at the spars Marty has spent the night cutting. It might be supposed that a pattern of analogy was going to be drawn between the natural and the human world, but if it is, it is with the lightest of touches and any attempt to make a story of evolutionary struggle out of the love-story would have to be conducted at a level of abstraction which denies the experience of reading. The book, despite its underlying and interlocking designs, is not schematic in effect at all. Thematic and verbal patterns suggest analogy and relationship of various kinds and emphases between the human and the natural, but in the larger structure only coexistence is suggested. The characters in the story and the setting of the story are in *The Woodlanders* shown in such a multiplicity of relationships that the variety itself becomes a structural feature.

Some of the freedom with which the narrator can move in the fictional space he creates comes from the separation of the characters' own consciousness from his perception of inner reality. They know the countryside thoroughly, but they do not interpret it. Giles and Marty share unthinking skill; Grace and her father move about the woods with the confidence of habit. Grace's sensibility is emotional not philosophical. Locked in Giles's cottage, waiting for him to come for his meal, she is aware of time passing, though since the clock has stopped it does so unrecorded except by her sharpened awareness of the tiniest sounds and movements. We are in no way given to understand that the weird similes ('Dead boughs scattered about like icthyosauri in a museum', or 'moss like malachite stars') represent Grace's consciousness. They are the narrator's means of making the reader conscious of analogy outside and irrelevant to the story as lived by the characters; the observations go beyond either the mood of the character or merely functional atmospheric description. Grace is frightened in the night, but the nature of her fear is superstitious:

> No sooner had she retired to rest that night than the wind began to rise, and after a few prefatory blasts to be accompanied by rain. The wind grew more violent, and as the storm went on it was difficult to believe that no opaque body, but only an invisible colourless thing, was trampling and climbing over the roof, making the branches creak, springing out of the trees upon the chimney, popping its head into the flue, and shrieking and blaspheming at every corner of the walls. As in the grisly story, the assailant was a spectre which could be felt but not seen. She had never before been so struck with the devilry of a gusty night in a wood, because she had never been so entirely alone in spirit as she was now. She seemed almost to be apart from herself – a vacuous duplicate only. The recent self of physical examination and clear intentions was not there.   (319–20)

The explanation in the clear light of morning is the narrator's:

> Next were more trees close together, wrestling for existence, their branches disfigured with wounds resulting from their mutual rubbings and blows.   (323)

Grace's own actions, observed sympathetically from the outside, are sketched with economy and in language of a different kind – simple, and unmetaphorical: 'Grace sighed, turned, and shut the door slowly', 'she continually peeped out through the lattice, but could see little', 'the strain upon Grace's mind in various ways was so great that on this most desolate day she had passed . . . '. And when she finally acts and goes in search of Giles the description is in language similarly appropriate to the description of limited and pragmatic action under emotional pressure:

> Suddenly rising from before the hearth of smouldering embers, where she had been crouching with her hands clasped over her knees, she crossed the room, unlocked the door, and listened. Every breath of wind had ceased with the decline of day, but the rain had resumed the steady dripping of the night before. (323)

The narrator's sense of the 'real' girl in the 'real' love-story is secure and his sympathy is never in doubt. Her night terrors are totally credible as is the ineffectual modesty with which she abandons her good intentions. The narrator's hold on his own position is equally secure; from it he can allow the strained images which give the situation its resonance beyond events and, even, the unrealistic theatricality which heightens Grace's moment of truth: – 'Can it be that cruel propriety is killing the dearest heart that ever woman clasped to her own!' – without any sacrifice of the reality of his heroine.

Romantic ideas commonly associated with the countryside have their place in *The Woodlanders*; the narrator is aware of their force for the reader and is himself beguiled by them even while he knows that they may be transitory for character and reader alike. The description of Grace as a wood-nymph indicates simultaneously the strength of her charms and their superficial hold in Fitzpiers:

> Just about here the trees were large and wide apart, and there was no undergrowth, so that she could be seen to some distance; a sylph-like greenish-white creature, as toned by the sunlight and leafage. She heard a footfall crushing dead leaves behind her, and turning hastily found herself reconnoitred by Fitzpiers himself, approaching gay and fresh as the morning around them.
>
> His remote gaze at her had been one of mild interest rather than of rapture. But she looked so lovely in the green world about her; her pink cheeks, her simple white dress, and the delicate flexibility of her movements acquired such rarity from their wildwood setting that his eyes kindled as he drew near. (191)

As far as Fitzpiers is concerned, the charms of Melbury's 'few golden hundreds' shape themselves in a similar pictorial way only two pages later, 'as a warm background to Grace's lovely face'. Grace's momentary guise as a wood-nymph is a flicker of light in the total picture, but has no status in the story beyond this confined moment. The glade in which Grace sits down after the fright over the mantrap is inviting, but there is to be no lingering in this idyllic spot. It is as though the narrator sets the scene for reconciliation but the heroine won't take his hint. The pastoral suggestions of enclosed peace are strong for the reader, but are independent of the story and unimportant to the characters. The strong suggestion of Giles as some kind of Nature spirit, however, belongs to Grace's consciousness. When Giles 'looked and smelt like Autumn's very brother' Grace has just watched her husband riding off on Darling, 'a Wouvermans eccentricity reduced to microscopic dimensions'. When he rises 'upon her memory as the fruit-god and the wood-god in alternation' she is convalescent. In both cases, while the narrator is describing strong feeling in Grace his verbalisation of it in these particular terms is his own rather than Grace's. Both times he describes and places the experience as springing from her earliest attachment to her home. As Giles joins her on the road 'her heart rose from its late sadness like a released bough'; the narrator's comment generalises that the smell of cider 'has such an indescribable fascination for those who have been born and bred among the orchards'. He shows Grace less aware of the mythic richness of her rooted association than he is; 'her senses revelled in the sudden lapse back to Nature unadorned', he says, but when Grace herself thinks, 'Nature was bountiful' a few lines later, she is only commenting on a fortunate natural economy which has brought one man to her side just at the moment of her disillusion with another. When 'during the days of her recovery' the image of Giles either 'leafy and smeared with green lichen' or 'cider-stained and starred with apple pips' appears to her, the narrator comments that 'her fancy wove about him a more romantic tissue than it could have done if he had stood before her with all the specks and flaws inseparable from concrete humanity'.

Giles in the story is portrayed 'in his concrete humanity'. He moves about the woods and does his work with an instinctive style which deserts him when he tries to arrange an evening party. Everything he does naturally goes well; socially, from the sturdy good sense of his encounter with Felice Charmond's carriage to the unfortunate meal in the inn and his two uncomprehending encounters with the law, his good qualities are inadequate. He is neither alert nor articulate enough to operate successfully. If such a life appears attractive to the reader, the response is often expressed in terms which cross the gap between the elements which Hardy, characteristically, keeps separate in the text. David Lodge, for instance, sees Giles descending from South's tree 'as if a "tree-spirit" is detaching itself'. But though the tree, as it seems first 'to shiver', then to 'heave a sigh' is responding to the lightest of movements, the trees are so described elsewhere in the book. As soon as a tree is planted it has its distinctive voice with which it speaks under the first breeze which catches it. Giles in the tree is the skilled workman; 'shrouding is not felling', he says with decision. He returns with billhook and ladder, and it is no tree-spirit which makes the boughs 'quiver' as they bend, crack, and then fall under his 'attack'. When he descends he puts away the tools and returns home to bed, his usual course as undisturbed by the doubtful legality of his afternoon's actions as by the rebuff from Grace. This last is the real experience of the afternoon for Giles and the natural phenomenon which unites all the characters involved in this part of the story is the fog. It makes Grace stop, it nearly hides Giles from view, the light of the cottage shines into it but does not illuminate Giles. The eyes of Marty and her father strain into it, but in this 'Niflheim' or fogland the characters are separated from one another physically as they are in understanding. The fog is a natural accident at one level, a visual effect at another, an atmospheric gloom at another. It shrouds a human scene in which emotions, motives, the past, Nature, the law, class and work come briefly together in the inexorable separateness of this sad story. It is tempting to take the Norse association further – to make, perhaps, a Hell of this little spot – but Hardy himself limits the range of association by his own alternative, 'Niflheim or fogland'; it functions rather like a brush-stroke of dark colour in the whole picture. It no more dominates the whole conception than do the strokes of brilliant light in the many skyscapes in the book or the warm radiance of the interiors.

The 'tragical mystery' of separateness is the distinctive underlying perception in *The Woodlanders* and it recurs alike in brief moments and in whole incidents. At the 'warm words' of Grace's father's attempted reparation Giles was 'much moved' and the narrator places the events of the story in their separate social and natural settings, in a poignant phrase:

Only a few short months ago completely estranged from this
family – beholding Grace going to and fro in the distance, clothed
with the alienating radiance of obvious superiority, the wife of the
then popular and fashionable Fitzpiers, hopelessly outside his
social boundary *down to so recent a time that flowers then folded were
hardly faded yet* – he was now asked by that jealously-guarding
father of hers to take courage; to get himself ready for the day
when he should be able to claim her. (290)   (my italics)

Nature, the narrator knows, can assume strange forms in a literate
mind, but when Melbury is searching for the fallen Fitzpiers it is not
he who makes such associations:

But though he threaded the wood hither and thither, his toes
ploughing layer after layer of the little horny scrolls that had once
been leaves, he could not find him. He stood still, listening and
looking round. The breeze was oozing through the network of
boughs as through a strainer; the trunks and larger branches
stood against the light of the sky in the forms of sentinels, gigantic
candelabra, pikes, halberds, lances, and whatever else the fancy
chose to make of them. Giving up the search Melbury came back
to the horses, and walked slowly homeward leading one in each
hand. (271)

So Melbury, Fitzpiers, the riderless horse and the boy who had 'read
about Death in the Revelation' pursue their separate ways in the
wood and at the same time the extraordinary scene of the three
women in Fitzpiers's bedroom takes place in the house. When the
narrator lets his own fancy loose he can be undercut by a character;
Marty, walking with Giles early in the story,

looked towards the western sky, which was now aglow like some
vast foundry wherein new worlds were being cast. Across it the
bare bough of a tree stretched horizontally, revealing every twig
against the evening fire, and showing in dark profile every beck
and movement of three pheasants that were settling themselves
down on it in a row to roost. (97)

Her comment is a prosy bit of country lore which prompts from this
strangely inward-looking girl a gloomy statement of disengagement
from the natural world:

'It will be fine to-morrow,' said Marty, observing them with
the vermilion light of the sun in the pupils of her eyes, 'for they are
a-croupied down nearly at the end of the bough. If it were going
to be stormy they'd squeeze close to the trunk. The weather is
almost all they have to think of, isn't it, Mr Winterbourne? And
so they must be lighter-hearted than we.'
'I dare say they are,' said Winterbourne.

Such disengagement is dramatically enacted in the scene between Grace and Felice in the wood. They have, as in their lives,
'zigzagged about without regarding direction or distance', and
there is more than one sense in which, since Grace 'traversed this,
the wildest part of the wood' in her childhood, 'the transformation
of outlines [has] been great'. But the climax of the scene is in the
expression, in astonishingly direct language, of Grace's emotional
discoveries: 'Then you *do* love him', and, finally, 'O my my great
God! . . . 'He's had you! Can it be – can it be!' Such baldness of
language suggests forcefully those moments of emotional revelation
in real life when surroundings seem to disappear and awareness is
only of the self in a momentously adjusted situation. The wood has
lost any symbolic reference it may have suggested. Instead,
intensely realised as it is, it becomes the situation which forces both
the revelations and the adjustment to them as the two women
huddle together to keep warm. Expectation of continuity and
connection, as of analogy and reference, continue to be aroused
then disappointed throughout the book. At the level of story, Grace,
who, with every evidence of sincerity, says she 'almost worships'
Giles and intends to stay in Little Hintock to keep grave and
memory green, departs for the uncertainties of married life with a
faithless man in a town, while Giles's grave is tended by a girl,
sexless to the point of sublimity, but of the homeliest understanding.
The real force of the final chapter, open-ended as it is, lies in the way
in which it enacts in uncompromising realism, the vision of
separateness and 'unfulfillment' which informs the novel. I have
sought to suggest the constant surprises of the interplay between
separate expectations and modes, between the narrator and his
material, which contributes to the rippled surface of the picture,
and to present *The Woodlanders* as an idyllic description in an
Impressionist style. It is not only the disenchanted view of the
human condition which pushes this novel to the very edge of the
potentialities of the idyllic mode, but the bold and innovative

technique, which holds a sharply focused realistic story in a difficult but highly successful suspension inside the same frame as the story's own stagey elements and the rich poetic suggestion of the setting. With an appearance of neutrality or mature acceptance the narrator presents a picture in many ways painful, but with a total effect of great mellowness. The steady central focus would seem to be at odds with a picture of broken, separate and uncertainly directed attention, but in fact the vision of separation and irresolution is repeated in large structural units and small details alike with such sureness that the multiplicity of ways in which parts of the picture relate creates its own coherence. The story of separated people is sad; the separate details of style and texture create a surface of shimmering variousness.

In contrast with *The Woodlanders, Far from the Madding Crowd* ends, as a story so extreme and so romantic should, in a complete resolution. It moves towards this end with an assurance and pace which Hardy was not to repeat. The writing has extraordinary richness and variety of effect. There is nothing elsewhere in Hardy quite like the swordplay among the ferns, for example. John Bayley has written brilliantly on this episode and very convincingly on the book as a pastoral in his introduction to the New Wessex Edition, in which he depicts it as basically a comic work.[31] He points in that introduction to the relationship of 'Character' and 'Environment' which characterises this novel, remarking that 'in contemplating this pastoral calm we are quite aware that those who experience it are not enjoying it as we are; its tranquillity lies in their unawareness of other possibilities and their inability to change their way of life'. The characters are in harmony with their world which is intact at the end as at the beginning. The conditions of rural life are hard; its economic and physical hazards are a part of the story. But the characters are not stunted by it, nor do they yearn for other things. The passion of their story exists side by side with this picture of farming life as though going mad for love was as natural for a middle-aged farmer as going to a cattle auction. To look closely at *Far from the Madding Crowd* is to discover how many different kinds of separation like the one John Bayley describes between reader and character go to make up this love-story in its remote setting. The unfamiliar rural world is made real by an element of conscious pleasure in the story-telling. The narrator is a delighted newcomer in an old tradition and tells us so with more frequent and more explicit pastoral references than in either *Under the Greenwood Tree* or

The Woodlanders.[32] But the references to the timeless pastoral accrue, paradoxically, around Gabriel, the one character who steadfastly and skilfully works. He plays his flute with 'Arcadian sweetness', but cures the sheep with an address which would do credit to a trained veterinary surgeon. This is a characteristic separation of effect in which the narrator and reader surrender to a given moment with an absorbed appreciation of effect which may not be picked up again any more than it will be contradicted by other effects.

The most intense and memorable moments of the book are heightened by just this isolation. Each one stands out from the context; we remember Gabriel's curing of the sheep or Bathsheba's first meeting in the dark with Troy clearly, the events which surround them more dimly. But internally their drama is composed of many small impressions. They make a total effect of simple theatrical sweep from separate perceptions not all of them naturally harmonious. The effect is in the first instance visual. We may consider the crucial scenes of the shearing supper, Troy's display of swordsmanship in the hollow and the rick-roofing in the thunderstorm. In each case the scene is unified by a defining light. The light intensifies but it does not harmonise; it encompasses figures and setting in a way which affects an observer (the reader directed by the narrator), but leaves the characters absorbed in quite other concerns. Something of the dehumanising clarity of the descriptions of the Mellstock choir is extended in this book to entire scenes with an effect which, however appropriately adjusted to the particular situation, may be seen in each one to have another purpose. While the violent thunderstorm and the improbable scene in the hollow may in their different ways seem to ask for a particularity which would enhance their strangeness, the same cannot be said of the shearing-supper where the undisturbed pictorial glow of traditional pastoral would seem to be most appropriate. The underlying restlessness of this scene springs partially, of course, from the tensions of the personal relationships in the story, but cannot be entirely accounted for in this way. The 'embrowning twilight' fixes the scene in the permanence of a beautiful picture, but the light which 'rakes' the earth has no warmth. Unease is only partly a reflection of the later events of the story; it extends to a sense that the seasonal recurrence of a full harvest is itself dependent on death:

It was still the beaming time of evening, though the night was stealthily making itself visible low down upon the ground, the

western lines of light raking the earth without alighting upon it to
any extent, or illuminating the dead levels at all. The sun had
crept round the tree as a last effort before death, and then begun
to sink, the shearers' lower parts becoming steeped in embrowning twilight, whilst their heads and shoulders were still enjoying
day, touched with a yellow of self-sustained brilliancy that
seemed inherent rather than acquired. (178)

The description suggests that the passions of the story are, like the
harvest scene, perenially renewable and so expendable. It continues
drawing its effects from an extraordinary range of weirdly assorted
sources, the harmony imposed by the flowing and compelling
rhythm of the narrative voice above the sinister undercurrents. The
sun goes down in a Turneresque 'ochreous mist'; Bathsheba, who
presides 'enthroned' as the company grows 'as merry as Gods in
Homer's Heaven', is quietly knitting like any country girl. As
Gabriel notices that Boldwood has withdrawn into the 'encircling
dusk', Liddy brings candles, 'and their lively new flames [shine]
down the table and over the men, and dispersed among the green
shadows behind'. Boldwood's bass part in the ballad with the
prophetic verse, 'For his bride a soldier sought her', adds 'shadow'
to the trio which only, at this point, enhances the strange beauty of
the scene along with the unnatural stillness of the listeners.

Ian Gregor, who sees the foreshadowing of events in the story as
principally the source of disruption to the pastoral calm of the
supper, thinks that the rick-roofing scene betrays a loss of authorial
control over the relationships of parts in the novel. The description
of storm and revel is characterised, he thinks, by a dark excess for
which there is no dramatic equivalent, as though Hardy were trying
'for a deeper explanation of his characters' and failing because 'this
particular novel cannot sustain this implied [psychological] complexity'.[33] This climactic sequence seems less different from other
comparable scenes than he suggests if the function of all of them is
seen as poetic rather than as dramatic, as an expression of the
narrative voice leading out of the drama rather than into it. Clearly
the traditional harmony of the communal supper is going to be
broken by the stark passions of the central figures. The sword-play
scene, too, is prophetic in its direct Lawrentian symbolism of sexual
attraction and imminent surrender. But there is in all these scenes
an excess of effect which catches up the consciousness of the reader in
references not only beyond the consciousness of the characters, but

beyond all the circumstances of this story. In so far as the shearing-supper scene is 'about' seasonal recurrence and the cycles of life and death, it sets the story in a time span which is irrelevant to the particulars of any human story at all. In so far as it is confined to one scene at one time it is as though the narrator were saying, 'Let us look for a moment as people have looked for generations at scenes like this.' He sees the 'real' or observed farm life and his own invented story briefly in a tradition of writing, itself both living and endlessly dying. In the scene in the hollow, Bathsheba's 'adventurous spirit' is part of her character, but the reader's implication in the whole scene is not confined to his sense of character. Indeed Troy in this episode is just a red coat and a flashing sword; having no consciousness at all he is as closed to the reader as he is to Bathsheba, and Bathsheba herself is not rising to the implications of the whole scene. The flashing sword for the reader is one gleam in the brilliantly lit hollow, along with the 'bristling ball of gold in the west', and 'the tall thickets of brake fern . . . radiant in hues of clear and untainted green'. The story, the event at the centre of this scene, functions partly by defining the intensity of this apprehension of a brilliant moment as sexual in nature. The strong story of *Far from the Madding Crowd* should not conceal the essentially static quality of the narrative comment. The visual and historical imagination of the narrator holds character and setting throughout in a harmony which, in both these scenes, is produced by fundamentally disjunctive means.

In this view of the nature of the outstanding visual scenes in the novel, the roofing of the ricks in the thunderstorm becomes central. It takes the same means to effect as the other two, but here, at the climax of the story, it has a major structural importance. It is here by a series of sharp stylistic contrasts that the nature of Gabriel's heroism is defined. As a person, of course, Gabriel is the ideal simple man at the centre of a story strong enough to throw his particular virtues into prominence and relief. He is modest, plain-spoken and patient, but these overriding virtues make even his bravey seem inward-turned. When he acts it is out of loyalty and knowledge. These are admirable qualities in real life and would yield literary 'heroism' to analysis and exploration of character. But in *Far from the Madding Crowd* there is statement but no exploration of character. Instead by expressive or outward-looking (which means in effect, reader-oriented) methods, the place in the story for a hero is etched and the nature of the 'heroism' which fills it is defined. This is finally accomplished, naturally enough, in the sequence which more than any other tries his loyalty.

As in the supper scene and the description of the sword-play in the hollow, the storm scene is mediated by the intense consciousness of the narrator set against the limited consciousness of the participants, from Gabriel's practicality to the oblivion of the drunken sleepers in the barn. Gabriel can work with unfearful concentration in the demonic fury, as the narrator sees it, of the storm, because he has in his knowledgeable and concerned way appraised the double danger of storm and cold rain, and assessed the value of the ricks to Bathsheba. The storm is heralded by the snail's trail, the fat toad and the geometrically huddled sheep – all signs which Gabriel correctly and unfussily interprets. The narrator interprets cloud and winds which prepares for the description of the height of the storm. The pattern of the whole sequence of storm, revel and roofing is one of juxtaposed, independent but thematically related incident. Between storm and revel stands Gabriel, with his homely knowledge and grasp of economic realities, a hero. The varied styles – heightened, explanatory and narrative – of the opening of chapter XXXVI, 'Wealth in Jeopardy – The Revel', set the pattern:

The night had a sinister aspect. A heated breeze from the south fanned the summits of lofty objects, and in the sky dashes of buoyant cloud were sailing in a course at right angles to that of another stratum, neither of them in the direction of the breeze below. The moon, as seen through these films, had a lurid metallic look. The fields were sallow with the impure light, and all were tinged in monochrome, as if beheld through stained glass. The same evening the sheep had trailed homeward head to tail, the behaviour of the rooks had been confused, and the horses had moved with timidity and caution.

Thunder was imminent, and, taking some secondary appearances into consideration, it was likely to be followed by one of the lengthened rains which mark the close of dry weather for the season. Before twelve hours had passed a harvest atmosphere would be a bygone thing.

Oak gazed with misgiving at eight naked and unprotected ricks, massive and heavy with the rich produce of one-half the farm for that year. He went on to the barn.

This was the night which had been selected by Sergeant Troy – ruling now in the room of his wife – for giving the harvest supper and dance. As Oak approached the building the sound of violins and a tambourine, and the regular jigging of many feet, grew more distinct. He came close to the large doors, one of which stood slightly ajar, and looked in. (254)

As the separate strands develop and the writing becomes more histrionic in its description of both storm and revel, so the description of Gabriel's deliberate actions as he goes about trying to rouse the revellers and then fetching his tools and getting on with the job alone, seems by contrast to get cooler and cooler, the bare description of action lent intensity by the accompanying extravaganza. Of course, the coolness rooted in practicality and directed towards the rescue of a bank balance is slightly comic, certainly incongruous, against the stereotypes of heroic action. But while as we read we have a comic vision of the disparity between his actions and the heavenly fireworks, we do not see Gabriel himself as comic.

In this sequence the relationship of the layered incidents makes an effect quite separate from that of any event singly. In such a method the intensity of the realisation of single moments is at constant odds with the movement of the story, which yet proceeds in this novel with characteristic sureness and speed. The narrator is not melancholy like the narrator of *The Woodlanders*, but he is similarly distanced. In his generalising way he sees correspondences within his story – passion in both the elements and his characters, for instance – but he does not seek to rationalise them inside a dramatic unity. Things do not have to be commensurate to reflect on one another,[34] and Gabriel is effective at the high moment of the storm because at this point farming and romance are linked inside the story. In *Far from the Madding Crowd*, as in other idyllic novels I have described, the appropriate depiction of the characters as 'figures in a landscape' is not a failure,[35] but a deliberate choice which throws the narrator into prominence as he makes his direct address to the reader. We may thus expect a different kind of consistency from the dramatic, since it will originate from the narrative point of view rather than, apparently, from the inner life of the characters. Curiously in this most obviously 'pastoral' of Hardy's novels, the consistency bears a strong resemblance to real life, full of loose ends, gaps and hard facts. This is life seen without a shaping religious sense but with a strong sense of its inexhaustible capacity both to prompt and to elude aesthetic shaping. At one end of the spectrum is

Troy, unmotivated even in a story remarkable for lack of exploration of motive. He is a figure whose 'history' is in fiction. But the
whole story resolves in the mode of realism, to which Troy does not
belong. As Bathsheba takes Gabriel at last, we know that there is
more love on one side than the other, but, too, that there is mutual
respect, a place in the community and plenty of energy.

Hardy must be the most inventive of modern writers of pastoral.
He pushes the genre to the edge of its possibilities, which is itself one
element in the tantalising quality of these novels. Other novels of
Hardy's provide stronger central characters, and some more
profound implications. But none equals that quality which defines
these three very different novels as 'idylls' – the clarity of narrative
focus over multiple planes of reality and fiction.

6 Conclusion: a Reflective Mirror

In my first chapter I attempted to illustrate the characteristic structures of the Victorian idyll from Clough's *The Bothie of Tober-na-Vuolich* and Tennyson's English Idyls. It seemed convenient first to show the patterns and methods as they operate in poetry since, simply by virtue of their length, the poems are more easily perceived as wholes. But the interdependence of prose and poetry inside the idyllic vision is closer in practice, as I have shown, than this might suggest. The idylls bridge a gap between poetry and prose fiction more obvious now than it was to contemporary readers. They bring the meditative and generalising tendencies thought proper to poetry to bear on the prosaic and disturbing circumstances of everyday life. Thus, though it derives from a poetic tradition, the Victorian idyll also belongs to the development of what in the mid-century came to be called 'Realism'.[1] It can be seen to respond to demands made in contemporary critical theory on poetry and on prose. Although a critical theory of the novel as a distinct form emerged in the middle years of the century, in many critical and aesthetic statements of the time poetry and prose remain, to a modern ear, strangely close. At one extreme they are inter-changeable terms; either 'poetry' or 'fiction' could be chosen, for instance, according to W. C. Roscoe, as 'the most comprehensive name for the art which has language as its medium'.[2] The history of mid-century novel criticism can be seen in one aspect as a pulling apart of these terms and a growth of some sense that they must be used to refer to works demanding different not similar response from a reader. Another way of putting it would be to see the classical derivation of Roscoe's vocabulary giving under pressure from new preoccupations and from the resulting new forms.

The process is slow. In the 1840s, for instance, prose and poetry are distinguished only at either end of the fiction-maker's subject-matter. In the demand for an art which would face the modern age with its railways, growing cities, disrupted social patterns and consequent emotional uncertainties, they are, in fact, one. W. E. Houghton in his book on Clough's poetry shows that *The Bothie* was an early outcome of the pressure for a 'modern poem'.[3] It incorporates into a poem what Carlyle called 'the barren prose of the nineteenth century . . . the vulgar life we are all leading'.[4] As a pastoral *The Bothie* holds within one frame the values of opposing worlds. As a nineteenth-century pastoral it characteristically chooses to do so in story. A. Dwight Culler says that the problem facing the would-be author of the 'modern poem' was 'not steam but the novel'.[5] As a poet Clough was aware of the competition from the novel. Why, he asked, attacking the use of 'classical models' and 'Oriental sources', did people 'much prefer' *Vanity Fair* and *Bleak House* to any poetry at all? The answer he thought was that the novels were clearly concerned with 'general wants' and 'ordinary feelings':

> The novelist does try to build us a real house to be lived in; and this common builder, with no notion of the orders, is more to our purpose than the student of ancient art who proposes to lodge us under an Ionic portico.

Clough takes for granted that contemporary interest is first and foremost in the ordinary or common. And just as he sees that such generality requires a specific and recognisable setting, so we can also see that the inhabitants of the 'real house' must be individualised in order to stand for the general. The 'commoner' the character the more specifically he must be drawn. The invention must include his circumstances and his history in enough detail to differentiate him from others and thus to render him, by metonymy, representative. An invented world is necessary to the reader's belief in the 'reality' of the character. However, although these remarks of Clough's may with hindsight seem to press the claims of the modern novelist as against those of the modern poet, he was in fact only praising one poet's invention of a freshly conceived fiction against another's reliance on ancient legend. Clough's joint review of Alexander Smith and Matthew Arnold endorses Smith's effort, despite its limited success, to address his poem *A Life Drama* to the contemporary scene.[6] In contrast, Matthew Arnold had escaped in *The Strayed Reveller* and *Empedocles on Etna* to a more easily held vantage-point. *A Life-Drama* (1853) is not as theatrical as the title leads one to expect, nor to a modern reader as vividly contemporary as Clough's criticism seems to imply, but, like *The Bothie* itself, and later *Aurora Leigh* and *Maud*, it confronts the stress of the times by means of a story, not a re-created legend, but a story of characters known only through the fiction and in a contemporary setting.

The necessity of narrative is implicit in the attempt at the 'modern poem' from the beginning. 'Locksley Hall', published with the English Idyls, was thought by Elizabeth Barrett Browning not, after all, to offer much 'in that way'; it lacked 'story' and 'manners', and she thought herself of writing 'a true poetical novel'.[7] 'Locksley Hall' describes the pressure of the modern world on individual feeling. Clearly interest in the individual in his own right, which the poem invites, raises questions of cause, effect and circumstance which the poem does not answer. Only the extension and continuity of a novel offers the space in which a character can be shown to find his place in the world and act out his life inside its complex and circumscribing circumstances. The poem contains the germ of such a story, but in place of the exploration in space and time which would satisfy curiosity about the person, it offers an intense perception of relationship. The Victorian idyll retains such a 'poetic' perception of the individual in a situation which is a given, and in that sense static, even when the story is extended to novel length. Figure and background are in a fixed relationship. The pictured figure cannot change the background, but the background, the living present, is itself shifting, erupting, or even, as in 'Locksley Hall', tumultuous.

Such a background, John Sterling thought, ought to have inspired poets. His review of Tennyson's *Poems* of 1842[8] expresses surprise that it has not yet done so and hails Tennyson as likely to become the Poet of the Age, just because he is fully engaged in feeling with contemporary life. Sterling's review is not by any means a plea for poetry to face any subject at all. Of 'St Simeon Stylites', for instance, he says that poetry has something better to do than 'wrap her mantle round a sordid, greedy lunatic' with his 'loathsome attempts at saintship'. The argument is more complicated than that poetry should be all-inclusive. The terms in which the argument is couched in this review make it as succinct and sustained an expression of Victorian idyllic feeling as I have read. Sterling advances the 'Idyllic kind' among the poems under review as the highest proof of Tennyson's potential. In them as in other 'better' poems of Tennyson 'there is this same character – the fusion of his own best feeling with the delightful affections, baffled or blessed, of others – and with the fairest images of the real world as it lies before us all today'. To retain the freshness of the heart's feelings and see beauty all around you is not to take refuge, to turn away from mechanical contrivances, bustle and commerce, but to confront and place them. The permanent morality of feeling and beauty is set in Sterling's review against the flux of history. He paints three pictures from contemporary life – the death of Mr Huskisson at the opening of the Manchester and Liverpool Railroad, a general election and a fund-raising meeting in Exeter Hall. They are in a mode which itself exemplifies the idyllic method. They have accuracy of observation and a humane awareness of permanent significance. They absorb both into a descriptive mode where noise and calm, falsity and truth, new and old are held in focus by a sense of the present as a part of history. The opening of the railroad is 'the inauguration of a new physical power'. 'The last human tragic touch to an event which would at any rate have retained for ever an historic importance' is the departure of 'a great statesman . . . on a darker and more distant journey'. The 'thrill of fear and pain' unite the onlookers even more closely than their interest and 'to a calm observer' it might have seemed that a sacrificial victim had been snatched, that 'in the most prosperous and peaceful of national triumphs the dark powers again claimed a share . . .'. In the second example the upheaval of a general election is undertaken, accompanied by a sustaining vision of the 'quiet [which] will spring out of tumult, and a government [about to] be born from a mob'. Most of the election talk is vapid if not fraudulent, but the 'mixture and spread of interests and faculties brought into action' is a wholly modern phenomenon, and the individual has become part of the 'throbbing business [of] the land', and his 'wishes and devices [are] braced' with those of others. In Exeter Hall, demagogic rhetoric and organised chicanery extract from the wealthy middle classes, represented largely by women of high minds, impeccable virtue and quiet tastes, large amounts of money for chimerical charities in remote places. The appeal, egregious and falsely expressed as it may be, reaches for and touches the very best in these 'warm and gentle breasts'. The individual's capacity for feeling and responsibility is in fact the centre of each episode. Sterling's heightened diorama of contemporary life began with a 'calm observer' of a dramatic scene reminded in the face of sudden death of the inscrutable darkness in ancient religion. From a sympathetic and reflective position like that of the pastoral narrator, he is moved to his vivid perception of the age-old pattern underlying the tragic death by the visible disturbance of a veteran soldier, in whom he saw, 'a quiver of the lip, a movement of the eye, such as have hardly been caused by the most unlooked-for and dreadful chances of his mighty wars'. He also saw the railroad itself as an achievement to set beside the pyramids, Cyclopean walls and the roads of the Roman Empire, carrying 'myriads of men . . . , travelling like the heroes of fairy-tales'. In the second 'scene' the 'calm observer' imagines the classic calm of patrician government which will emerge from the democratic tumult. 'At last the tailor's and brazier's voice does really influence the course of human affairs', even though it can only be raised amid 'fraud, folly and noise'. In Exeter Hall, the third scene, where the imperturbably good ladies are inspired to charity by the 'raving folly of some declaimer', the calm is internalised in the sanctity of the individual conscience.

In Sterling's view Tennyson surpasses in his Idyllic poems even his own other work, because in them, 'the heartfelt tenderness, the glow, the gracefulness, the strong sense, the lively painting', are 'drawn from the very heart of English life'. Other great modern poets have turned away from the world of everyday things, Scott to Romance, Byron to foreign lands and ways, Wordsworth to lofty speculation. Crabbe, who offered so much promise as a Poet of the Age in ranging 'so widely through the classes' and employing 'so many divers elements of circumstance and character', lacked the 'enthusiastic sympathy and jubilant love whose utterance is melody'. As the Gaskells saw, he had no 'seeing-beauty spirit'. Tennyson achieves 'melody' everywhere, but his potential status as Poet of the Age is clearest in the Idyls. There, though their scale is small, the present is made to seem a part of history, as worthy of observation and representation in art as the past. In following their classical models so closely the Idyls not only 'turn to fixed beauty [a] part of the shifting and mingled matter of our time', but actually show, 'all the gain that Christianity and civilization have brought to the relation of the sexes and the characters of women'. Sterling's representative vignettes make very clear that he sees the melodious, descriptive art of the Idyls as value-laden, and the values carried by the average or ordinary individual. Idyls and illustrative review together present the intrinsic worth of the individual as the means of making a pattern out of the confusions of the modern world. In his own right the private person is emerging into a central role on a new but still heroic scale. As an object of contemplation he is the means by which an observer assesses the scale and sees the relationships in the composition of a modern picture. Both as actor and as represented figure he stands for values which may be found as well in humble as in more exalted walks of life – sympathy, perception of worth in others and an openness to beauty. Such values are those which may be cultivated by staying still in a 'throbbing' world. They are, of course, those most readily and widely associated at the time with women and domesticity. So Victorian pastoral becomes, amongst other things, a celebration of domesticity inside a world of business.

While there is no mention of prose in Sterling's review – he is seeking a Poet of the Age – his central point presses towards what was increasingly to become, indeed was largely already, the province of prose. The 'conflicting energies' of contemporary life, he thought, should provide inspiration for a 'truly great' poet, and yet his elaboration of how these energies might present themselves to an artist reads like a skeleton of a novel by Dickens:

> The fierce, too often mad force, that wars itself away among the labouring poor, the manifold skill and talent and unwearied patience of the middle classes, and the still unshaken solidity of domestic life among them – these are facts open to all, though by none perhaps sufficiently estimated. And over and among all society the wealth of our richer people is gathered and diffused as it has never been before anywhere else, shaping itself into a thousand arts of luxury, a million modes of social pleasure, which the moralist may have much to object against, but which the poet, had we a truly great one now rising among us, would well know how to employ for his own purposes.

There is, in fact, an in-built tension in the concept of the 'modern poem', between the perception of relationship or connection, what might be called the 'germ' of story, and the means by which it can be realised. If those generalised figures at the heart of Sterling's vignettes – the veteran, the tailor, the brazier, the charitable lady – were to be explored in sufficient depth in their own right to focus the pressures of the modern world, they would have to be shown in appropriate action, through time, exercising judgement, responding to circumstances, making choices. 'Their passions and foibles' would have to be allowed, in the way James found lacking in *Adam*

Bede, to 'play themselves out'.[9] Logically the impressionistic techniques which alone would suggest the 'fierce, too often mad force, that wars itself away among the labouring poor' would have to give way to a manner more suited to the investigative and scientific temper of the time. The 'story' of the protagonist, his fictitious biography, would then approach the condition of history and show as few signs of a creator other than God as possible.[10]

To some extent the tension I am describing is that between the general and the specific, but, of course, that is endemic in any realist project. Certainly the perception of relationships, which is central to the idyll, is inextricably tied to a degree of generality. The combination of relationship and representativeness is not picturable without narrative distance. A common contemporary view was that such distance was proper for poetry and, conversely, if distance could not be achieved the proper medium was prose. That critical theory was not always abreast of artistic practice is made clear by an uneasy review by W. E. Aytoun in *Blackwood's Magazine* of *Aurora Leigh*.[11] Aytoun thinks that Mrs Browning made the mistake of allowing 'fancy to be trammelled in its work by perpetual reference to realities'. In this review narrative distance and distance in time are conflated. Contemporary events should be handled in prose, he thinks; poetry can step in when time has done the distancing:

> It is curious to observe that poets in all ages have shrunk from the task of chronicling contemporaneous deeds. These are first consigned to the tutelage of the muse of history; nor is it until time has done its consecrating office, that poetry ventures to approach them. The bards of old touched their harps, not for the glorification of their compatriots, but in memory of the deeds of their ancestors. No one supposes that the time has yet arrived when the Peninsular War or the sea-victories of Britain can be taken up as proper epical themes, though Nelson and Wellington have both entered into the famous mansions of the dead. This universal repugnance to the adoption of immediate subjects for poetical treatment, seems to us a very strong argument against its propriety; and certainly Mrs Browning has not succeeded, by practice, in establishing her theory.

In seeming to ask for the distance given by time he is also asking for the narrative distance which allows the detail to be submerged in a pattern imposed by an observer remote from the distortions of close involvement. He prefers, for instance, the descriptions of Italy which recall Aurora's childhood over those of London, which he finds over-wrought and reminiscent of Turner. Nevertheless, he can approve the portrait of Marian Erle, 'a daughter of the people', since, 'the course of poetry' being in 'the empyrean or in the fresh and wholesome air', the poet can avoid the mean without by-passing the humble.

Two aspects of this single exception are worthy of note here. In the first place the example maintains distance. Neither writer nor sophisticated reader are assumed to be so familiar with humble life as to cause distortion of the picture by proximity. Further it is assumed that the reader's interest is in the sameness not the difference between themselves and those in circumstances so humble as to be almost foreign. 'The most sanctified affections', Aytoun says, 'the purest thoughts, the holiest aspirations are as likely to be found in the cottage as in the castle'. Poetry finds its interest in the continuity and permanence perceivable from a distance. If the central interest of Marian Erle's story had been her circumstances he would have seen prose as the more suitable medium as he thought it would have been for the contemporary story of *Aurora Leigh* as a whole. All mid-Victorian realist fiction assumes the individual worth of ordinary people, but as con-temporary critics observed of Thackeray, for instance, a scrupulous effort to portray things as they are can omit a whole dimension of life and character.[12] Concern for the worth rather than the circum-stances implies a measure of generality. *Aurora Leigh* is a 'modern poem'. Its verse confers a representativeness on its contemporary subject-matter. The idyllic novels tell 'poetic' stories of permanent values seen in their relation with 'prosaic' facts of life.

Victorian novel theory calls the generality achieved by distance and reflection 'Idealism', the opposite of 'Realism'. It was difficult then, as now, to write of 'Idealism' without sliding into an assumption of 'ought', a moral imperative rather than the aesthetic 'ought', which implies the consistency of the typical. But for G. H. Lewes the critic who writes most lucidly on the subject, the true opposite of 'Realism' is 'Falsism'. 'Idealism', for Lewes, was a means not an end. By the methods of Idealism it was possible to reach the *inner* reality, to pass beyond the 'vulgarities of life' to its 'more impassioned moments'.[13] The antithesis commonly assumed to exist between Realism and Idealism is parallel, Lewes sees, to the false distinction between Art and Reality:[14]

A distinction is drawn between Art and Reality, and an antithesis established between Realism and Idealism which would never have gained acceptance had not men in general lost sight of the fact that Art is a Representation of Reality – a Representation which, inasmuch as it is not the thing itself, but only represents it, must necessarily be limited by the nature of its medium; the canvas of the painter, the marble of the sculptor, the chords of the musician, and the language of the writer, each bring with them peculiar laws; but while thus limited, while thus regulated by the necessities imposed on it by each medium of expression, Art always aims at the representation of Reality, i.e. of Truth; and no departure from truth is permissible, except such as inevitably lies in the nature of the medium itself. Realism is thus the basis of all Art, and its antithesis is not Idealism, but *Falsism.* When our painters represent peasants with regular features and irreproachable linen; when their milkmaids have the air of Keepsake beauties, whose costume is picturesque, and never old or dirty; when Hodge is made to speak refined sentiments in unexceptionable English, and children utter long speeches of religious and poetic enthusiasm; when the conversation of the parlour and the drawing-room is a succession of philosophical remarks, expressed with great clearness and logic, an attempt is made to idealize, but the result is simple falsification and bad art.

The peculiar stamp, and probably the most antipathetic to modern readers, of the prose idylls I have discussed is the distance between the narrator and his material. The falsification of which Lewes speaks certainly gives an impression of distance, but there is a distinction to be drawn between the distance from which Nature is, as Lewes says, 'beautified', and that from which general or representative truths can be depicted. I have tried to establish that by means of a creative narrative distance, at the time commonly thought to characterise poetry, the novels I have discussed focus simultaneously, and so in relation, the permanent truths accessible to 'idealism' and the shifting 'realities' of the contemporary scene. Though in our time these novels have been neglected as history and insufficiently appreciated as poetry, in their own time they were received as pictures of recognisable 'real' life. Nevertheless, their Realism is subject to two significant restraints, which in fact characterised Idealism, or what with Lewes one might see as a higher kind of Realism. In the first place they show the 'analytic perception' which W. C. Roscoe thought Defoe, with his apparent truth to life, lacked, but which was necessary for any depiction of realities beyond the mere truth of surfaces.[15] To reflect on simplicity is to see it in relation to the complex, and as we saw in examining the views of Arnold and Schiller, the presentation of this reflection must itself be complex. By their juxtapositioning of new and old, permanent and changing, simple and sophisticated, the idyllic novels offer the perceptions which have arisen from reflection without resolving inherent oppositions. The reader is required to respond with reflection himself. Secondly, while as in other Realist fiction the relation in these novels with other kinds of story-telling is frequently parodic, they also in compensating balance, draw an unironic attention to their own handling of familiar, sometimes commonplace material. 'Those', says Archbishop Whately in his well-known review of Jane Austen's work, 'who look with pleasure at Wilkie's pictures, or those of the Dutch school, must admit that excellence of imitation may confer attraction on that which would be insipid or disagreeable in the reality.'[16] The self-absorbed and lingering attention to detail – whether of Miss Matty's well-scrubbed shop-floor, the red hassocks in Hayslope church or the ticking clock in the Holmans' kitchen – asserts in these idyllic novels a set of opposing values, social and aesthetic, 'real' and 'ideal'. While the protagonists are pointedly unheroic in many ways, they conform to the standards by which Lewes found Charlotte Brontë's Robert Moore wanting as a hero. They are never 'sordid, mean [or] wanting in the statelier virtues of our kind'.[17] These novels reinstate 'heroism' by restating its terms. And the characters are shown in harmony with a carefully pictured background, with which they share the focus of attention.

The idealising cast of the Victorian idyllic novel brings it near to the condition of poetry in two hardly separable senses. Structurally the novels approach poetry because of the static nature of their vision and the meditative position of the narrator in the face of what is depicted. The relation of parts, figure against background, and opposed worlds or values, remains static. The characters will move in time, events will affect them and they will influence events – which is only to say that the narrator is telling a story. In relation to this story-content, however, the narrator is less interested in the story *qua* story than in the thoughts to which its situations may give rise. The Victorian idyll might be described as a mode in which reflection is aroused by relationships or juxtapositioning, and held inside the frame of a slight or largely unresolved story. The presence of story in the idyllic representation of simple life has been remarked. The narrative nature of the reflection aroused by such depiction brings us back to genre painting. It can be well illustrated by Ruskin's famous description of Landseer's 'The Old Shepherd's Chief Mourner', where, quite apart from the fact that this is a picture, there can be no possibility of even imagined words from the protagonist's own mouth since he is a dog. The 'language' of the picture is described by Ruskin as lying in the high finish of the detail and the relationships established by composition and technique together. It is, he claims, a language both precise and expressive, but his own version, his translation as it were, is dependent for its 'expressiveness' on hints of narrative. Only by extending the impressions in time can he convey the 'inner reality' of this picture:[18]

Take, for instance, one of the most perfect poems or pictures (I use the words as synonymous) which modern times have seen: – the 'Old Shepherd's Chief-mourner'. Here the exquisite execution of the glossy and crisp hair of the dog, the bright sharp touching of the green bough beside it, the clear painting of the wood of the coffin and the folds of the blanket, are language – language clear and expressive in the highest degree. But the close pressure of the dog's breast against the wood, the convulsive clinging of the paws, which has dragged the blanket off the trestle, the total powerlessness of the head laid, close and motionless, upon its folds, the fixed and tearful fall of the eye in its utter hopelessness, the rigidity of repose which marks that there has been no motion nor change in the trance of agony since the last blow was struck on the coffin-lid, the quietness and gloom of the chamber, the spectacles marking the place where the Bible was last closed, indicating how lonely has been the life, how unwatched the departure, of him who is now laid solitary in his sleep; – these are all thoughts – thoughts by which the picture is separated at once from hundreds of equal merit, as far as mere painting goes, by which it ranks as a work of high art, and stamps its author, not as the neat imitator of the texture of a skin, or the fold of a drapery, but as the Man of Mind.

This passage leads Ruskin into one of his castigations of the Dutch school, who, he says, use language divorced from thought. In other words, the Dutch paintings are 'realistic' to the exclusion of all 'idealism', or, concerned with the prose rather than the poetry of the subject. In the review of recent German fiction from which I have already quoted, Lewes uses a parallel argument. He compares Landseer and Snyders as animal painters, both equally faithful to external realities but Landseer's animals 'express their inner life' because he 'throws a sentiment into his groups'. In painting people, Lewes thinks, Teniers is as realistic and unpoetic as Snyders in his treatment of animals. He asks his reader to 'suppose two men equally gifted with the perceptive powers and technical skill necessary to the accurate representation of a village group'. We are to suppose them equally skilful, but one, moved by sympathy to paint 'a mother's tenderness' as well as the 'graceful attitude' in a young mother, 'tender' lovers and 'venerable' old people, will 'without once departing from strict reality . . . have thrown a sentiment into his group which every spectator will recognise as poetry'. The novelist, Lewes says, will not choose humble subjects if he finds them 'prosaic and uninteresting', but once he has chosen he is under an obligation to paint them with both their 'reality' and their 'poetry'. 'Poetry' or 'sentiment' is a quality which translates for the spectator or reader into generalised thought. It exists in the work in relationships or abstractions and not in individual character as such. It follows that analysis of character or extended history of persons pulls representation of humble life towards accuracy of rendering externals rather than towards the reflections they may generate, or, in Lewes's terms, towards the reality of humble life rather than its poetry. In so far as it reflects on simplicity, idyllic representation tends to 'Idealism' in the terms of contemporary novel theory, but to 'Realism' in so far as it seeks to paint with truth. As in the face of its other oppositions, it holds a delicate balance.

If the mid-nineteenth century presented the 'perfect pastoral moment'[19] it did so partly because an aesthetic of human passion found ready expression in the depiction of simple people in humble and rustic life. In the words of Wordsworth's preface, 'in that condition of life our elementary feelings coexist in a state of greater simplicity, and consequently, may be more accurately contemplated, and more forcibly communicated'. Ruskin, of course, also thought that it was nobility of subject which made for great art, though the artist had to be aware of and dwell on the nobility. He is referring to religious subjects, but such notions transfer easily to more socially oriented ideas of greatness in event and social class.

Wordsworth's preface was written in place of the elaborated defence he thought really necessary, which would have involved not only going into the 'present state of public taste in this country' but 'retracing the revolutions, not of literature alone, but likewise of society itself'. In France, as we have seen with George Sand, these 'revolutions' of society were perceived in explicitly political terms. However untouched the life described in her stories, George Sand saw it with a sharp political sense of its relation to a disturbed society. As late as 1864 the brothers Goncourt in their famous preface to *Germinie Lacerteux* defend their 'clinical study of love' as a serious novel, not simply one intended to shock taste, on similarly political grounds:[20]

Living in the nineteenth century, in a time of universal suffrage, democracy, and liberalism, we asked ourselves whether what are called 'the lower classes' did not have a right to the Novel, whether this world beneath a world, the people, must remain under literary interdict and the disdain of authors, who up to now have kept silence about whatever heart and soul the people might have. We asked ourselves whether in this era of equality in which we live there could still be, for writer or for reader, any classes too unworthy, any miseries too low, any dramas too foul-mouthed, any catastrophes insufficiently noble in their terror.

Wordsworth, on the other hand, is remarking neutrally on the connection of art and life, and his passage would not be substantially altered if we substituted 'change' for 'revolutions'. A similar acceptance of concurrent change and continuity informs Sterling's review of Tennyson's *Poems* of 1842. He is no more politically embattled than Wordsworth, and he only reflects the actual course of English history between the dates of the preface and his review in seeing the changes as having more social than political impact. The democratisation of England, for its comparative gradualness among other reasons, could be perceived as placing the individual citizen in a new personal relation to circumstances and to other people. The necessary adjustments are seen as moral rather than political. In both countries aesthetic taste is seen to lag behind social and political facts. The Goncourts paint themselves as engaging in something like a scientific investigation:

We became curious to know . . . whether in a country lacking castes and legal aristocracy the misfortunes of the little people and the poor could arouse interest, emotion, and pity to the same degree as the misfortunes of the great and the rich.

Twenty years earlier and in another country Sterling's call for a Poet of the Age is so absorbed in the observed phenomena that it provides a structural prose model of the poetic handling it envisages. In fact, inside and outside the idyll, the characteristic English statement of the potentially explosive idea that the simplest human being has all the essential human characteristics is unscientific and a-political, stoical rather than revolutionary. In its portrait of a gentle soul surviving in a social scene described with bitter fantasy, *Little Dorrit*, for instance, seems to me to make a very English approach to the fictional representation of the ills of society. The Marshalsea has spread its metaphoric shade over nine hundred pages of indictment and black comedy before, in the last two, Arthur and Little Dorrit stand in the rays of the burning paper and then are married 'with the sun shining on them through the painted figure of Our Saviour on the window', passing to 'a modest life of usefulness and happiness' through 'the roaring streets, inseparable and blessed'. Such a narrowing down of political implication to the spiritual and emotional survival of two individuals may be seen as a gesture of political helplessness or as an ennobling expression of faith in the ultimate significance of the individual as he is known by his feelings. A reader who does not feel the end of *Little Dorrit* to be on a disproportionately small scale for the size and weight of the complexities it resolves would be, I think, the ideal reader of the idylls I have discussed.

The Victorian idylls are, above all, explorations of basic human emotions; the springs of feeling are sought in simple surroundings and an isolable network of family and community relationships. The novels grow out of a perception of the inevitable connection of opposites and present, as far as they can, a moment of conscious equilibrium. While conservatism is thus of their nature, it is hardly the main distinguishing feature between them and other great nineteenth-century realist novels. Exploration of life at a given point in time is unlikely to be transformed into an art which presses for general changes or offers the possibility of solution. When George Eliot and Thomas Hardy, whose last writings show more political awareness than their earlier ones, in the end abandon their pastoral strategies, they do not, even then, write of social change as if they or their characters had the capacity to affect the course or the direction of change. *Middlemarch* is, among other things, a wonderful description of man as a political animal, but the situation in which he operates is a given. The emergence of Jewish self-consciousness into the possibility of action offers a correlative in *Daniel Deronda* for the public identity of an individual, held in focus with Gwendolen's story of a search for private identity. Tess and Jude, no less than Michael Henchard, have the stubborn grains of their own characters to contend with as well as the indifference of society.[21] Nevertheless, while the realist position is basically conservative, the idyll seems, by the roundness of its picture, positively to repudiate change. This is a difference more apparent than real. The effect of engagement with the central figure in *Tess of the d'Urbervilles* or *Jude the Obscure*, for instance, is to arouse a desire for change, however unspecified. Things should not be like this, we feel. But this is a direct effect of closure in the story; the novels point no clear direction for change. The idyll asks for acceptance of the whole picture with all its related parts intact, the balance preserved, the irresolution left poised in all its doubts.

In another sense, of course, the idylls in prose and poetry, were an innovatory effort to come to terms with startling change. Tennyson's English Idyls, as we have seen, were perceived to have achieved this status by rewriting an ancient mode with a modern sensibility. But obviously inspired by ancient pastoral or not, the effect of the works I have described was of freshness and immediacy. Blackwood felt he 'knew' the characters in *Adam Bede*, Ruskin wanted more and more of Miss Matty, Dickens kept thinking about Hetty, and in 1925, before the character of nineteenth-century rural life had entirely evolved into twentieth-century patterns, 'Q' recognised the authenticity of observation in *Cousin Phillis*. But as with 'Q', who saw that the structure of feeling was rooted in pastoral, the responses to these novels are rarely far from a consciousness of the works as art. Forster resigned himself to the 'death' of Captain Brown because it led to the delightful scenes with the bereaved daughter, the reviewer in the *Spectator*, whom Hardy was happy to quote, was irresistibly reminded of Wilkie and 'even more of Teniers' by the rustic scenes in *The Poor Man and the Lady*. Jane Carlyle, on the other hand, had 'fresh and happy remembrances' in reading *Adam Bede*, as though she had revisited Scotland. It would seem that these works impressed not so much by what they showed as by the invitation to look freshly. At this point the psychological and aesthetic roots of pastoral coincide. The idyllic narrator, who knows more about the people he describes and about his audience than either side knows of the other, mediates between them by establishing an aesthetic common ground. In the first place, he shares with his audience an act of personal memory. The artist draws on childhood memory but any autobiographical element is subsumed in what gives the appearance of being a truthful picture of a remote way of life. Set in a past which roughly corresponds to the far span of living memory, the idyllic novel seems to revert to both psychological and communal origins. Secondly, his story proceeds with constant reference to other ways of telling and other representations of simple life. Literature and painting are used to place and communicate; they constitute if not a language at least a set of signs or signals.

The way in which a sympathetic and indubitably 'competent' contemporary reader finds means of placing his first reading of *Adam Bede* reveals how the immediacy of the book can be traced to an adjustment of focus. Reviewing the novel in 1859 John Forster finds an impression of 'reality' to be its most conspicuous feature.[22] But his review makes clear that he means that the illusion of reality is created by the inner consistency of its system of signs not by its correspondence with the known. His effort to characterise and place it is done in relation to other art. George Eliot resembles Hawthorne 'in a certain minute, yet not tedious, habit of description'. 'He' is superior to Thackeray in that 'Thackeray's chief power lies in describing the sort of world we live in, and the author of *Adam Bede* leads us into the world we do *not* live in'. His account of the 'festival and village games . . . [is] worthy the pen of the Author of 'Tom Brown's Schooldays' and 'The Scouring of the White Horse'.' Adam's 'agony' recalls Dickens, the descriptions of children Gainsborough. Above all, in his praise of Mrs Poyser's talk, given a high proportion of space in his review, Forster is explicit about the relation between art and life. Mrs Poyser is so real and so attractive a character that 'we thirst to *know* her'. To describe her proverbial talk Forster refers the reader to George Herbert's *Jacula Prudentum*, and quotes from it 'at random'. *Unlike* anyone in real life who might 'lace his talk' with the occasional old saw, Mrs Poyser 'creates and multiplies proverbs for her own use'. Though he nowhere so aligns himself, Forster is here taking the 'Idealist' position, where the typical is seen as more interesting than the particular. Further, being creative and inventive herself, Mrs Poyser is seen as a source of life in the book. For Forster she is 'the very sunlight by which we read the story of *Adam Bede*'. He sees no contradiction in asserting both her lifelikeness and the artfulness of her portrayal. If it were not that modern criticism often raises the question of the way characters speak in order to disapprove of the art this would seem almost too obvious to be worth mentioning. But the book creates an illusion of reality within its own world largely by means of the clear pattern in the speech modes represented. The gap between upper- and lower-class speech, between the language of countryman and townsman, is an undoubted fact of social life. It is rendered with accuracy even if the speech of any individual character in the book could not be transferred from the page to life.

These idyllic novels demand that we accept them whole. Inside their own world they present, like other pastoral, a finely balanced set of interdependent oppositions. Novels like *Cranford* and *Under the Greenwood Tree* explore process as realistic novels always do, but the tendency is grafted on to a meditative poetic structural pattern of great antiquity, which may be rephrased and repossessed whenever circumstances alter the relation of the simple and the sophisticated. Where contemporary readers saw the modernity, modern readers all too often see only simple-minded escapism in these evocations of simple worlds. We should not, I think, be so deceived. The complex pressures of a shifting world are not absent from these novels. They are present in the fleeting perceptions of duality and mutually mitigating truths and in the impossibility of final resolution. Their implied presence is the reason why the end effect of works as different as *Adam Bede*, *Cousin Phillis* and *The Woodlanders* is not cloying but delicate.

Notes

NOTES TO THE INTRODUCTION

1. Raymond Williams, *The City and the Country* (New York and London, 1973) ch. 16.
2. Ibid., p. 206.
3. And other general studies, notably Michael Squires, *The Pastoral Novel: Studies in George Eliot, Thomas Hardy and D. H. Lawrence* (Charlottesville, 1974). Relevant individual studies are listed in n. 2 to Chapter 4 below.
4. Even *Emma* has recently been shown to have absorbed the Gothic of *Northanger Abbey* into its own psychological realism. See Judith Wilt, *Ghosts of the Gothic: Austen, Eliot and Lawrence* (Princeton, 1980) ch. 3, pp. 121–72.
   Frankenstein is seen as 'a pattern and a metaphor' by George Levine in *The Realistic Imagination: English Fiction from Frankenstein to Lady Chatterley* (Chicago and London, 1981) p. 23.
5. The word 'idyll' is generally synonymous with 'pastoral' in critical literature since the Renaissance. (See J. E. Congleton, *Theories of Pastoral Poetry in England: 1684–1759* (Gainesville, Fla, 1952) p. 6.) The more widespread use of 'idyll' in Victorian times is obviously related to the preference for Theocritus over Virgil which characterises Romantic and pre-Romantic poets and critics. (See Congleton, ch. VI and passim.)
6. See Angus Easson, 'John Chivery and the Wounded Strephon: A pastoral element in *Little Dorrit*', *Durham University Journal*, vol. LXVII (n.s., XXXVI) (June 1975) pp. 165–9.
7. A. Quiller-Couch, 'Mrs Gaskell', *Charles Dickens and Other Victorians* (Cambridge, 1925) p. 214. Quoted by J. G. Sharps, *Mrs Gaskell's Observation and Invention: A Study of her Non-Biographic Works* (Sussex, 1970) p. 427.
8. Ernst Gombrich, *Art and Illusion* (1959).
9. See R. Goodwin-Jones, 'The Representation of Economic Reality in George Sand's Rural Novels', *Studies in the Literary Imagination* (Fall 1979) pp. 53–60, where the journalism and the fiction is compared. George Sand did not herself include *Le Meunier d'Angibault* in the series of *romans-champêtres* which began with *Jeanne* and, according to the 1852 Notice to *Jeanne*, later included *La Mare au Diable*, *François le Champi* and *La Petite Fadette*. These novels are 'idylls' in the terms I shall develop, as is *Les Maîtres Sonneurs*, not yet written at the time of the Notice to *Jeanne*.
10. Cf. Quentin Skinner, 'Language and Social Change', in *The State of the Language*, ed. Leonard Michaels and Christopher Ricks (Berkeley, Los Angeles, and London, 1980) pp. 562–78. In this essay, a review of Raymond Williams's *Keywords* and first published in *Essays in Criticism* (July 1979), Professor Skinner

argues a case for the interdependence of words and culture, querying the assumption underlying *Keywords* that words reflect social values in a one-way traffic. His essay is concerned, as is *Keywords*, with single words, but a parallel and related case for verbal structures as both reflecting and forming social attitudes may be made and is assumed throughout this study.

Robert Weimann in *Shakespeare and the Popular Tradition in the Theater: Studies in the Social Dimension of Dramatic Form and Function* (Baltimore and London, 1978) p. xii, writes of what he calls 'the dialectics of interdependence' between 'the receptivity of the audience' and the 'artistry of the drama':

> If, as Marx noted, 'art' is 'one of the special modes of production', then surely Shakespeare's theater and his society were interrelated in the sense that the Elizabethan stage, even England, was also a potent force that helped to create the specific character and transitional nature of that society. Thus, the playgoers did not determine the nature of the plays, for although the latter certainly responded to the assumptions and expectations of the spectators, the audience itself was shaped and educated by the quality of what it viewed.

Weimann shows the traditional thinking on which Shakespeare drew as actually embodied in the theatrical conventions he used.

11. See H. Toliver, *Pastoral Forms and Attitudes* (Berkeley, 1971).
12. Rosalie Colie, *The Resources of Kind: Genre Theory in the Renaissance*, ed. Barbara K. Lewalski (Berkeley, 1973) p. 8.
13. E. D. Hirsch Jr, *Validity in Interpretation* (New Haven, 1967) pp. 86 and 88.
14. *Art and Illusion*, p. 211.
15. H. Toliver shows how pastoral may deploy contrasts inside elements of these basic oppositions, e.g. idyllic nature and anti-pastoral nature: op. cit. p. 3.
16. By Raymond Williams, for instance, op. cit. p. 208, where the 'patronage' is thought to consist of giving the characters her own consciousness. The problem centres on the language the characters speak, and the charge so widely accepted it need only be referred to. Cf Gillian Beer's comment on the language of *Mary Barton*: 'Although the narrative style is kept distinct from the speech of the characters there is remarkably little sense (as there is in some early George Eliot novels) of pity masking condescension.' 'Carlyle and Mary Barton: Problems of Utterance', *1848: The Sociology of Literature*. Proceedings of the Essex Conference on the Sociology of Literature (July 1977) ed. F. Baker, J. Coombes, P. Hulme, C. Mercer and D. Musselwhite (University of Essex, 1978) p. 254.
17. John F. Lynen, *The Pastoral Art of Robert Frost* (New Haven, 1960) passim.
18. Op. cit. introduction, p. ix.
19. David Masson, *British Novelists and their Styles: Being A Critical Sketch of the History of British Prose Fiction* (Boston, 1859). Lecture 1 begins by distinguishing the range of prose and poetry in fiction, but ends by illustrating how they overlap and how many of the effects of 'realistic' prose are poetic.
20. *Quarterly Review* (September 1842) lxx 385–416. Reprinted in *Tennyson: the Critical Heritage*, ed. J. D. Jump (1967). See Chapter 6.
21. See above, p. 2.

22. R. H. Horne, *A New Spirit of the Age* (Oxford, 1907) pp. 132–3 (first published 1844).
23. *Our Village* was published in five volumes between 1824 and 1832. The early volumes were made up of sketches which had been previously published in *The Ladies' Magazine* and which had increased the circulation of that magazine from 250 to 2000 copies a month. The first two volumes were in further editions before the later ones were written. Besides being an instant success they created a fashion. The first two volumes contain most of what is of interest now; they formed what was called a 'new edition' in 1865 (ten years after the author's death) in Bohn's Standard Library. After that, volumes of selections appeared drawn from all five volumes with some regularity, sometimes restricted in subject, e.g. 'children' or 'characters'. The most recent of these appeared as late as 1947.

NOTES TO CHAPTER I—THE VICTORIAN IDYLL

1. First published in 1848 as *The Bothie of Toper-na-Fuosich*. The story behind the change is told in *The Poems of Arthur Hugh Clough*, ed. H. F. Lowry, A. L. P. Norrington and F. L. Mulhauser (Oxford, 1951) p. 497.
2. *Letters of Matthew Arnold 1848–88*, ed. G. W. Russell, in 2 vols (1859) vol. I, pp. 379–80.
3. Charles Kingsley, unsigned review in *Fraser's Magazine* (January 1849) vol. XXXIX, pp. 103–10. Reprinted in *Clough: The Critical Heritage*, ed. Michael Thorpe (1972) pp. 37–46. G. H. Lewes in *The Life and Works of Goethe* (Everyman Edition, 430) puts *Hermann and Dorothea* in appropriate company and makes a critical comment interesting in relation to *La Mare au Diable* (pp. 62–5) 'on comparing it [*Hermann and Dorothea*] with Theocritus or Virgil, with Guarini or Tasso, with Florian or Delille, with Gessner or Thomson, the critic will note with interest the absence of ornamentation, its freedom from all "idealisation".' I do not understand Kingsley's inclusion of *Bernard Leslie*; a tale of the mistakes of a young clergyman and his eventual self-discovery as a pastor of a middle-of-the-road position in Church doctrine and practice, it seems neither pastoral nor comic.
4. Unsigned review in *Saturday Review* (30 November 1861) pp. 564–5. Reprinted in *Clough: The Critical Heritage*, pp. 101–6.
5. Compare Arnold's view that *Thyrsis* would not be popular.
6. The metre is discussed in the introduction to *The Poems* (Oxford) pp. x–xiii. Contemporary opinion was divided. Kingsley and Rossetti thought it interesting and appropriate. Whewell ('English Hexameters', *North British Review* (May 1853) pp. 143–6; *Critical Heritage*, pp. 65–8) thought it might 'be made the vehicle of a representation of the realities of life, better than any more familiar form', in spite, or perhaps because, of being to a cultivated reader 'uncouth and licentious'. Arnold (*On Translating Homer*) thought similarly that 'needlessly rough' as they may be the hexameters do produce 'the sense of having, within short limits of time, a large portion of human life presented to him [the reader] instead of a small portion' (*Critical Heritage*, pp. 69–70). The anonymous reviewer in *The Literary Gazette* (18 August 1849) vol. LXVI,

606–7, thought 'the ridiculous versifying' only one of the blemishes of the poem (*Critical Heritage*, pp. 49–52).

7. W. M. Rossetti, review of *The Bothie* in *The Germ*, I (January 1850) pp. 34–46; *Critical Heritage*, pp. 54–64.

8. Clough to Emerson, 10 February 1849: 'Will you convey to Mr. Longfellow the fact that it was a reading of his Evangeline aloud to my Mother and sister which, coming after a reperusal of the Iliad, occasioned this outbreak of hexameters. Evangeline is very popular here.' – *The Correspondence of Arthur Hugh Clough*, ed. F. L. Mulhauser (Oxford, 1957) vol. I, pp. 240–1.

9. I quote from *The Poems of Tennyson*, ed. C. Ricks (1969) (Annotated English Poets), hereafter referred to as Ricks. All textual information is derived from the annotations and apparatus of this edition. Tennyson spelt English Idyls with one 'l', *Idylls of the King* with two.

10. Specific reference is given by Ricks.

11. Robert Pattison, *Tennyson and Tradition* (Cambridge, Mass., and London, 1979) passim.

12. E. C. Stedman, *Victorian Poets*, revised edition (Boston and New York, 1897) pp. 342–3.

13. Op. cit. chs 3 and 4.

14. J. W. Mackail, *Lectures on Greek Poetry* (1910) pp. 218–35. Page references are given in the text.

15. A. Dwight Culler, *The Poetry of Tennyson* (New Haven and London, 1977) 114.

16. Ricks, 508.

17. Culler, 119.

18. John Dixon Hunt, 'Story Painters and Picture Writers', in *Writers and their Backgrounds: Tennyson*, ed. D. J. Palmer (1973) pp. 180–202.

19. Ricks, 641.

20. 'On Translating Homer', *The Complete Prose Works of Matthew Arnold*, vol. I, *On the Classical Tradition*, ed. R. H. Super (Ann Arbor, 1960) p. 206.

21. Op. cit. p. 116.

22. See above, p. 2.

23. For example, the matching 'domestic' pictures in *Adam Bede*, ch. L, show a pattern of relationships between the people and their surroundings which is very like the final picture of 'Dora'. We may compare the 'picture' of Dorothea in *Middlemarch*, ch. LXXX, which Hugh Witermeyer compares to Friedrich's 'Frau am Fenster' (*George Eliot and the Visual Arts* (New Haven and London, 1979) p. 155). The use of this picture is not idyllic within the terms of my argument. The narrator both sees and identifies with Dorothea. Further, the incident represents a realistic length of time in the story when Dorothea comes in, pauses and looks through the window. The picture represents a moment shown partly as the sensibility of the figure.

24. *Alfred Lord Tennyson. A Memoir by his Son*, 2 vols (1897) vol. I, p. 265.

25. Loc. cit. 206 n. I.

26. Unsigned review, *Church of England Quarterly Review* (October 1842) vol. XII, pp. 361–76. Reprinted in *Tennyson: The Critical Heritage*, ed. J. D. Jump (1976) pp. 126–36.

27. Cf. John F. Lynen, *The Pastoral Art of Robert Frost*, pp. 23–4, defining the consciousness of separate worlds as essential to pastoralism.

28. *The Prose Works of William Wordsworth*, ed. W. J. B. Owen and J. W. Smyser, 3 vols (Oxford, 1974) vol. III, p. 28.

29. Ibid., vol. III, pp. 76 and 98.

30. I quote from Friedrich von Schiller, 'Naïve and Sentimental Poetry', *Two Essays Translated with Introduction and Notes*, by Julius A. Elias (New York, 1966). Page references are given in the text to the paperback edition, 1975. The German text is quoted at crucial points in my argument; page references are to Schiller, *Über Naïve und Sentimentalische Dichtung*, ed. W. F. Mainland, Blackwell's German Texts (Oxford, 1957).

31. I am arguing only the relation of the views, not the question of influence. There is no evidence that Wordsworth knew the essay, but Coleridge did. See *The Notebooks of Samuel Taylor Coleridge*, ed. Kathleen Coburn (Princeton, 1973) vol. I, no. 1705 and appendix A, n. 453.

32. See *The Poems of Matthew Arnold*, ed. Kenneth Allott (1965) p. 49, n. 5. I have not found any evidence that Arnold knew the essay at first hand, but Schiller's views in general were widely diffused. See René Wellek, *A History of Modern Criticism 1750–1950 in Five Volumes* (New Haven and London, 1955 and 1965) vol. II passim. Ruskin's discussion 'Of the Pathetic Fallacy' (*Modern Painters*, III, ch. XII) divides poets similarly into 'Creative' and 'Reflective'.

33. Salomon Gessner, 1730–88, Swiss landscape painter and engraver as well as author. His *Idyllen* (prose poems) were first published in 1756. An English edition of 1886 calls him 'The Swiss Theocritus'.

34. That is to say that the idyllic mode of perception, or in the terms of my Introduction, the pastoral 'genre' in this Victorian transformation, arises from and presents circumstances of sufficient tension between the 'ideal' of innocence and the reality of a simple life to give rise to reflection on, or ideas *about* innocence or simplicity. A recurring difficulty in this area is the ordinary usage of 'ideal' and the idealism which could be more accurately rendered as generalisation. Pater (see p. 51) slips from one reference to the other and contemporary critics of the novel range across a spectrum of meaning between the two (see Ch. 6).

35. Toliver, op. cit.

36. *Selected Writings of Walter Pater*, ed. H. Bloom (New York and Scarborough, 1974) pp. 67–8.

37. Max J. Friedländer, *Landscape, Portrait, Still Life. Their Origin and Development*, trans. R. F. C. Hall (New York, 1963) p. 158.

38. Richard and Samuel Redgrave, *A Century of British Painters* (1866). A new edition, 1947, p. 319.

39. Redgrave, 301.

40. Redgrave, 313–14.

41. 'Letters on the Fine Arts No. 3: The Royal Academy', *Stray Papers by William Makepeace Thackeray Being Stories, Reviews, Verses and Sketches 1821–1847*, ed. Lewis Melville (1901), pp. 214–17.

42. Frederick Wedmore, *The Masters of Genre Painting: being an Introductory Handbook to the Study of Genre Painting* (1880) pp. 46 ff. Most of Wedmore's published work is art criticism; amongst a small amount of fiction he has some idylls. One collection of three stories, *Pastorals of France*, 1878, is prefaced with the usual pastoral disclaimers of high intention. The 'period of social change' in which we live 'is especially baffling to the somewhat fettered chronicler of our daily

ways' (2) so it is natural for many writers to turn to 'such rural or outland life as by reason of its remoteness can hardly be deemed contemporary'. Such life keeps values of the past alive in the present, 'only Time and the settlement of things disturbed can show whether it may also belong to the Future'. (4). In 'A last love at Pornic' (the first story), an elderly art dealer and a young rural beauty make contact through their mutual appreciation of landscape pictures and the history of the neighbourhood.

43. *The Champion* (5 March 1815) in *The Complete Works of William Hazlitt in Twenty One Volumes*, Centenary Edition, ed. P. P. Howe (London and Toronto, 1933) vol. XVIII, pp. 96–100. 'On Mr. Wilkie's Pictures'. The letter is itself an interesting example of the habit of thinking in patterns established by contemporary painters.

44. *Works*, vol. XVIII, pp. 36.

45. Redgrave, 400.

46. E. Adams, *Francis Danby: Varieties of Poetic Landscape* (New Haven, 1973) p. 26.

47. This is not a problem which goes away. Reviewing a recent novel, *At the Shores* by Thomas Rogers, Josh Rubins (*New York Review of Books* (18 September 1980) pp. 63–4) describes this 'memory-book' set 'in a lakeside vacation spot' as a 'perilous balancing act'. He defines the author's task in placing his adolescent hero thus:

> For every archetypal gesture he makes, he needs to make a dozen that plant Jerry on rough, specific, verifiable ground. One false move and the whole idyllic confection will turn into treacle. Fortunately, Rogers has the narrative abilities required for such a chancy proposition, and his near-fable has the textured authenticity of a photo-essay.

NOTES TO CHAPTER 2 – GEORGE SAND AND MARY MITFORD:
POLITICS AND POETRY

1. There is one modern biography: Vera Watson, *Mary Russell Mitford* (1949). The most interesting source is the letters. There are two substantial collections: *The Life of Mary Russell Mitford, Related in a Selection of her Letters to her Friends*, ed. Rev. A. G. L'Estrange, in 3 vols (1870) (abbreviated *LL*, followed by volume and page number in the two-volume edition, 1870); *Letters of Mary Russell Mitford*, 2nd series, ed. Henry Chorley, in 2 vols (1872) (Chorley). There are other collections and many unpublished. Page references to the sketches are not given since there are so many editions and the sketches are short.

2. *Foscari* (1826) excited 'rapturous applause' and no disapprobation even 'without a single order in the house' (*LL* II 232). *Rienzi* (1828) 'passed the twentieth night which . . . insures the payment of 400 pounds from the theatre (the largest price any play can gain)' and sold 'eight thousand copies in two months' (*LL* II 259). The plays and 'dramatic scenes' were collected in *The Dramatic Works of Mary Russell Mitford* (1854).

3. Published in 1834.

4. *Life and Letters of Leslie Stephen*, ed. F. W. Maitland (1906) p. 290.

5. See Patricia Thomson, *George Sand and the Victorians* (1977) ch. 6, 'Arnold's "Days of Lélia" '.

6. In the Notice to *Jeanne*, written for Hetzel's 'édition populaire', (1852), Sand identifies this novel as a first attempt, 'Qui m'a conduit à faire plus tard *La Mare au Diable, Le Champi* et *La Petite Fadette*'. *La Mare au Diable*, according to the preface of 1851, was to be the first in a series, 'sous le titre de Veillées de Chanvreur'. The narrator of *Les Maîtres Sonneurs*, not written at the time of the 1852 preface to *Jeanne*, is Étienne Depardieu, who was the *chanvreur* at Nohant.
7. The language of the Berrichon novels has been the subject of detailed study, the most extensive by Marie-Louise Vincent, *La Langue et le Style rustiques de George Sand dans les roman-champêtres* (Paris, 1916).
8. 1852 preface to *Jeanne*.
9. G. S. Haight, *George Eliot: A Biography* (Oxford, 1968) p. 60.
10. Page references which follow the text are to the Garnier Frères édition of *La Mare au Diable*, ed. P. Salamon and J. Mallion (Paris, 1962).
11. See below, p. 78.
12. See above, Introduction, n. 9.
13. Chorley, vol. i, p. 11.
14. Mary Howitt, *Wood Leighton: Or a Year in the Country* (The Parlour Library, 1847) p. 309. First published in 3 vols, 1836.
15. *LL* ii 126, dated 22 March 1821.
16. Percy Lubbock, *Elizabeth Barrett Browning in her Letters* (1906) pp. 32–3.
17. [George Procter] *'Our Village Sketches of Rural Character and Scenery* By Mary Russell Mitford, Author of Julian, a Tragedy', *The Quarterly Review*, vol. XXXI (December 1824–March 1825) pp. 166–74.
18. *LL* i 181–2.

NOTES TO CHAPTER 3 – ELIZABETH GASKELL: HISTORY AND FICTION

Reference to the novels and stories is in the text; it is to chapter or part followed by page reference to *The Works of Mrs Gaskell*, ed. A. W. Ward (The Knutsford Edition, reprinted 1919–20 by John Murray, from the Smith, Elder first edition, 1906). *The Letters of Mrs Gaskell*, ed. J. A. V. Chapple and A. Pollard (Manchester, 1966), is abbreviated *GL*; reference is in the notes and is to letter number followed (in brackets) by page number. I am generally indebted for references and information to J. G. Sharps, *Mrs Gaskell's Observation and Invention: A Study of her Non-Biographic Works* (Fontwell, Sussex, 1970).

1. Raymond Williams, *Culture and Society 1780–1950* (London and New York, 1958).
2. John Lucas, *The Literature of Change: Studies in the Nineteenth Century Provincial Novel* (Sussex and New York, 1977).
3. John Gross, 'Mrs Gaskell', *The Novelist as Innovator*, ed. W. Allen (1965) pp. 49–63. Reprinted in *The Victorian Novel: Modern Essays in Criticism*, ed. Ian Watt (London, Oxford and New York, 1971) pp. 217–28.
4. John Lucas, 'Mrs Gaskell and Brotherhood', *Tradition and Tolerance in Nineteenth Century Fiction*, ed. D. Howard, J. Lucas and J. Goode (1966) pp. 141–205.
5. Published in *Blackwood's Edinburgh Magazine*, XLI (1837) 48–50.

Notes

6. *GL* 12 (28) to Mary Howitt about the survival of old customs in Lancashire and Cheshire.
7. *GL* 42 (74). Samuel Greg was a philanthropist whose 'Utopian' schemes cost him dear – *GL* 72(a) (120). For Elizabeth Gaskell's response to comments and reviews see *GL* 35 (66), 36 (67), 37 (68) – 'Half the masters here are bitterly angry with me – half (and the best half) are buying it to give to their work-people's libraries.' For an annotated survey of opinion see R. L. Selig, *Elizabeth Gaskell: A Reference Guide* (Boston, 1977).
8. Published in *Sartain's Union Magazine* (July 1849). Reprinted in *Cranford*, ed. E. P. Watson (Oxford English Novels, 1972).
9. Published in *The Ladies Companion and Monthly Magazine*, vol. III (February–April 1851).
10. Criticism has been sceptical of *Cranford's* status as a novel. It has been called 'a series of vignettes' (Coral Lansbury, *Elizabeth Gaskell: The Novel of Social Crisis* (1975) p. 7), 'a string of coloured beads' (A. B. Hopkins, *Elizabeth Gaskell: Her Life and Work* (1952) 108) 'a type of novel half-way between the informal essay and the novel' (G. Sanders, *Elizabeth Gaskell*. With a bibliography by C. S. Northrup. Cornell Studies in English, vol. IX (New Haven and London, 1929) 46). But there have been other voices; Edgar Wright sees the 'historical' unity of the description (*Mrs Gaskell: The Basis for Reassessment* (1965) ch. VII) and Barbara Hardy describes the appropriate naturalness of the 'piecemeal method' of narration, in which 'we accumulate impression in a continuous process of slight shocks and revisions' ('Mrs Gaskell and George Eliot', *The Victorians*, ed. A. Pollard, in History of Literature in the English Language, **6** (1970) 179). Since this chapter was written, W. M. Kendrick ('The Novelization of *Cranford*', *Structuralist Review*, II I (Winter 1980) 1–19) has described the evolution of the fictional elements in the first paper as they take over from the descriptive or historical elements. *Cranford*, he says, 'becomes a novel when it gives up innocent repetition for a self-knowledge that may deserve to be called guilty' (9). The 'guilt' ('self-exploitation' is another term used) is ascribed to the text not the author, but seems to me to arise from a suspicion on Mr Kendrick's part of art as necessarily a falsification of reality. It is on the question of the relation of art and history in this book, which we agree is a novel, that, as my chapter makes clear, I would take issue with him. Art is, of course, one mode of perception, and in this novel as in other idylls it indicates a version or view of reality. It is, too, part of the element of 'play' in a book which is, though one would never guess it from Mr Kendrick's article, funny.
11. *GL* 562 (748) to Ruskin.
12. Knutsford, vol. II, pp. xxiii–iv.
13. Margaret Tarratt, 'Cranford and the Strict Code of Gentility', *Essays in Criticism*, **18**, no. 2 (April 1968) 152–63.
14. W. M. Kendrick (op. cit. 18) sees the continuation of *Cranford* into 'The Cage at Cranford' as indicating that 'the truth of the world is, finally, superior to the beauties of literature'.
15. *GL* 42 (74) 'tragic' is an editorial emendation of 'magic'. The phrase 'tragic poem' is also used of *Mary Barton* in *GL* 37 (68), 39 (70).
16. Michael Wheeler ('Dives versus Lazarus: *Mary Barton*', *The Art of Illusion in*

Victorian Fiction (London and Basingstoke, 1979) ch. IV) shows how Barton and Carson are alike in distorting the Bible stories they rely on. This interesting study reveals how class relations in *Mary Barton*, and the Barton/Carson confrontation which is their climax, are mediated by allusion.

17. Peter Brooks, *The Melodramatic Imagination: Balzac, Henry James, Melodrama, and the Mode of Excess* (New Haven and London, 1976) p. 5.
18. *Culture and Society*, p. 89.
19. 'Mrs Gaskell and Brotherhood', p. 172.
20. *Culture and Society*, p. 91.
21. As in the opposition of the title and the complicating oppositions within the description of each region, e.g. Helstone is rooted but restrictive, Milton forceful but lacking in heart and culture.
22. An account of the composition and serialisation of *North and South* is given by D. W. Collin, 'The Composition of Mrs Gaskell's *North and South*', *Bulletin of the John Rylands Library*, **54**, no. 1 (Autumn 1971) 67–93.
23. E.g. *GL* 192 (282), 200 (294).
24. *GL* 195 (282).
25. Collin, 72, gives Dickens's computation of manuscript into printed pages.
26. *GL* 192 (282).
27. Verbal pictures have various functions in Elizabeth Gaskell's work; they mirror emotion, for example, as in *Ruth* (landscapes and interiors) or 'The Moorland Cottage' (Maggie's retreat or Maggie after Frank's absence in a dress 'the exact tint of which a painter would have admired'.) Recalled pictures as in 'Mr Harrison's Confessions' or *Cousin Phillis* carry values and foreshadow event. A structural picture such as I am describing in *North and South* has a distinct and perhaps more problematic function.
28. For another view of the narrator's relationship with her heroine see P. N. Furbank, 'Mendacity in Mrs Gaskell', *Encounter*, **40**, no. 6 (June 1973) 51–5.

NOTES TO CHAPTER 4 – GEORGE ELIOT: 'ADAM BEDE' – THE BOUNDS OF THE IDYLL

Page references which follow the quotations from *Adam Bede* are to the Penguin English Library edition, edited by Stephen Gill (1980).

1. Ian Gregor and Brian Nicholas, *The Moral and the Story* (1962) ch. 1, pp. 13–32.
2. *Adam Bede* is much written about. Amongst modern critics those who consider its elaborate organisation and those who consider it as a pastoral are particularly germane to my subject. These include: G. S. Creeger, 'An Interpretation of *Adam Bede*', *English Literary History*, XXIII, no. 3 (September 1956) 218–38; R. A. Foakes, '*Adam Bede* Reconsidered', *English*, XII (1958–9) 174–5; John Goode, '*Adam Bede*', *Critical Essays on George Eliot*, ed. Barbara Hardy (1970) pp. 19–41; W. J. Harvey, *The Art of George Eliot* (Oxford, 1969); Barbara Hardy, *The Novels of George Eliot* (1959); M. Hussey, 'Structure and Imagery in *Adam Bede*', *Nineteenth Century Fiction*, x (September 1955) 115–29; K. Marotta, '*Adam Bede* as a Pastoral', *Genre*, **9** (1976) 59–72; Michael Squires, *The Pastoral Novel* (Charlottesville, 1974) ch. 3. This is not a comprehensive list of views of *Adam Bede*; my chapter deals only with aspects of the book related to

my present argument and makes no claim for comprehensiveness as a study, but I hope it may modify views of *Adam Bede*.

3. Op. cit. p. 31.
4. Cf. 'It is as though he [the reader] had made acquaintance with real human beings: the story is not a story, but a true account of a place and people who have really lived. . . .' (*The Athenaeum*, no. 1635 (26 Feb 1859) 284): 'We do not know whether our literature anywhere possesses such a closely true picture of purely rural life as *Adam Bede* presents.' (Anne Mozley, unsigned review, *Bentley's Quarterly Review* (July 1859) 1 433–56, reprinted Carroll, *George Eliot: The Critical Heritage*, pp. 86–103.) But the *Athenaeum* reviewer also represents some who thought there was too much reality: in 'the whole scene of proceeding to execution . . . the brutal facts are not softened to fit them for their place in a work of Art . . .'.
5. *The George Eliot Letters*, ed. G. S. Haight, 7 vols (New Haven and London, 1954–5) (hereafter abbreviated *GEL*) III 6.
6. *GEL* III 42.
7. *GEL* III 114–15.
8. *GEL* III 17–18.
9. *GEL* III 24.
10. *GEL* III 18.
11. *Critical Heritage*, 77–8.
12. *The Atlantic Monthly*, 18 Oct 1866. Reprinted in G. S. Haight (ed.) *A Century of George Eliot Criticism* (1965) (University Paperbacks, 1966) pp. 43–54.
13. *Century*, p. 51.
14. *GEL* II 503.
15. *GEL* II 504.
16. *GEL* II 488.
17. *GEL* III 374.
18. *GEL* II 480.
19. *Essays of George Eliot*, ed. Thomas Pinney (1965) pp. 268–9.
20. Further implications of this choice of historical time are central to John Goode's argument, '*Adam Bede*', *Critical Essays*, ed. Hardy.
21. *GEL* II 419.
22. E. H. Corbauld's illustration of this scene, 'Dinah Morris Preaching on Hayslope Green' [Hugh Witermeyer, *George Eliot and the Visual Arts* (New Haven and London, 1979) plate 25] is interesting in this connection. It includes the traveller in the scene, thus confining the point of view to the author. The landscape is misty and idealised, the gentlemanly traveller and Dinah herself drawn in a different style from the surrounding villagers who are roundly and robustly characterised.
23. Op. cit. p. 22.
24. See T. G. Rosenmeyer, *The Green Cabinet: Theocritus and the European Pastoral Lyric* (Berkeley, 1969) ch. 4 on 'Otium'.
25. Op. cit. p. 31.
26. *GEL* III 264.
27. See P. Brooks, 'The Melodramatic Imagination: The Example of Balzac and James', *Romanticism: Vistas, Instances and Continuities*, ed. Thorburn and Hartman (Ithaca and London, 1973) pp. 198–220.
28. Haight, 249–50.

29. Ibid., p. 313.
30. J. Hillis Miller, 'Optic and Semiotic in *Middlemarch*', in *The Worlds of Victorian Fiction*, ed. J. H. Buckley (Cambridge, Mass., and London, 1975) pp. 125–45.
31. Always seen implicitly as two sides of the same coin, the pastoral and the heroic emerge in explicit juxtaposition in single works in the Renaissance. For an interesting discussion of their relation in Sidney's *Arcadia*, see Toliver, op. cit. ch. 3, 45–62. Donald Cheney, who sees Spenser's Fairyland as a version of pastoral which becomes explicitly so in book VI says: 'In offering a study of Spenser's treatment of pastoral motifs I am trying to suggest still another controlling force in the poem: A force which might be called a generic allegory in analogy to the moral, theological, and historical allegories. This force makes itself felt in repeated assertions of conflict between epic and pastoral, public and personal, idealist and realist. Though Spenser is not the first to introduce such controlling forces in his epic (Homeric simile and Virgilian melancholy have much the same role), he does develop them with unprecedented complexity and self-consciousness, in proportion as his poem is more directly concerned with a study of the imaginative process.' *Spenser's Image of Nature: Wild Man and Shepherd in 'The Faerie Queene'* (New Haven and London, 1966) p. 8. In Henry James, *The Bostonians* reference to the two modes of pastoral and heroic is explicit, in a way that it is not, of course, in *Daniel Deronda*.
32. Henry James, '*Daniel Deronda*: A Conversation', *The Atlantic Monthly* (December 1876). Reprinted in *A Century of George Eliot Criticism*, ed. G. S. Haight (1965) pp. 97–112.

NOTES TO CHAPTER 5 – THOMAS HARDY: CHARACTER AND ENVIRONMENT

Page references which follow extended quotation in the text are to the New Wessex Edition, 1975.

1. For the letters to Macmillan discussing publication see *The Collected Letters of Thomas Hardy*, ed. R. L. Purdy and Michael Millgate, vol. 1, 1840–92 (Oxford, 1978) pp. 11–12. Hardy thought 'a pastoral story would be the *safest* venture', presumably because of the familiarity of the subject-matter.
2. He was thought at the time to owe much to George Eliot. See Hardy's comment on the attribution of *Far from the Madding Crowd* to her: F. E. Hardy, *The Life of Thomas Hardy 1840–1928* (1962) (paperback) p. 98 (hereafter abbreviated *The Life*). For a modern view on her influence see Norman Page, 'Hardy's Dutch Painting: *Under the Greenwood Tree*', *Thomas Hardy Yearbook*, no. 5 (1975) pp. 39–42.
3. J. H. Miller, *Thomas Hardy: Distance and Desire* (1970) p. 106.
4. For an analysis of changes made at proof stage in the paragraph in part I, chapter VIII which describes their falling in love during the Christmas dance see Simon Gatrell, 'Thomas Hardy and the Dance', *Thomas Hardy Yearbook*, no. 5 (1975) 42–7.
5. Lloyd Fernando, 'Thomas Hardy's Rhetoric of Painting', *Review of English Literature*, VI (October 1965) 62–73, says Hardy gives us 'pictures of pictures' rather than 'pictures of reality'. Many critics are uneasy with Hardy's use of named pictures; even a generally approving critic like Joan Grundy thinks

thematic relevance and suggestion mark his greatest success with the method. I think this tidies up his art too much; we can appreciate the grotesque disjunction, for example, when Jude's Aunt turns upon the cousins 'a countenance like that of Sebastiano's Lazarus', without being able to call the picture to mind (Joan Grundy, *Hardy and the Sister Arts* (1979) pp. 26–7).

6. See below, n. 17.
7. Michael Millgate, *Thomas Hardy: His Career as a Novelist* (1971) pp. 249–50.
8. P. J. Casagrande, 'The Shifted "Centre of Altruism"', in *The Woodlanders*: Thomas Hardy's third "Return of a Native"', *English Literary History*, **38** (1971) 104–25, accepts 1874 as the likely date of conception, and sees *The Woodlanders* as a monistic, Darwinian handling of the 'return' motif, which yields comedy in *Under the Greenwood Tree*, tragedy in *The Return of the Native*; the handling of the material in *The Woodlanders* 'is guided steadily by the desire to dull the sharp edges of dramatic contrast and conflict'.
9. *The Life*, p. 96.
10. These are most succinctly listed by Millgate, op. cit. p. 260.
11. As a description of the complicated interconnection of theme, character and setting, Ian Gregor's elaboration of Hardy's notion of the web of human life is, in my view, illuminating on all the novels. *The Great Web: The Form of Hardy's Major Fiction* (1974) passim.
12. Robert Drake Jr, '*The Woodlanders* as traditional pastoral', *Modern Fiction Studies*, **6** (1960) 251–7.
13. Op. cit. p. 348. His explanation of the 'pastoral stance' is based on John Lynen, *The Pastoral Art of Robert Frost* (1960).
14. Op. cit. p. 260.
15. *Spectator* (26 March 1887) pp. 419–20. Reprinted in *Thomas Hardy: The Critical Heritage*, ed. R. G. Cox (1970) pp. 142–5.
16. *Dial*, VIII (July 1887) 68. Noted in *Thomas Hardy: An Annotated Bibliography of Writings about Him*, ed. H. E. Gerber and W. E. Davis; de Kalb (1973) no. 119.
17. Dale Kramer, *Thomas Hardy: The Forms of Tragedy* (1975) p. 104. Joseph Warren Beach, *The Technique of Thomas Hardy* (1922). Richard Carpenter, *Thomas Hardy* (1964).
18. Ibid. p. 47.
19. Op. cit. introduction, p. x.
20. *The Life*, pp. 185 and 358.
21. Op. cit. pp. 15–18.
22. Ibid. pp. 110–12.
23. Op. cit. p. 142 and, in the present connection, p. 168.
24. Ibid. p. 170.
25. *The Life*, pp. 184–6.
26. Mr R. N. Peers, Curator of the Dorset Natural History and Archaeological Society, informs me that this Bonington has not been identified and that its present whereabouts is unknown.
27. Alastair Smart, 'Pictorial Imagery in the Novels of Thomas Hardy', *Review of English Studies*, n.s. XII (1961) 279. Cf. Penelope Vigar, *The Novels of Thomas Hardy* (1974) p. 27: 'The "Impressionistic" effect [of *The Woodlanders*] gives form and coherence to the story simultaneously as it furthers the action, and gives an "atmosphere" which holds our attention and partially directs our appreciation of a given situation.'

28. T. S. Eliot, *After Strange Gods: A Primer in Modern Heresy* (1934) p. 54. Quoted by many modern critics, e.g. Millgate, op. cit. p. 281. A particularly interesting use is made of it by P. N. Furbank in the introduction to the New Wessex *Tess of the d'Urbervilles*.
29. Op. cit. pp. 168–9.
30. S. F. Johnson, 'Hardy and Burke's Sublime' in *Style in Prose Fiction: English Institute Essays 1958*, ed. H. C. Martin (New York, 1959).
31. I am greatly indebted to this introduction and to the chapter on *Far from the Madding Crowd* in John Bayley, *An Essay on Thomas Hardy* (1978).
32. Millgate, op. cit. pp. 92–3.
33. Op. cit. pp. 69–71.
34. Gregor, op. cit. pp. 59–62, quotes Ruskin from *The Stones of Venice*, vol. III, ch. 45, and *Modern Painters*, vol. III, ch. 8, part IV, on the grotesque. The 'beholder' has to make the links himself between juxtaposed symbols over the gaps 'left or overleaped by the master of the imagination'.
35. See above, p. 2. Raymond Williams on *Adam Bede*.

NOTES TO CHAPTER 6 – CONCLUSION: A REFLECTIVE MIRROR

1. For contemporary thinking on the novel this chapter draws on R. Stang, *The Theory of the Novel in England 1850–1870* (New York and London, 1959) and on two articles by J. D. Jump, 'Weekly Reviewing in the Eighteen Fifties', *RES*, **24** (January 1948) no. 93 pp. 42–57, and 'Weekly Reviewing in the Eighteen Sixties', *RES* n.s. III (July 1952) pp. 244–62.
2. Stang, op. cit. p. 52.
3. W. E. Houghton, *The Poetry of Clough: An Essay in Revaluation* (New Haven and London, 1963) pp. 92–118.
4. In the preface to *Wilhelm Meister* (1824) quoted by Houghton, op. cit. p. 93.
5. Op. cit. p. 112.
6. 'Review of some poems by Alexander Smith and Matthew Arnold', *The Poems and Prose Remains of Arthur Hugh Clough*, ed. by his wife (1879) vol. I, pp. 359–83. First published in *The North American Review* (July 1853) vol. LXXVII, no. 160.
7. *Letters*, ed. Kenyon (1897) vol. I, p. 204, quoted by Houghton, op. cit. p. 95.
8. *Quarterly Review* LXX (September 1842) 385–416. Reprinted in *Tennyson: The Critical Heritage*, ed. J. D. Jump (1967) from which I quote.
9. See above, Chapter 4.
10. On the novel as 'fictitious biography' Stang (op. cit. p. 150) quotes Fitzjames Stephen (1855) in what Stang calls 'a thoroughgoing statement of the realist position', which would allow the novel 'no more plot than a bona-fide biography'.
11. *Blackwood's Magazine*, **81** (1857) 23–41.
12. Stang (52–3) quotes W. C. Roscoe (*The National Review*, II (January 1856)), who says, for example, that Thackeray 'never penetrates into the interior, secret, *real* life that every man leads in isolation from his fellows'. Cf. J. R. Findlay, *Scotsman* (18 December 1850) reprinted *Thackeray: The Critical Heritage*, ed. Geoffrey Tillotson and Donald Hawes (1968) p. 95), who thought there was no need for truth 'to taste in the mouth like a dose of bitters', or David Masson ('Pendennis and Copperfield', *North British Review* (May 1851), *Critical*

Heritage, pp. 111–27), who saw Thackeray's work as 'real', Dickens's as 'ideal'. Thackeray replied (*Critical Heritage*, p. 128) that Dickens's work was not 'real' but 'exaggerated'.

13. 'Principles of Success in Literature', *Fortnightly Review*, vol. I, 187.

14. G. H. Lewes, 'Realism in Art: Recent German Fiction', *Westminster Review*, LXX (October 1858) 488–518. In *The Life of Goethe* Lewes praises *Hermann and Dorothea* ('of all idylls the most truly idyllic') for its truthful picture 'of country life and country people' and its freedom from all 'idealisation'. He is clearly here (*The Life of Goethe*, introduction by Victor Lange (New York, 1965) p. 420) referring to the falsification or beautifying of nature described in the review of German fiction.

15. Stang, op. cit. p. 179.

16. Richard Whately, unsigned review of *Northanger Abbey* and *Persuasion*, *Quarterly Review*, XXIV (January 1821) 352–76. Reprinted in *Jane Austen: The Critical Heritage*, ed. B. C. Southam (London and New York, 1968) pp. 87–105.

17. Stang, op. cit. p. 175.

18. *The Works of John Ruskin*, Library Edition, ed. G. T. Cook and A. Wedderburn, (1903) vol. III (*Modern Painters*, I) pp. 88–9. When Ruskin later modified his view of Landseer (see Cook and Wedderburn, IV 302) he excepted this picture 'and many others, in which the soul, if we may call it, of animals, has been explained to us in modes hitherto unfelt and unexampled'. Ruskin's references to Landseer are brought together in Cook and Wedderburn, II 334 n 1.

19. Culler, op. cit. p. 114.

20. *Documents of Modern Literary Realism*, ed. G. J. Becker (Princeton, 1963) pp. 118–19.

21. Hardy's one extended, non-fictional comment on the social scene, 'The Dorsetshire Labourer', takes a characteristically idyllic stance of emotional involvement and objectivity of judgement. Michael Millgate (op. cit. p. 210) describes it as reflecting 'a scrupulous determination to eschew the kind of blinkered simplification essential to the politician or to the preacher, and to try instead to see and present things as they are or were, in all their dense and often confusing perplexity'.

22. *The Edinburgh Review* (July 1859) pp. 223–46.

Index